Finite-State Computational Morphology

Irina Lobzhanidze

Finite-State Computational Morphology

An Analyzer and Generator for Georgian

Springer

Irina Lobzhanidze
Institute of Linguistic Studies
Ilia State University
Tbilisi, Georgia

ISBN 978-3-030-90247-6 ISBN 978-3-030-90248-3 (eBook)
https://doi.org/10.1007/978-3-030-90248-3

This Springer imprint is published by the registered company Springer Nature Switzerland AG
The registered company address is: Gewerbestrasse 11, 6330 Cham, Switzerland

This book is dedicated to my parents for their love and support.

Preface

Georgian presents a lot of different morphological features and is a highly interesting language for NLP systems, especially from the viewpoint of computational morphology. Modeling Georgian presents us with an opportunity to adapt and to test computational techniques, to build applications and to develop interdisciplinary approaches to languages with rich morphology. This book can be seen as an attempt to demonstrate how technology can be used for the processing of highly agglutinative language types like Georgian.

This book also brings together most of the work done in Georgian in the last 8 years. It covers the compilation of corpora of Georgian texts and the development of tools including a tokenizer, a rule-based morphological analyzer, and a generator of Georgian. The computational model presented here, which is implemented by means of finite-state technology, specifically *lexc* and *xfst,* encodes the morphosyntactic features of Georgian language, while the transducer, which has been tested on the Georgian Language Corpus, can be used as a component of other NLP applications for lemmatizing or tagging other resources.

It is also our hope that this book will assist other researchers in advancing their knowledge of Georgian and, possibly of other Kartvelian languages sharing similar features, and in using technology for their processing activities.

Oxford, UK
December, 2019

Irina Lobzhanidze

Acknowledgments

This work is the result of 8 years of research projects financed by the Shota Rustaveli National Science Foundation (SRNSF): Projects No. AR/320/4–105/11, Corpus Annotation and Analysis Software for the Modern Georgian Language, and No. DP2016_23, Digital Humanities: Digital Epigraphy, Computational Linguistics, Digital Prosopography. Additional funding was provided by Ilia State University.

Many people have contributed to this book. My special gratitude goes to Dr. Nino Doborjginidze, who encouraged me to preserve with it from the very beginning, and to Dr. Damana Melikishvili, who contributed a great deal to the development of verbal module from a theoretical perspective. I would also like to thank Irakli Gunia, who has contributed significantly to the online version of the Georgian Language Corpus (GLC) and to the dictionary of idioms developed since.

I would also like to thank the corpus supervisors: Svetlana Berikashvili, Nato Bilanishvili, Tsira Khakhviashvili and George Tadumadze, programmer George Mirianashvili, and many research assistants: S. Abralava, N. Chichikoshvili, M. Dadunashvili, T. Damenia, M. Damenia, N. Datashvili, N. Donadze, T. Gavashelishvili, T. Getiashvili, K. Gilashvili, N. Gogichaishvili, M. Ishkhanova, T. Kalkhitashvili, T. Karosanidze, T. Khubashvili, T. Kitoshvili, L. Kitsmarishvili, L. Kupreishvili, M. Kvaskhvadze, M. Kvinikadze, E. Kvirkvelia, N. Latibashvili, I. Lobjanidze, Z. Machavariani, S. Margvelashvili, K. Maridashvili, E. Mdinaradze, S. Nozadze, M. Rukhadze, L. Sergia, A. Sturua, G. Shubitidze, L. Tetrashvili, A. Tkebuchava, S. Tumanishvili, and L. Vashakmadze, who contributed extensively to the project and participated in the testing and development of corpus annotation. Without their efforts, most of the work described here would not have been possible.

Finally, I would like to express my gratitude to two anonymous reviewers for their helpful comments and suggestions and Geoffrey Gosby, who assisted with the editing and proofreading of the final manuscript.

Contents

About the Author

Irina Lobzhanidze is Professor of Linguistics at Ilia State University, Georgia, where she is also the Director of MA program in Applied Linguistics. She received her PhD in Linguistics from Ilia State University, Georgia. She held visiting Georgian studies fellow position at the Oxford School of Global and Area Studies (2019–2020). Her main research interests lie in the areas of morphology and syntax, and their interface. She has worked extensively on developing language processing tools and resources for Georgian, including the morphological analyzer and generator of Georgian. She is the Linguistic Coordinator of the *Georgian Language Corpus (GLC),* a co-author of *the Dictionary of Idioms* (2014–2017) and the Principal Researcher in the construction of the *Wardrops' Collection Online (WCO).* Previously, Irina conducted research on various aspects of Georgian idioms and degree of their "frozenness."

List of Figures

List of Tables

Abbreviations

ALA-LC	American Library Association – Library of Congress
AP-CH	Aphridonidze-Chkhaidze Transliteration System
CxG	Construction Grammar
Degr	Degree marker
Dial	Dialect form
EGIDS	Expanded Graded Intergenerational Disruption Scale
FSA	Finite-state automata
FST	Finite-state transducer
GLC	Georgian Language Corpus
GPSG	Generalized Phrase Structure Grammar
HPSG	Head Phrase Structural Grammar
IPA	International Phonetic Alphabet
IS	Indirect speech marker
LFG	Lexical Functional Grammar
Nbr	Number marker
NLP	Natural Language Processing
PARC	Palo Alto Research Center
Pers	Person marker
PoS	Part of speech
Posp	Postposition
Prev	Preverb
Ptl	Particle
R	Root
TAM	Tense-Aspect-Mood
TEI	Text Encoding Initiative
Tns	Tense marker
Vers	Version marker
XFST	Xerox Finite-State Tools
XRCE	Xerox Research Centre Europe

Chapter 1
Introduction

Keywords Finite-state transducer · Tokenization · Morphological analysis · Georgian

The present work describes a morphological analyzer and generator for the Georgian language developed with the financial support of the Shota Rustaveli National Science Foundation (Project Nos. DP2016_23, LE/17/1-30/13, AR/320/4-105/11, Y-04-10) and important aspects of the language that may be of interest to whose wishing to use technology for the processing of Old and Modern Georgian. The book focuses on the challenges presented by the complex morphology of Georgian and on the application of finite-state technology - specifically, *lexc* and *xfst* - to processing of the language. The morphological rules presented here have been encoded to generate inflected word-forms from a list of dictionary entries.

The book comprises three chapters and accompanying appendices. The aim of the first chapter is to describe the morphosyntactic structure of Georgian, focusing on differences between Old, Middle and Modern Georgian. The second chapter focuses on the application of finite-state technology to the processing of Georgian and on the compilation of a tokenizer, a morphological analyzer and a generator for Georgian. The third chapter discusses the testing and evaluation of the analyzer's output and the compilation of the GLC, which is now accessible online and freely available to the research community. The ALA-LC transliteration system for Georgian scripts (Johnson 2011) is used in current research, while the International Phonetic Alphabet (IPA) issued by (International Phonetic Association 1999) is adapted for phonological representation only.

The appendices include the list of morphosyntactic tags used for annotation and of triggers and flag diacritics used to establish long dependencies and to trigger the processing of changes and mutations.

I. Lobzhanidze, *Finite-State Computational Morphology*,
https://doi.org/10.1007/978-3-030-90248-3_1

References

Johnson, Bruce. 2011. *ALA-LC Romanization Table: Georgian*. https://www.loc.gov/catdir/cpso/romanization/georgian.pdf. Accessed 16 July, 2019.

International Phonetic Association. 1999. https://www.internationalphoneticassociation.org/. Accessed 16 July, 2019.

Chapter 2
The Georgian Language

Abstract This chapter aims to describe the status of the Georgian language and its main characteristics, principally in terms of the differences between Old and Modern Georgian, which reference some important aspects of the complex morphology of Georgian and how morphology interacts with syntax. The chapter comprises of four sections, the first of which is a short introduction providing a description of the language and its origins. Section 2.2, "Alphabets and Phonology", describes the alphabets used to write Georgian, its consonantal and vocalic system and syllable structure, which affects the modeling of the language. Section 2.3, "Morphology", outlines the morphological structure of Old and Modern Georgian in terms of the parts of speech already modeled in the analyzer. Finally, Section 2.4 summarises the information provided in the preceding sections.

Each section is based primarily on references to the grammar of Modern Georgian and a comparison with Old Georgian adapted with the purpose of providing a modeling of Georgian natural language as a whole and representing these differences in the morphological analyzer, which will be separately discussed in Chap. 3. Special tags: +OGE and + MGE are used to represent forms belonging to Old Georgian and Modern Georgian respectively.

Keywords Georgian scripts · Phonology · Morphosyntax

2.1 Introduction

The Modern Georgian language is one of the official languages of Georgia (the other being Abkhazian spoken in the Autonomous Republic of Abkhazia). While spoken it is predominantly there, its geographical area covers historical Tao-Klarjeti (on the territory of present-day Turkey), Saingilo (on the territory of Azerbaijan) and Fereydan (on the territory of present-day Iran) (Kurdiani 2008). Georgian, which has been further subdivided into two major dialect groups,[1] is a member of the Kartvelian

[1]Various classifications are presented in scholarly research with regard to the dialect groups of Georgian: Shanidze (1984) describes 6 groups of dialects, Dzidziguri (1982) - 5 groups, Jorbenadze (1998) – 2 groups subdivided into smaller subgroups, and so on. For a corpus of Georgian dialects (Beridze 2006), see http://www.corpora.co/#/, last accessed 17 November, 2019.

I. Lobzhanidze, *Finite-State Computational Morphology*,
https://doi.org/10.1007/978-3-030-90248-3_2

(also known as Iberian (Gamkrelidze and Gudava 1998) or South Caucasian (Boeder 2002–2005)) language family, which also includes the Mingrelian (Megrelian), Laz and Svan languages and can be attributed some 4.2 million speakers overall. The Expanded Graded Intergenerational Disruption Scale (EGIDS) level for Georgian in Georgia is 1, meaning that the language is used in education, work, mass media and government at the national level (Eberhard et al. 2019).

Common features shared by Georgian and the other Kartvelian languages include:

- A relatively uniform sound system;
- A well-developed system of word inflection and derivation;
- Agglutinating and inflecting systems that make use not only of a large variety of grammatical affixes, but also of ablaut and other types of processes typical of internal stem inflection;
- The ergative construction[2] of the sentence.

All of these features and characteristics pose unique problems at all levels of language processing and present interesting challenges for the compilation of robust language processing systems, from a huge diversity of possible tagsets to syntactic models. In addition, Georgian can be considered a good case study for the discussion of changes in and the development of languages with mixed (fusional/agglutinating) morphology and free constituent order in syntax; among the Kartvelian languages only Georgian has an extensive literary tradition dating back to the fourth century, which enables us to develop natural language processing systems not only for Modern, but also for Old Georgian. While, in recent years, various research groups (Datukishvili 1997a, 1997b; Margvelani 1999–2001; Gurevich 2006a, 2006b; Meurer 2007; Kapanadze 2009 and others) have developed some tools for the processing of Modern Georgian morphology, many challenges remain unsolved.

The literary tradition of Georgian is generally subdivided into three stages (Sarjveladze 1997)[3]:

1. Old Georgian, from the fourth to the ninth centuries;
2. Middle Georgian, from the ninth to the eighteenth centuries;
3. New (Modern) Georgian since the nineteenth century.

---

[2] Opinions with regard to the extent of ergativity in Georgian differ, see (Boeder 1979; Harris 1982, 1985; Hewitt 1983, 1987; Amiridze 2006; Tuite 2017; Baker and Bobaljik 2017; Nash 2017 and others). These differences stem from the fact that case morphology does not coincide with verbal alignment and behaves as if some constructions use ergative-absolutive syntax (e.g in the screeves of the second series), while others use nominative-accusative syntax. The ergative construction is therefore referred to hereinafter in the sense of split ergativity.

[3] Opinions as to this periodization differ greatly Chikobava (2008) differentiates two periods: Old (fifth – eleventh centuries) and Modern (from twelfth century to the present day); Shanidze (1976), three periods: Old (fifth – eleventh centuries), Middle (twelfth – eighteenth centuries) and Modern (from nineteenth century to the present day); and Jorbenadze (1998), five periods: the first (fifth – nineth/eleventh centuries), the second (eleventh/twelfth – seventeenth/ eighteenth centuries), the third (from eighteenth – nineteenth centuries from the middle of the second half of the century), the fourth (from the sixties of the nineteenth century until the beginning of the twentieth century) and the fifth (from the beginning of the twentieth century to the present day), etc. For a full comparison of different periodizations, see (Gogolashvili 2004).

The differences between the languages of these three periods are not significant; readers of Modern Georgian are able to read and understand Old Georgian texts, grasping the language in them at a morphological, syntactic and semantic level. The main differences observed between the texts which cause difficulties in comprehensions are as follows: (a) alphabets; (b) vocabulary; (c) some phonological items; (d) some morphological elements.

2.2 Alphabet and Phonology

2.2.1 The Alphabet and Scripts

Georgian literary tradition is based on the three scripts of the Georgian alphabet: *Asomtavruli* (from the fifth century), *Nuskhuri* (from the ninth century) and *Mkhedruli* (from the tenth century). There are many theories describing the origin and development of these scripts: Javakhisvhili (1949) and Pataridze (1980) connect them to Semitic alphabet, while Gamkrelidze (2006, 2011) considers the Classical Greek writing system a prototype script for Georgian, and Chkhenkeli et al. (1977) and Machavariani (1982, 2015) describe the Georgian alphabet as a stylistically whole and complete graphic system that was created independently of other scripts. Despite their graphical differences, the Georgian scripts are interconnected in the manner depicted in Fig. 2.1.

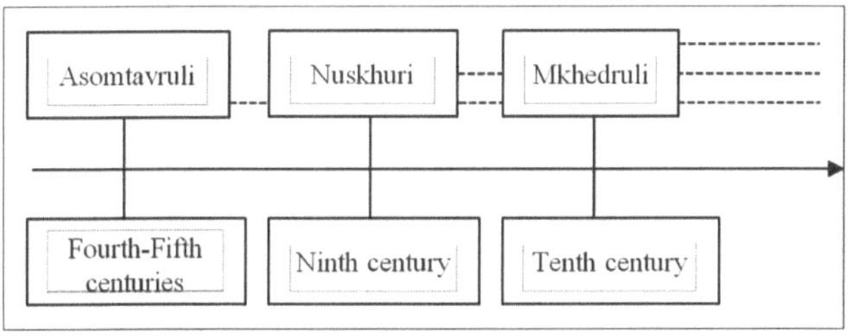

Fig. 2.1 The origin of the Georgian scripts

The oldest extant samples of Georgian script are three *Asomtavruli* inscriptions found at a site near Bethlehem in Palestine and dated to 430–532 AD and another *Asomtavruli* inscription found at Bolnisi Sioni Cathedral in Georgia and dated to 494 AD; one *Nuskhuri* inscription found in the Ateni Sioni Church and dated to 835 AD; one *Mkhedruli* inscription found, also, in the Ateni Sioni Church and dated to 982–986 AD.

Consisting of 38 characters, Georgian nowadays preserves 33 written from left to right without any upper-lower case distinctions (Table 2.1), the Georgian orthography belongs to the so-called 'phonemic' type, in which the graphemes correspond to the phonemes. Although Georgian does not have capital letters, from the ninth century onward, *Asomtavruli* (*Mrgvlovani*) was systematically used in *Nuskhuri* and *Mkhedruli* manuscripts to demarcate titles and/or the beginning of paragraphs, sentences and sometimes words. This tradition persevered in some printed books (Chikobava and Vateishvili 1983; and others) as well.

The standardized forms of the Georgian scripts are reflected in Unicode Ranges 10A0–10FF and 2D00–2D2F,[4] in which the *Asomtavruli* script is described as the majuscule of the old ecclesiastical alphabet under the title 'Capital Letters (*Khutsuri*)' without taking into consideration that from the fifth until the ninth century, the *Asomtavruli* (*Mrgvlovani*) script was not used in opposition to any other. It was only from the ninth century onward that religious texts were written in a combination of *Asomtavruli* and *Nuskhuri* called *Khutsuri* ('ecclesiastical'), whereby *Asomtavruli* was employed as a majuscule in opposition to *Nuskhuri*. This use of *Asomtavruli* script also continued in secular literature after the eleventh century, when secular

Table 2.1 Georgian Alphabets: Asomtavruli, Nuskhuri, Mkhedruli

Asomtavruli[a]	ALA-LC[b]	Nuskhuri[c]	Mkhedruli[d]	ALA-LC	Numerical Value
Ⴀ	A	ⴀ	ა	a	1
Ⴁ	B	ⴁ	ბ	b	2
Ⴂ	G	ⴂ	გ	g	3
Ⴃ	D	ⴃ	დ	d	4
Ⴄ	E	ⴄ	ე	e	5
Ⴅ	V	ⴅ	ვ	v	6
Ⴆ	Z	ⴆ	ზ	z	7
Ⴡ	Ē	ⴡ	ჱ	ē	8
Ⴇ	T′	ⴇ	თ	t′	9
Ⴈ	I	ⴈ	ი	i	10
Ⴉ	K	ⴉ	კ	k	20
Ⴊ	L	ⴊ	ლ	l	30
Ⴋ	M	ⴋ	მ	m	40
Ⴌ	N	ⴌ	ნ	n	50
Ⴢ	Y	ⴢ	ჲ	y	60
Ⴍ	O	ⴍ	ო	o	70
Ⴎ	P	ⴎ	პ	p	80
Ⴏ	Ž	ⴏ	ჟ	ž	90
Ⴐ	R	ⴐ	რ	r	100

(continued)

[4]Before the creation of the Unicode standard, a very large number of Georgian fonts, including *AcadNusx*, *LitNusx*, and others, employed an ASCII-based mapping, which was insufficient and awkward to use online if users were not able to find and install additional fonts for reading purposes.

Table 2.1 (continued)

Ⴑ	S	ⴑ	ს	s	200
Ⴒ	T	ⴒ	ტ	t	300
Ⴣ	W	ⴣ	ჳ	w	400
Ⴓ	U	ⴓ	უ	u	-
Ⴔ	P′	ⴔ	ფ	p′	500
Ⴕ	K′	ⴕ	ქ	k′	600
Ⴖ	Ġ	ⴖ	ღ	ġ	700
Ⴗ	Q	ⴗ	ყ	q	800
Ⴘ	Š	ⴘ	შ	š	900
Ⴙ	Č′	ⴙ	ჩ	č′	1000
Ⴚ	C′	ⴚ	ც	c′	2000
Ⴛ	Ż	ⴛ	ძ	ż	3000
Ⴜ	C	ⴜ	წ	c	4000
Ⴝ	Č	ⴝ	ჭ	č	5000
Ⴞ	X	ⴞ	ხ	x	6000
Ⴤ	X̣	ⴤ	ჴ	x̣	7000
Ⴟ	J	ⴟ	ჯ	j	8000
Ⴠ	H	ⴠ	ჰ	h	9000
Ⴥ	Ō	ⴥ	ჵ	ō	10000

[a]*Asomtavruli* and *Mkhedruli* scripts are represented in the Unicode Standard, Version 12.1, Range 10A0–10FF, see (Everson 1991–2019).
[b]Transliteration of Georgian alphabets associated with representation of Georgian characters by the characters of *Latin* script is not unique. There are different types of transliterations developed in different years and for different purposes, especially, ALA-LC: American Library Association – Library of Congress's Romanization table for Georgian language developed in 2011; ISO 9984:1996, BGN/PCGN romanization for Georgian, last confirmed in 2015; AP-CH: Aphridonidze-Chkhaidze's transliteration system developed by the Institute of Linguistics (Georgian Academy of Sciences) in 2004 etc.
[c]*Nuskhuri* script is represented in the Supplement to the Unicode Standard, Version 12.1 as well, Range 2D00–2D2F, see (Everson 1991–2019), where it is considered as the lowercase of the old ecclesiastical alphabet as opposed to Asomtavruli capitals.
[d]As it was mentioned above, *Mkhedruli* script is represented in the same chart with *Asomtavruli* Script, Range 10A0–10FF, but on the basis of the Proposal for the addition of Georgian characters to the UCS prepared by Everson et al. (2016), it was extended by so called *Mtavruli* letters as the upper-case pair to *Mkhedruli.*

manuscripts were written using the *Asomtavruli* and *Mkhedruli* scripts in such a way that the former served as the majuscule to the minuscule of its descendant.

The principal difference between the *Asomtavruli, Nuskhuri* and *Mkhedruli* scripts (in addition to the aforementioned differences) relates to the following characters: ჱ (he), ჲ (hie), ჳ (vic), ჴ (qari), ჵ (hoc), ჶ (fi) and უ̂ (non syllabic u), which have not formed part of the Modern Georgian alphabet since 1879,[5] although they are occasionally encountered in Modern Georgian texts.

2.2.2 *Phonology*

Overviews of the Georgian phonological system can be found in Akhvlediani (1949), Vogt (1961), Aronson (1997), Butskhrikidze (2001, 2002) and others. The phonemic inventory of Modern Georgian consists of 5 vowels and 28 consonants, to which the letters of the Modern Georgian alphabet correspond closely, and has changed little in comparison with Old Georgian; the main changes are the loss of semivowels, the merging of bilabial /w/ with labiodental /v/ and the convergence of velar /q/ with spirant /x/ (Vogt 1961; Butskhrikidze 2002 and others). Some of these features can still be found today in Georgian dialects.

2.2.2.1 Vowels

There are 5 vowels in Standard Modern Georgian, which can be characterized by the two parameters of position and openness. While Akhvlediani (1949) observes vowel lengthening before voiced fricatives, voiced stops and nasal sonants, length does not play a distinctive role within the vowel system of Standard Modern Georgian (Butskhrikidze 2002), although both length and umlaut have been identified as distinctive features in Georgian dialects. The Georgian vowel system can be represented as a triangle and is generally described as follows (Table 2.2):

Table 2.2 Georgian vowel system

IPA	Description
i	Front, near close, close
ɛ	Front, open-mid
a	Front, open
o	Back, close-mid
u	Back, close

One of the principal phonotactic restrictions identified in Standard Modern Georgian that two adjacent vowels are disallowed and result in so-called *hiatus*, as described by Butskhrikidze (2002). Exceptions to this rule are found in loanwords

[5] These letters were removed from the Modern Georgian alphabet as the result of a reform launched by the Society for the Spreading of Literacy among Georgians in 1879 based on the work of David Chubinashvili, who argued in *A Brief Grammar of Georgian* (Chubinashvili 1855) that the letters ჱ (he), ჲ (hie), ჴ (qari) and ჵ (hoe) were inserted into the Georgian alphabet only to correspond to numerical values, while ჳ (vie), ჶ (fi) and ჷ (non-syllabic û) were used only for the writing of loan words.

and in some compound words, as described by Uturgaidze (1976). *Hiatus* is resolved at the morpheme boundary by means of epenthesis of the sonant /v/, but is permitted at the boundary between a prefix and a stem, or between a prefix and another prefix, see (1).

(1) a. *ušno-∅*
ugly-SG.NOM
'ugly'

b. *da-a-ušno-v-a*
PV-PRV-ugly-3SGSBJ:AOR.IND
made smb. ugly'

All of these restrictions were present in Old Georgian as well, but with some exceptions with regard to loanwords chiefly from Greek and the representation of allophones with special characters for their representation in the alphabet. In Old Georgian, these allophones can be viewed as morphologically conditioned positional variants used at the end of the syllabic structure of a word (Shanidze 1976; Sarjveladze 1997). For instance, /i/ was represented by two alophones: [i] and [y]. The [y] was morphologically conditioned, and from the ninth century onward was gradually replaced by [i]. The main restriction on the use of [y] as opposed to [i] was that it could not appear before vowels, but only follow them. The following morphologically conditioned cases were attested:

- In the nominative case after stems ending in the vowels /a/, /o/, /u/ and, from the ninth century onward, occasionally after /e/ as opposed to /ē/, for instance (2–4)

(2) a. *cqaro-∅-y*
srping-SG.NOM
'spring'

b. *cqaro-∅-i*
srping-SG.NOM
'spring'

(3) a. *żma-∅-y*
brother-SG.NOM
'brother'

b. *żma-∅-i*
brother-SG.NOM
'brother'

(4) a. *ru-∅-y*
torrent-SG.NOM
'torrent'

b. *ru-∅-i*
torrent-SG.NOM
'torrent'

- In the genitive and instrumental cases at the end of non-syncopating stems (5–7)

(5) *cqaro-∅-ys*
spring-SG.GEN
'of spring'

(6) *żma-∅-ys*
brother-SG.GEN
'of brother'

(7) *ru-∅-ys*
torrent-SG.GEN
'of torrent'

- In the superlative degree of adjectives (8)

(8) a. *xup'ro-ys-i*
best-SUP-NOM
'best'

b. *xup'ro-is-i*
best-SUP-NOM
'best'

c. *up'ro-ys-i*
best-SUP-NOM
'best'

Very rarely, the use of /y/ was conditioned phonologically, as for example in *saydumloy* 'secret, mistery'.

/o/ was represented by two allophones: [o] and [ō]. The [ō] was used only in a form of interjection and, sometimes, for the transliteration of Greek -*ω*- in loanwords. Since 1879 it has been replaced in all cases with [o]. The frequent alternation between -*o*- (ⴍ) and -*u*- (ⴓ) encountered in Old Georgian texts is conditioned by their graphematic similarity rather than by any allophonic relationship.

/ɛi/ is a morphologically conditioned descending diphthong represented in the Georgian alphabet by the special characters Ⴡ (in *Asomtavruli*), ⴡ (in *Nuskhuri*) and ჱ (in *Mkhedruli*). From the ninth century onward, this diphthong was sometimes substituted with [e], sometimes with [ey] and sometimes with [eē]. The principal contexts in which it is found are:

- In the nominative case (9–10)

(9) a. *kldē-∅*
rock-SG.NOM
'rock'

b. *klde-y*
rock-SG.NOM
'rock'

c. *kldeē-∅*
rock-SG.NOM
'rock'

(10) a. *żē-∅*
son-SG.NOM
'son'
b. *że-y*
son-SG.NOM
'son'
c. *żeē-∅*
son-SG.NOM
'son'

- In the superlative degree of adjectives (11–12)

(11) a. *x-umjob-ēs-i*
3SGSBJ-good-SUP-NOM
'best'
b. *x-umjob-eys-i*
3SGSBJ-good-SUP-NOM
'best'
c. *umjob-ēs-i*
good-SUP-NOM
'best'
d. *umjob-es-i*
good-SUP-NOM
'best'

(12) a. *udid-ēs-i*
biggest-SUP-NOM
'biggest'
b. *udid-eys-i*
biggest-SUP-NOM
'biggest'
c. *udid-es-i*
biggest-SUP-NOM
'biggest'

- In some adverbs, such as *esrēt'*| *esreyt'* 'thus', *egrēt'* | *egreyt'* 'thus', etc.
- For the transliteration of Greek loanwords with diphthongs, for instance *israēli* 'Israel', *ierusalēmi* 'Jerusalem', etc.

In Old Georgian, non-syllabic /û/ (so-called *ubrjgu*), which stood in opposition to /u/, is not encountered word-initially, but is encountered in the stem between a consonant and a vowel (*t'ûali* 'eye', *sitqûay* 'word', etc.), between consonants (*t'k'ûmay* 'speaking', *mkûdari* 'dead', etc.) and following a consonant word-finally (*nażû* 'spruce', *t'agû* 'mouse', etc.).

From the ninth century onward, non-syllabic /û/ was partially substituted, initially by the bilabial spirant /w/ represented by Ⴣ (in Asomtavruli), ⴣ (in Nuskhuri) and ჳ (in Mkhedruli), and then by the consonant /v/, which appeared word-initially before a vowel (*vec'xli* 'silver coin', *varc'li* 'small boat', etc.) or a consonant (*vlineba* 'sustaining', *vrdoma* 'falling down', etc.), between vowels (*aġzaveba* 'blending', *aġmavali* ‘ascending’, etc.), between a vowel and a consonant (*bčevri* ‘elegant’, *gavrc‘oba* ‘spreading’, etc.) and in word-final position following a consonant (*gamoxatav* ‘you express’, *vklav* ‘I kill’, etc.) (Shanidze 1976; Sarjveladze 1997). The mergence of the spirant /w/ with labi-dental /v/ in Modern Georgian is the result of the aforementioned phonetic transformations (*nażû* → *nażw* → *nażvi* ‘spruce’, etc.).

The majority of vowel alternations in Georgian are morphologically conditioned as follows:

- Alternation in the nominal paradigm in the genitive, instrumental and adverbial cases: *a* → ∅ (13), *e* → ∅ (14), *o* → ∅ | *v* (15–16)

(13) a. *merc‘xal-∅-i*
swallow-SG-NOM
‘swallow’

b. *merc‘xl-∅-is*
swallow-SG-GEN
‘of the swallow’

c. *merc‘xl-∅-it‘*
swallow-SG-INS
‘with the swallow’

d. *merc‘xl-∅-ad*
swallow-SG-ADV
‘(in)to the swallow’

(14) a. *mgel-∅-i*
wolf-SG-NOM
‘wolf’

b. *mgl-∅-is*
wolf-SG-GEN
‘of the wolf’

(15) a. *limon-∅-i*
lemon-SG-NOM
‘lemon’

b. *limn-∅-is*
lemon-SG-GEN
‘of the lemon’

(16) a. *nior-∅-i*
garlic-SG-NOM
‘garlic’

b. *nivr-∅-is*[a]
garlic-SG-GEN
‘of the garlic’

[a]Substitution of the vowel *-o-* with *-v-* does not occur where it is followed by the bilabial sonant *-m-*

- Alternation in the verbal paradigm in the aorist: *e* → *i* (17)

(17) a. *grex-s*
twist-2SGSBJ:PRS.IND
'twists smth.'
b. *mo-grix-a*
PV-twist-3SGSBJ:AOR.IND
'twisted smth.'

There are no diphthongs in Modern Georgian, while Old Georgian is characterized by two types of diphthong: falling (descending) and rising (ascending), represetned by means of the phonemes /y/ and /û/:

/i/, which possessed two allophones, [i] and [y], actively participated in the formation of descending diphthongs and could be added to /a/, /o/, /u/ and /e/;

Non-syllabic /û/ (so-called *ubrjgu*) actively participated in the formation of ascending diphthongs and could be added to /a/, /e/ and /i/, which triggered the process of its substitution with /v/.

2.2.2.2 Consonants

There are 28 consonants in Modern Standard Georgian, which can be subdivided into stops, affricatives, fricatives, vibrants and laterals (Zgenti 1965–1956; Gamkrelidze and Machavariani 1965; Nebieridze 1974; Aronson 1997; Butskhrikidze 2002; Shosted 2006 and others) and characterized by manner and place of articulation as follows (Table 2.3):

Table 2.3 Georgian consonant system

		Bilabial/labial	Dental	Alveolar	Velar	Postvelar	Glottal
Nasal		m	n				
Stop	Voiced	b	d		g		
	Voiceless	p^h	t^h		k^h		
	Glottalised	p'	t'		k'	[q^h][a] q'	
Affricative	Voiced		d͡z	d͡ʒ			
	Voiceless		$\widehat{ts}^h$	$\widehat{tʃ}^h$			
	Glottalised		t͡s'	t͡ʃ'			
Fricative	Voiced	[w][b] v	z	ʒ		ʁ	
	Voiceless		s	ʃ		x	h
	Glottalised						
Vibrant				r			
Lateral				l			

[a]/q^h/ does not exist in the sound system of Modern Georgian, but still remains in Khevsurian dialect
[b]Non-syllabic /û/ does not exist in the sound system of Modern Georgian; it is generally substituted by /v/ or /u/

The major constraints of consonant phonotactics, which are already described in the academic literature (Akhvlediani 1949; Aronson 1997–1990 and others) and summarised in Butskhrikidze (2002), are as follows:

- No minimal word ends in consonant, and grammatical affixes with a final consonant which can be added to the end of a stem undergo the phonetic process of devoicing word-finally;
- The consonants of Modern Standard Georgian can be subdivided into those which occur in both lexical and grammatical morphemes: /b/, /tʰ/, /d/, /g/, /k'/, /tsʰ/, /s/, /ʁ/, /v/, /m/, /l/, /r/, /n/ and those in which occur in lexical morphemes only: /p/, /p'/, /t'/, /k/, /t͡ʃʰ/, /d͡ʒ/, /t͡s'/, /t͡ʃ'/, /j/, /ʃ/, /š/, /ʒ/, /q/, /x/, /h/. The inflectional affixes feature only the following consonants: /v/, /m/, /n/, /s/, /t/, /d/, /g/, /b/;
- The distribution patterns of grammatical affixes are as follows: (1) word-initial consonants: /v/, /m/, /n/, /s/, /d/, /g/; (2) word-internal consonants: /v/, /m/, /n/, /l/, /r/, /n/, /t'/, /d/, /g/, /b/, /k/, /ʁ/; (3) word-final consonants: /v/, /m/, /n/, /s/, /d/, /t'/, /b/, /tsʰ/;
- While the following sequences of adjacent alveolar consonants are not permitted: /*tʃ/, /*dd͡ʒ/, /*dt͡sʰ/, etc., the reverse sequences are permitted: /ʃt/, /d͡ʒd/, /t͡sʰd/ etc.;
- /v/ before a voiceless consonant is substituted with the labiodental fricative /f/ in spoken Georgian. In Old Georgian manuscripts and published material, the allophone [f] is sometimes represented using the character -*φ*-, particularly in loanwords from Greek and Russian;
- The occurrence of /v/ as a part of the thematic suffix in verbal forms gives rise to a process of metathesis in accordance with the constraint that the stem should end in a sonant and should not begin with a labial (18)

(18) a. *kit'xva-∅*
reading-SG.NOM
'reading'

b. *h-kit'x-av-s*
2SGIOBJ-ask-TS-3SGSBJ:FUT.IND
'will ask smb.'

The process of metathesis has played an active role in the formation of Georgian numerals; for instance, *rûa* 'eight' → *at'rûameti* → *at'ûrameti* || *at'vrameti* → *t'vrameti* 'eighteen', etc.

- /v/ may not occur in combination with bilabial consonants within the stem or on the boundary between stem and suffix. Such combinations trigger the phonetic process of *v*-loss (19)

(19) a. *u-t'k'v-am-s*
PRV.3IOBJ-said-TS-1SGSBJ:PLUP
'said smth'

b. *t'k'ma-∅*
saying-SG.NOM
'saying, speaking'

This sequence is however permitted at the boundary between prefix and stem (20)

(20) *v-mogzaur-ob*
1SGSBJ-travel-TS:PRS.IND
'I travel'

- The occurrence of sonants in stem-final positions, as for example in /al/, /ar/, /an/, /am/, /el/, /er/, /en/, /em/, /ol/, /or/, /on/, often gives rise to vowel-deletion processes: principally, syncope in nominal paradigms (21)

(21) a. *ked**e**l-i*
wall-SG.NOM
'wall'
b. *kedl-is*
wall-SG.GEN
'of the wall'

Syncope in verbal paradigms occurs more rarely (22)

(22) a. *še-i-pq**a**r-i*
PV.PFV-PRV.3OBJ-seize-TS:AOR.IMP
'seizes/grabbed smth'
b. *še-i-pqr-ob-s*
PV.PFV-PRV.3OBJ-seize-TS:FUT.IND
'will seize/grab smth.'

- Although voiceless glottal (sometimes referred to as laryngeal) /h/ tends to occur in word-initial position, tendencies in Modern Georgian are leading toward its disappearance.

The majority of the processes described above can be found in Old, Middle and Modern Georgian. As for possible combinations between consonants and the syllablic structure of the Georgian word, while separate mention should be made of the so-called 'system of consonant clusters', consonant clusters should also be considered with regard to the syllabic structure of the Georgian word, taking into consideration its initial and final positions.

2.2.2.3 Syllable Structure and Consonant Clusters

Georgian word structure is closely connected to two types of representation: morphological and lexical, meaning that the structure of the Georgian word reflects a distinction between lexical morphemes (*l-morphemes*) and functional morphemes (*f-morphemes*). Following the principles described by Harley and Noyer (2000), *l-morphemes* are the terminal nodes of featureless roots, whereas *f-morphemes* are feature-oriented nodes that include zero elements.

The structure of a word in Georgian can be as follows: (a) pure stem belonging to the *l-morpheme* type; (b) stem with appropriate affixes belonging to the *f-morpheme* type. A stem alone can act as an independent so-called 'free' morpheme, while affixes require some conditions to be attached to a stem and can be considered bound morphemes. The structure of the stem and of affixes should be determined prior to the description of word structure and the generation of paradigms, because the use of distinctive suffixes, syllable structure, and the initial and final positions of characters in the stem allow us to identify possible nouns, adjectives, verbs and foreign words in the text (if the text includes words not represented in the lexicon).

The historical structure of the Georgian stem can be described following Gamkrelidze and Machavariani (1965), Aronson (1997) and others in terms of C- and CV(R)C- structure, where C is a consonant, a consonant with *-v-*, a harmonic cluster or a harmonic cluster with *-v-*, a non-harmonic cluster; V is a vowel; and R a sonant. Prefixes are considered to have CV- structure, while suffixes are considered to have -V(C) structure.

Modern Georgian includes many stems consisting of consonant + vowel (CV) or consonant + vowel + consonant (CVC) (Zgenti 1956; Ertelishvili 1970, 1980 and others); while the first stem type consists of vowel-final structures like CV, CCV, CCCV, etc., the second CVC type requires vowel-initial affixes to create disyllabic structures of type CVCV. The maximum number of consonants per root varies from one to six, and the specific sequence of these consonants is considered a part of a consonant cluster's – a syllabic constituent's – determining phonotactic constraints.

There are two types of harmonic (decessive) cluster: Type A, which consists of two consonants whereby the second is a velar consonant, and Type B, which consists of two consonants whereby the second is a postvelar consonant (Table 2.4):

Table 2.4 Consonant clusters

Type A (C + velar)			Type B (C + postvelar)		
bg	pʰkʰ	p'k	bʁ	pʰχ	p'q'
dg	tʰkʰ	t'k	dʁ	tʰχ	t'q'
dzg	tsʰkʰ	ts'k	dzʁ	tsʰχ	ts'q'
dʒg	tʃʰkʰ	tʃ'k	dʒʁ	tʃʰχ	tʃ'q'

As described in (Vogt 1961; Aronson 1997; McCoy 1999; Kehrein 2002), non-harmonic (accessive) clusters, which provide back to front sequences of phonemes, occur primarily in morpheme-initial position: *t'be* 'dough', *gdeba* 'throwing', etc.

Following Zgenti (1956), Uturgaidze (1976), Butskhrikidze (2002) and others, the possible combinations of consonants at stem-initial and final positions can be summarised as follows:

- Clusters found in stem-initial position only: /t'b/, /k'b/, /χb/, /tʰb/, /gd/, /χd/, /gdz/;
- Clusters found both in stem-initial and in stem-final positions: (a) harmonic clusters: /bʁ/, /dʁ/, /zʁ/, /ʒʁ/, /pʰχ/, /sχ/, /ʃχ/, /ts'q'/, /tʃ'q'/; (b) fricatives + sonants: /zv/, /zr/, /zl/, /pʰr/, /tʰr/, /sl/, /ʃl/, /ʒr/, /ʃn/, /zn/, /χl/, /χr/, /ʁl/, /ʁr/;
- Clusters used neither in stem-initial, nor in stem-final positions: /zb/, /χb/, /q'p'/, /ʒb/, /rpʰ/, /rʒ/, /lʒ/, /lʃ/, /ldz/.

This information on clusters allow us to constrain some issues with regards to the analyzer's functionality concerning additional guessers of nominal and verbal paradigms, if stem structure has to be defined prior the generation of inflectional forms for words, which are not represented in the lexicon of the transducer, as shown in Fig. 2.2.

```
define ST [b|p‘|p|d|t‘|t|g|k‘|k|q|x] ;   ! Stops
define AF [ż|c‘|c|j|č‘|č] ;              ! Affricates
define FR [z|s|ž|š|ġ|x|h] ;              ! Fricatives
define SN [m|n|r|l|v|w|f] ;              ! Sonants
define V [a|e|o|u|i|ē|y|ō] ;             ! Vowels

# Allow up to 2 consecutive consonants in accordance
with schemes represented by Butskhrikidze (2002) for
stem initial positions
define ISEQ2 [ [ ST ST | ST AF | ST FR | ST SN | AF ST
| AF FR | AF SN | FR ST | FR AF | FR FR | FR SN | SN ST
| SN AF | SN FR | SN SN ] ] ;

# Allow up to 3 consecutive consonants
define ISEQ3 [ [ ST ST ST | ST AF ST | ST FR SN | ST SN
ST | ST SN AF | ST SN SN | AF ST SN | AF FR SN | AF SN
ST | AF SN AF | AF SN FR | AF SN SN | FR ST SN | FR AF
SN | FR FR SN | FR SN ST | FR SN AF | FR SN FR | FR SN
SN | SN ST SN | SN AF SN | SN AF FR | SN FR SN | SN SN
AF ] ] ;

# Allow up to 4 consecutive consonants
define ISEQ4 [ [ ST ST SN SN | ST FR FR SN | ST FR SN
SN | ST SN ST FR | ST SN ST SN | ST SN AF FR | ST SN AF
SN | AF FR SN ST | AF FR SN SN | AF SN ST SN | FR FR SN
SN | FR SN AF SN | FR SN FR SN | SN ST FR SN | SN AF FR
SN | SN FR SN SN ] ] ;

# Allow up to 5 consecutive consonants
define ISEQ5 [ [ AF SN SN ST SN ] ] ;

# Allow up to 6 consecutive consonants
define ISEQ6 [ [ST SN AF ST SN SN] ] ;

# Define monosyllabic nominal stems ended with eliding
vowels in accordance with Ertelishvili (1970)
Define N4 [ [ ISEQ2 | ISEQ3 | ISEQ4 | ISEQ5 | ISEQ6 ] [
a | e ] %+Guess%+N:0 ] ;

# Define monosyllabic nominal stems ending with vowels
Define N5 [ [ ISEQ2 | ISEQ3 | ISEQ4 | ISEQ5 | ISEQ6 ] [
o | u ] %+Guess%+N:0 ] ;

read regex [ N4 | N5 ] ;
```

Fig. 2.2 Formation of syllables and determination of monosyllabic nominal stems

Despite the aforementioned, the determination of a monosyllabic stem is insufficient because of the nature of minimal word structure in Georgian. As described in (Broselow 1982; McCarthy et al. 1986/1996), a minimal word is determined on the basis of the prosodic hierarchy and foot binary (segment – stem + (affix) – word). Every lexical word corresponds to a phonological word, which contains at least one foot, and every foot must be bimoraic or disyllabic. As proved by Butskhrikidze (2002), in Georgian the minimal word is disyllabic and consonant sequences are restricted to the stem domain in the form of harmonic clusters, sequences of C + *v* and sequences of *s* + fricative. All of these possibilities for identifying the Georgian stem must be additionally tested and evaluated from a computational point of view, however.

2.2.3 Word Structure

It is well known that languages differ with regards to the morphological processes affecting word formation. Some languages reveal a full correspondence between a word and its meaning and do not need any additional features to show this correspondence, while in others, words consist of several morphemes which have different meanings, and it is the sum of these morphemes that creates firstly the structure and secondly the meaning of a word. Following (Comrie 1989; Harris et al. 2006 and others), languages can be classified on this basis as fusional (flectional or inflecting); that is, using a single inflectional morpheme to express different features; agglutinating – that is, made up of morphemes, each of which represents only one grammatical category; and isolating languages, which are considered to be languages without morphology. What, then, is the principal structure of the Georgian word, and which parts of this structure must be considered with respect to the morphological analysis of Georgian by computer?

Georgian can be viewed as a "combined-type" language that does not fit well into any of the types described above. Some Georgian morphemes are of the agglutinating type (23), while others are of the fusional type (24). This combined type may also be referred to as "quasi-polysynthetic" – a term used by (Wier 2011a, 2011b) to identify a language with a great number of possible word-formation strategies such as affixation, modification and stem compounding. Comparing the features characterizing fusional, agglutinating types of languages (Iacobini 2006) with the structure of Georgian reveals both structures in Georgian characteristic of agglutinating languages – that is, affixes, morpheme-by-morpheme correspondence, a tendency for monosyllabism, nouns marked for number and case, an absence of nouns marked for gender, and the synthetic expression of comparison on adjectives; and structures in Georgian characteristic of fusional languages, including affixes, clear distinctions between parts of speech (PoS), and the presence of inflectional classes in verbs.

Word structure consists of so-called 'independent morphemes', which include the aforementioned stem, and bound morphemes, which include the affixes which attach to the stem. Some affixes can be attached to a nominal stem and participate in the formation of a nominal paradigm, while others attach to a verbal stem only and participate in the formation of a verbal paradigm.

(23) *k'al-eb-ma*
woman-PL-ERG
'women'

(24) *saxl-∅=ši*
house-SG=in.DAT
'in the house'

Affixation (25) is used in Georgian for the expression of grammatical functions and for the production of new grammatical classes, modification (26), for the expression of grammatical functions, and compounding (27), for the formation of 'compounding lexemes'.

(25) a. *kac'-∅-ma*
man-SG-ERG
'man'

b. *kac'-ur-∅-i*
manly-SG-NOM
'manly'

(26) a. *rże-∅*
milk-SG.NOM
'milk'

b. *rż-∅-is*
milk-SG-GEN
'of milk'

(27) a. *enat'mec'niereba-∅*
linguistics-SG-NOM
'linguistics'

b. *ena-t'-mec'niereba-∅*
language-PL+science-SG.NOM
'linguistics'

Well known affix types in Georgian include: (1) prefixes attaching to the beginning of the stem (28) or to the beginning of other prefixes (29), suffixes attaching to the end of the stem or to the end of other prefixes (29), (2) infixes which are inserted within the body of the stem (30) and (3) circumfixes consisting of two affixes: one placed at the beginning and the other at the end of the stem (31).

(28) Inflectional prefixes: *cer-s* ‘he writes smth.’ → *u-cer-s* ‘he writes smth. to smb.’ → *mi-s-cer-s* ‘he will write smth. to smb.’, etc.

a. *cer-s*
write-3SGSBJ:PRS.IND
‘he writes smth.’

b. *u-cer-s*
PRV.3IOBJ-write-3SGSBJ:PRS.IND
‘he writes smth. to smb.’

c. *mi-s-cer-s*
PV.PFV-3SGIOBJ-write-3SGSBJ:FUT.IND
‘he will write smth. to smb.’

Derivational prefixes: *cer-s* ‘he writes smth.’ → *na-cer-∅-i* ‘piece of writing’, etc.

d. *na-cer-∅-i*
piece_of_writing-SG-NOM
‘piece of writing’

(29) Inflectional suffixes: *a-c‘xad-eb-s* ‘he declares smth.’ → *gamo-a-c‘xad-a* ‘he has declared smth.’, etc.

a. *a-c‘xad-eb-s*
PRV-declare-TS-3SGSBJ:PRS.IND
‘he declares smth.’

b. *gamo-a-c‘xad-a*
PV.PFV-PRV-declare-3SGSBJ:AOR.IND
‘he has declared smth.’

Derivational suffixes: *k‘al-∅-i* ‘woman’ > *k‘al-ur-∅-i* ‘womanly’, etc.

c. *k‘al-∅-i*
woman-SG-NOM
‘woman’

d. *k‘al-ur-∅-i*
womanly-SG-NOM
‘womanly’

(30) Derivational infixes: *xnav-s* ‘ploughs smth.’ → *x<v>na-∅* ‘ploughing’, etc.

a. *xnav-s*
plough-3SGSBJ:PRS.IND
‘ploughs smth.’

b. *x<v>na-∅*
ploughing-SG.NOM
‘ploughing’

(31) Inflectional circumfixes: *lamaz-∅-i* 'beautiful' → *u>lamaz<es-∅-i* 'most beautiful', etc.

a. *lamaz-∅-i*
beautiful-SG-NOM
'beautiful'

b. *u>lamaz<es-∅-i*
DIM>declare<DIM-SG-NOM
'most beautiful'

Derivational circumfixes: *k'alak'-∅-i* 'city'→ *mo>k'alak'<e-∅* 'citizen', etc.

c. *k'alak'-∅-i*
city-SG-NOM
'city'

d. *mo>k'alak'<e*
citizen-SG.NOM
'citizen'

All of these affix types are described in detail in the academic literature (Martirosov 1958; Manjgaladze 1963; Glonti 1964; Pochkhua 1974; Shinjiashvili 1984; Aronson 1969, 1989 and others). They are used to express different functions, including the formation of different lexemes. While the inflectional affixes can be considered a closed class of morphemes and can be easily constrained in a finite-state calculus, the quantity of derivational affixes is large and their formation models cannot be described precisely, although, generally speaking, they are constrained by their meaning; form example, diminutive forms (32), possessive forms (33), and so on.

(32) *c'xen-uk-a* 'little horse' as opposed to *c'xen-i* 'horse', *mam-ik-o* 'daddy' as opposed to *mama-∅* 'father', etc.

a. *c'xen-uk-a*
horse<DIM>:SG.NOM
'little horse'

b. *c'xen-i*
horse-SG.NOM
'horse'

c. *mam-ik-o*
father<DIM>:SG.NOM
'daddy'

d. *mama-∅*
father-SG.NOM
'father'

(33) *c'xen-osan-i* 'with horse', *zec'-ier-i* 'heavenly', etc.

a. *c'xen-osan-i*
horse-POSS-SG.NOM
'with horse'

b. *zec'-ier-i*
heaven-POSS-SG.NOM
'heavenly'

The criteria for this distinction, which is described in Anderson (1992), Aronoff (1994), Booij (2006) and others, are generally satisfied by the structure of Georgian as follows: (a) derivation is optional, while inflection is obligatory; (b) derivation may change the PoS of initial forms, while inflection cannot; (c) inflection is always associated with grammatical paradigms.

The following peculiarities of Georgian inflectional affixation should also be mentioned:

(a) 'portmanteau' morphs, where an affix conveys several grammatical features and there is no one-to-one correspondence between a grammatical feature and its representation (34).

(34) *gv-cer-s*
1PLOBJ-write-3SGSBJ:PRS.IND
's/he is writing us smth.'

(b) 'zero' morphs, where an affix is expected to exist but does not; for instance, a zero morph representing singular forms in nominals, which is identified only to preserve parallelism between number forms (35).

(35) a. *saxl-∅-i*
house-SG-NOM
'house'

b. *saxl-eb-i*
house-PL-NOM
'houses'

(c) 'empty' morphs with no content, whereby an affix occurs which does not represent any grammatical feature. In the majority of cases, the existence of this type of morph is connected to the existence of functional morphs in Old Georgian and their substitution with 'empty' ones in Modern Georgian (36).

(36) Modern Georgian:
a. *s-żin-av-s*
PV-sleep-TS-3SGSBJ:PRS.IND
'he is sleeping'

Old Georgian:
b. *s-żin-av-s*
3SGOBJ-sleep-TS-3SGSBJ:PRS.IND
'he is sleeping'

These types of morphs have a great influence on the formation of morphosyntactic paradigms and increase the number of generated forms. As a result, the use of inflectional and derivational affixes for the formation of word structure leads to a great number of possible forms that can be generated from only one noun or verb, using up to three derivational morphemes supplemented by inflectional affixes: on average, a Georgian noun root without derivational affixes generates approximately 3750 units per paradigm, while a verb root generates approximately 33,260 units per subject and object paradigm. In fact, a verb root can generate about one and a half million different word forms, the majority of which are rarely used in spoken Georgian and are semantically constrained. This results in an enormous lexicon and poses numerous challenges for the development of resources for the Georgian language.

Each of the affixes discussed adds additional material to the word stem, which can in addition undergo several changes, including the following:

- Reduplication as a part of lexical derivation (Moravcsik 1978; Marantz 1982) doubles part of a word and is used to create new words, including verb-to-noun (37) and noun-to-verb derivation (38)

(37) *kiv-i-s* 'shrieks' → *kiv+kiv-∅-i* 'noise made by an eagle, crake, duck, etc.'

a. *kiv-i-s*
shriek-PRS.IND-3SGSBJ
'shrieks'

b. *kiv+kiv-∅-i*
shriek+shriek-SG-NOM
'noise made by an eagle, crake, duck, etc.'

(38) *kiv+kiv-∅-i* 'noise made by an eagle, crake, duck, etc.' → *kiv+kiv-i-s* 'gobbles like a turkey'

a. *kiv~kiv-∅-i*
shriek+shriek-SG-NOM
'noise made by an eagle, crake, duck, etc.'

b. *kiv~kiv-i-s*
shriek+shriek-PRS.IND-3SGSBJ
'gobbles like a turkey'

- Ablaut (apophony), or the internal modification of a stem vowel, is found in the vocalic alternation *e* > *i* in the formation of the aorist in the verbal paradigm. Such cases are not frequent and are not recoverable elsewhere in the verbal paradigm, so that ablaut is an additional to other markers of aorist (39).

(39) a. *drek-s*
bend-3SGSBJ:PRS.IND
'bends smth.'

b. *drik-a*
bend-3SGSBJ:AOR.IND
'bent smth.'

- Midclipping (syncope) triggers deletion of the vowels *-a-*, *-e-* and *-o-* in the stem. This process takes place in nominals ending with the sonants *-l-*, *-r-*, *-m-* and *-n-* in the genitive, instrumental and adverbial cases in singular and in all cases in plural (40–42), although exceptions to this rule exist (43).

(40) a. *kalam-∅-i*
pen-SG-NOM
'pen'

b. *kalm-∅-is*
pen-SG-GEN
'of the pen'

c. *kalm-eb-is*
pen-PL-GEN
'of the pens'

(41) a. *kedel-∅-i*
wall-SG-NOM
'wall'
b. *kedl-∅-it'*
wall-SG-INS
'with the wall'
c. *kedl-eb-it'*
wall-PL-INS
'with the walls'

(42) a. *p'ot'ol-∅-i*
leaf-SG-NOM
'leaf'
b. *p'ot'l-∅-ad*
leaf-SG-ADV
'to the leaf'
c. *p'ot'l-eb-ad*
leaf-PL-ADV
'to the leaves'

(43) a. *bal-i*
wild_cherry-SG-NOM
'wild cherry'
b. *bal-is*
wild_cherry-SG-GEN
'of the wild cherry'

- Truncation (clipping) (Mester 1990) causes deletion of the vowels *-a-* and *-e-* stem-finally. Like syncope, truncation is encountered very frequently in the nominal system in the genitive and instrumental cases (44–45). Where words end in two sonant-final syllables, syncope and truncation are triggered simultaneously (46).

(44) a. *mze-∅*
sun-SG.NOM
'sun'
b. *mz-∅-is*
sun-SG.GEN
'of the sun'
c. *mz-∅-it'*
sun-SG.INS
'with the sun'

(45) a. *deda-∅*
mother-SG.NOM
'mother'
b. *ded-∅-is*
mother-SG.GEN
'of the mother'
c. *ded-∅-it'*
mother-SG.INS
'with the mother'

(46) a. *pepela-∅*
mother-SG.NOM
'butterfly'
b. *pepl-∅-is*
mother-SG.GEN
'of the butterfly'
c. *pepl-∅-it'*
mother-SG.INS
'with the butterfly'
d. *pepla-d*
mother-SG.ADV
'(in)to the butterfly'

- Stem suppletion reflects a relation between grammatically similar, but phonologically different forms and is used to fill gaps in the verbal paradigm. Stem suppletion is a highly irregular process (47).

(47) a. *e-ubn-eb-a*
PRV-say-TS-3SGSBJ:PRS.IND
'says smth. to smb.'
b. *e-tqv-i-s*
PRV-say-TS-3SGSBJ:FUT.IND
'will say smth. to smb.'
c. *u-t'xr-a*
PRV-say-3SGSBJ:AOR.IND
'said smth. to smb.'
d. *u-t'k'v-am-s*
PRV-say-3SGSBJ:PF.IND
'apparently says smth. to smb.'

The process of word-formation by the compounding of two or more stems (Bauer 2006) should also be mentioned. In Georgian this process forms part of lexical derivation and does not affect the formation of inflectional paradigms. A compound stem behaves like a single stem (48).

(48) a. *t'avis+up'leba-∅*
of_head+right-SG.NOM
'freedom'
b. *c'xvir+pir+dasisxlianebul-i*
nose+mouth+bloodied-SG.NOM
'with a face covered in blood'

2.3 Morphosyntax

The theoretical framework followed in this section has its basis in construction-dependent morphology (Gurevich 2006b; Booij 2010 and others), and in construction grammar (CxG) developed by Lakoff (1987), Kay and Fillmore (1999), Kay

(2002) and others, which determines 'form and function pairings' and represents a return in some sense to a 'taxonomic' approach to grammatical analysis. The theory of construction morphology is based on the assumption that the mapping between form, meaning and function is expressed in terms of words and schemes which form part of the lexicon. At the same time, sets of words represent paradigmatic relations, and each construction is associated with a concrete meaning. Only those morphosyntactic aspects of this approach will be considered which are crucial for understanding the data for the purpose of their representation in the analyzer, paying special attention to constraints on form and interpretation which depend on the grammatical constructions and their internal complexity.

The peculiarities described in the previous section make it possible to subdivide Georgian morphology into two parts: derivational and inflectional. In all cases, the derivational and inflectional peculiarities of morphological items depend on their semantic correspondence with the root. Derivation, which occurs in the lexicon, concerns the formation of new types of words; that is, the substitution of one class of a word with another, and the generation of open classes of items, for example adjectives from nouns (49) or verbal nouns from verbs (50), while inflection, which is a component of syntax, concerns the generation of concrete paradigms by means of concrete affixes within pre-determined classes and the triggering of concrete phonological processes by the addition of morphosyntactic features to those features already represented in an open class of items.

(49) *c'xen-∅-i* 'horse', *c'xen-ian-∅-i* 'horse owner, with a horse', etc.
(50) *xat-av-s* 'paints', *m-xat-var-∅-i* 'painter', *da-xat-ul-∅-i* 'painted', etc.

In the majority of languages, causatives are lexical, morphological, or syntactic in type. Georgian causatives can be considered to belong to the morphological and syntactic types, because they are expressed by special morphologically-derived causation markers and affect the argument structure of the verb (51).

(51) a. *a-cer-s*
PRV-write-3SGSBJ:PRS.IND
'he/she writes smth. on smth.'
b. *a-cer-in-eb-s*
PRV-write-CAUS-TS-3SGSBJ:PRS.IND
'he/she forces smb. to write smth.'

Inflectional morphology is always constrained by a closed class of affixes and highly strict paradigm formation rules. Paradigm formation rules are closely connected to word formation rules as described by Sproat (1992), which limit affix attachment to hosts on the basis first of phonological and then syntactic and semantic restrictions, and to the understanding of paradigm function morphology rules stated by Stump (2001, 2002) and Zwicky (1985a, 1985b–1990), which assumes linking of cells between syntactic and morphological paradigms.

The Georgian word-class system is subdivided into nine individual elements used to provide mapping between the meaning and the syntactic function of a word. The existing nine PoS-es are divided into open and closed classes of items:

- Open classes of items can easily be supplemented with new members to refer to recently created items in a process which is constant;

- By contrast, closed classes of items acquire new members very rarely and consist of strictly defined words.

Nouns, adjectives, verbs and adverbs belong to the open class of items. New members can easily be added to these PoS-es via derivational processes or borrowings from other languages. The adaptation and incorporation of foreign words and abbreviations from other languages with or without their translation is very frequent in Modern Georgian; while loan words were generally introduced into Old and Middle Georgian under the influence of Persian, Arabic, Greek and Turkish, of the majority have been introduced into Modern Georgian under the influence of Russian and English. Formation principles and tests for foreign borrowings are addressed in the literature (Danelia 1975; Amiridze 2018; Amiridze et al. 2019 and others); it can be said in summary that foreign words in Georgian are of two types:

(a) Stems that are borrowed from a foreign language preserving the alphabet of the donor language;
(b) Stems that are borrowed from a foreign language without preserving the alphabet of the donor language.

While stems of the first type remain unchanged, stems of the second type fully conform to the inflectional and derivational morphology of Georgian and participate in the formation of nominal or verbal paradigms (52).

(52) a. *ZED-ma*
ZED-SG.ERG
'ZED'

b. *p'asilitator-Ø-i*
facilitator-SG-NOM
'facilitator'

c. *m-i-laik'-eb-s*
1SGIOBJ-PRV.RFL-like-TS-3SGSBJ:PRS.IND
'he likes my post'

Although abbreviations generally make up the majority of so-called 'graphic shortenings' (Lopez Rua 2006), which in the majority of languages do not require additional morphological description with regard to PoS and morphological categories, in Georgian, abbreviations follow the principles of foreign word formation mentioned previously, appearing in the text like any other borrowings and behaving accordingly (53), or like any other original Georgian words (54).

(53) *gaero-Ø* 'United Nations Organization, UNO'
(54) *ix. nax.* 'see drawing'

Mention should also be made of the frequent use in Old Georgian texts of the titlo diacritic specifically for the marking of abbreviated words. The use of this diacritic in Old Georgian corresponds closely to the general rules of scribal abbreviations followed not only in Georgian manuscripts, but also in the majority of Medieval manuscripts worldwide, which employ the following strategies:

- Suspension, whereby only the first part of a word is written and the final part is replaced with a diacritic mark. Although suspension is not attested in the majority of Old Georgian Manuscripts, the Kala-Boinisi inscriptions are viewed as an exception (Danelia and Sarjveladze 1997);
- Contraction, whereby the middle part of a word is omitted; in its 'pure' form only the initial and final letters of the word are present, while 'impure' contractions feature one or more letters in the middle part. In *the Corpus of Georgian Chronicles* (Doborjginidze et al. 2014) we encounter both types of contraction implemented in different ways depending on the context (55–56).

(55) a. *r̅i̅* for *romeli*
which:SG.NOM
'which'
b. *q̅i̅* for *qoveli*
every:SG.NOM
'every'

(56) a. *k̅q̅n-s-a* for *k'ueqansa*
Country-SG.DAT-EMPH
'which'
b. *s̅p̅'l̅v̅-i* for *sap'lavi*
grave-SG.NOM
'every'

In Greek Manuscripts, abbreviations of this kind are generally encountered in the nomina sacra.

- Truncation, whereby only the first letter of the word is written, while its other letters are substituted by a titlo diacritic. In Old Georgian texts this kind of abbreviation is very common (57).

(57) r̅ for *rom* 'for, because', x̅ for *xolo* 'but', etc.

The contracted forms of scribal abbrevations follow the formation rules of open class items, while suspended and truncated forms belong to the closed class. The closed class includes numerals, pronouns, conjunctions, particles, postpositions and interjections. These PoS-es can be simply listed in the form used to represent them in dictionaries and undergo changes in accordance with inflectional rules appropriate to their PoS; numerals and pronouns, for example, follow the general inflectional rules of the nominal paradigm.

The inflectional morphology of Georgian reflects the following categories:

(a) Number: singular, plural;
(b) Case: nominative, ergative[6], dative, genitive, instrumental, adverbial and vocative for the Modern Georgian paradigm and, additionally, absolute for the Old Georgian paradigm;
(c) Degree: diminutive, positive, comparative, superlative;

[6] Referred to as the narrative in (Gurevich 2006b; Wier 2011a, 2011b and others).

(d) Person: first, second, third;
(e) TAM series, in which the following are represented:

- Tense: present indicative, imperfect indicative, present subjunctive, future indicative, future conditional, future subjunctive, aorist indicative, aorist subjunctive, aorist imperative, perfect indicative, pluperfect, perfect subjunctive;
- Aspect: perfective, imperfective;
- Mood: indicative, conditional, subjunctive, imperative;

(f) Voice (diathesis)[7]: active, autoactive, inactive (inversial active), passive, autopassive (mediopassive);
(g) Agreement[8]: subject, direct object and indirect object.

The rules of derivational morphology are also taken into consideration with respect to the formation of numerals with the purpose of simplifying the generation of cardinal and ordinal numerals. The aforementioned information can be summarised as follows (Table 2.5):

Table 2.5 Type of stems, processes and features

PoS	Types of stems	Processes	Features
Noun	Consonant-final, vowel-final	Syncope, truncation	Case Number
Adjective	Consonant-final, vowel-final	Syncope, truncation	Degree Case Number
Verb	Consonant-final, vowel-final	Ablaut, suppletion (rarely)	TAM Voice Agreement Number Person
Pronoun	Consonant-final, vowel-final	Syncope, truncation	Case Number Person
Numeral	Consonant-final, vowel-final	Truncation	Case
Conjunction	Consonant-final, vowel-final		
Particle	Consonant-final, vowel-final		
Postposition	Consonant-final, vowel-final		Case
Interjection	Consonant-final, vowel-final		

[7] The traditional approach adopted by the majority of Georgian grammarians (Gogolashvili et al. 2011, Wier 2011a, 2011b and others) distinguishes three voices: active, passive and middle. In this context, Georgian grammars define voice as a grammatical category described for monopersonal verb systems and commonly studied in European languages.

[8] Generally, subject-object agreement is considered a part of syntax, but the existence of concrete morphological markers for this category compels us to describe it as a part of inflectional morphology. Subject-object agreement in Georgian can be considered an interplay between morphological and syntactic aspects with concrete morphological markers affecting syntactic relations.

In addition to the PoS-es discussed above, punctuation marks should be mentioned. Punctuation is used to disambiguate the meaning of sentences, but not the morphological structure of a word. Taking into account that punctuation rules in Georgian have changed over time and that Modern Georgian employs a variety of punctuation symbols, these are worth of describing from the point of view of computer processing.

2.3.1 Noun Inflection

Nouns, which refer to things, persons etc., belong to the open class of items and can be classified in various ways. In Georgian nouns are subdivided into proper and common nouns, both of which can be inflected for case and number (Shanidze 1973; Tuite 1998–1984; Hewitt 1995 and others). While the distribution into proper and common nouns is purely semantic, in contrast to common nouns, proper nouns form plural forms rarely (Abesadze 1956). A semantic distinction can likewise be drawn between animate and inanimate common nouns (Comrie 1989); although the category of animacy does not have special morphological markers in Georgian, it affects verbal number agreement at the syntactic level, in that plural number agreement occurs obligatorily in the case of animate nominals bearing the *-eb-*, *-n-* and *-t'-* plural markers and very rarely in the case of inanimate NPs bearing the *-eb-* marker (see Sect. 2.3.6.3).

Case and number are the most important and morphologically specified characteristics of the Georgian nominals. These serve chiefly to indicate the relationship of a noun to a verb, to an adjective, or to other types of attributes. In the singular, case and number are represented by a combination of an empty morph occupying the slot for number followed by the case marker. This combination involves changes at the boundary between a vowel-final stem and affixes.

Nominal inflection in Georgian follows the scheme: type → number markers → case markers and/or clitics [postpositions] → extension vowel → clitics [auxiliary verb, markers of indirect speech]. In Modern Georgian the maximum possible number of slots is nine (Vogt 1971; Shanidze 1973; Hewitt 1995; Boeder 2005 and others); these consist of the following units (Table 2.6):

Table 2.6 Distribution of slots of noun frame in Modern Georgian

0	1	2	3	4	5	6	7	8
Root (R)	Number marker (Nbr)	Case marker (Case)	Extension vowel (Ext)	Post-position (Posp)	Extension vowel (Ext)	Particle (Ptl)	Auxiliary verb (Aux)	Indirect Speech marker (IS)
	eb	*i*	*a*	*vit'*	*a*	*c'*	*a*	*met'k'i*
	n	*ma, m*		*ze*		*c'a*		*t'k'o*
	t'	*s*		*t'an*		*ġa*		*o*
		is		*ši*		*ġac'*		
		it'		*gan*		*ve*		
		d, ad		*t'vis*		*me*		
		v, o		*ken*		*mc'*		
				ebr				
				t'anave				
				urt'				
				dan				
				mde				

1. *The Nominal root*, on the basis of the final phoneme of which Georgian nouns can be subdivided into different declension types, including those which undergo syncope and those which undergo truncation;
2. *Number*;
3. *Case*;
4. *Emphatic vowel*;
5. *Postposition*;
6. *Extension vowel*;
7. *Particle*;
8. *Auxiliary verb*; and
9. *Indirect speech markers* (58).

(58) *cxen-Ø-is-a=t'vis-a=ca=a=met'k'i*
horse-SG-GEN-EMPH=for.GEN-EMPH=PTCL=be.
3SG.AUX=1.QUOT:PRS.IND
'is also for the horse as I said'

By adding the aforementioned markers to a single root, it is theoretically possible to generate approximately 2772 inflected word forms, including forms which are not realized in Georgian. The sequence of slots in Old Georgian is as follows (Table 2.7):

Table 2.7 Distribution of slots in the nominal frame in Old Georgian

0	1	2	3	4	5	6	7	8	9	10	11	12
R	Case	Emph	Nbr	Nbr	Case	Emph	Case	Emph	Posp	Emph	Ptl	Aux

The primary difference between Old and Modern Georgian with respect to the nominal frame concerns the first six slots, which in Old Georgian are occupied by a combination of case and number markers constituting a doubling of plural number markers (59–60) and a doubling or sometimes tripling of case markers generated on the basis of the genitive case (61–62).

(59) a. *sop'l-eb-n-i*
village-PL-PL-NOM
'villages'

b. *sop'l-eb-t'a*
village-PL-PL.NNOM
'of villages'

(60) *k'ueqan-a-t'-a-ys-a-n-o*
country-EMPH-PL-EMPH-GEN--
EMPH-PL-VOC
'of the countries as it was said'

(61) *kac'-is-a-t'-a*
man-GEN-EMPH-PL.DAT-EMPH
'of men'

(62) a. *kac'-Ø-is-a*
man-SG-GEN-EMPH
'to the man'

b. *kac'-Ø-is-ad*
man-SG-GEN-ADV
'for a man'

2.3.1.1 Case

In Modern Georgian there are seven cases: nominative, ergative, dative, genitive, instrumental, adverbial and vocative. Case-marking theories draw a distinction between grammatical and structural case and, broadly, between those languages possessing a nominative-accusative case-marking strategy and those possessing an ergative-absolutive case-marking strategy (Anderson 1976; DeLancey 1981; Dixon 1994 and others). In Georgian, with regards to noun-verb concord, nominative and dative cases mark either subject or oblique grammatical functions, while the ergative case always marks subjects (63). In addition to their use to mark the agent of an action, the nominative and dative cases are also used to mark the patient (64–65).

(63) *kata-Ø-m* *t'agv-Ø-i*
cat-SG-ERG mouse-SG-NOM
da-i-čir-a.
PV.PFV-PRV.RFL-catch-3SG.SBJ:AOR
'The cat caught a mouse.' (Doborjginidze et al. 2012)

(64) a. *gamxdar-Ø-i* *bič-Ø-i* *ga-rb-od-a*
thin-SG-NOM boy-SG-NOM PV.IPFV-run-EM-3SGSBJ:IMPF
'the thin boy was running' (Doborjginidze et al. 2012)

b. *xma-Ø* *mi-a-cvdin-a*
voice-SG-NOM PV.PFV-PRV.3IOBJ-give- 3SGSBJ:AOR.IND
bič-Ø-ma
boy-SG-ERG
'the boy said smth.' (Doborjginidze et al. 2012)

(65) a. *bič-Ø-s* *ga-e-c'in-a*
boy-SG-DAT PV.PFV-PRV-smile-3SGSBJ:AOR.IND
'the boy smiled' (Doborjginidze et al. 2012)

b. *igi* *surat'-eb-s*
s/he picture-PL-DAT
u-xat-av-d-a
PRV.3IOBJ-draw- TS-EM-3SGSBJ:IMPF
patara-Ø *bič-Ø-s*
small-SG.DAT boy-SG-DAT
's/he drew pictures for a small boy' (Doborjginidze et al. 2012)

In Modern Georgian the genitive case is generally used to mark the dependent of a nominal, while in Old Georgian it is also used as a base for secondary cases (so-called 'Suffixaufnahme' (Plank 1995)) to indicate its attributive relationship together with agreement with other nouns in number and case.

The instrumental case reflects the instrument, while the adverbial case reflects a state of being or temporary location. In Modern Georgian, the marker of the adverbial case is used as a derivational suffix to derive adverbs from nouns (66–67) or adjectives (68–69) and, syntactically, forms in the adverbial case are used as adverbial modifiers.

(66) a. *kac'-i*
man-SG.NOM
'man'

b. *kac'-ad*
man-SG.ADV
'as a man'

(67) *pativsac'em-∅* *kac'-ad*
honourable-ADV man-SG.ADV
v-i-t'vl-eb-i.
1SGSBJ-PRV.RFL-consider-TS-PRS.IND
'I am an honourable man' (Doborjginidze et al. 2012)

(68) a. *lamaz-i(*
beautiful-SG.NOM
'beautiful'

b. *lamaz-ad*
beautiful-SG.ADV
'beautifully'

(69) *ulvaš-eb-i* *lamaz-ad*
moustache-PL-NOM beautiful-SG.ADV
u-xd-eb-od-a.
PRV.3IOBJ-build-TS-IMPERF-3SGSBJ
'the moustache suited him' (Doborjginidze et al. 2012)

As can be observed, forms in the adverbial case express a relation of place, time, manner, etc. and meet the often-given definition of adverbs as words or phrases used to modify and/or qualify nouns, adjectives and verbs. Despite the fact that the adverbial case is considered a part of Georgian nominal declension, its position in the declension system of nouns and adjectives is questionable. In the morphological analyser of Georgian presented here, adjectives in the adverbial case marked by the *-ad* or *-d* markers are treated as adverbs.

Opinions with regard to the case status of the vocative vary; some scholars do not consider it a case, but instead a form (Topuria 1956a, 1956b; Chikobava 1968–2008 and others), while others on the contrary discuss it as a case (Shanidze 1956a, 1956b and others) (Table 2.8).

Table 2.8 Case markers

Cases	Modern Georgian	Old Georgian
Absolutive	-	-
Nominative	-∅, *-i*	-∅, *-i, -y*
Ergative	*-ma, -m*	*-man*
Dative	*-s*	*-s*
Genitive	*-is*	*-is, -ys*
Instrumental	*-it'*	*-it', -yt'*
Adverbial	*-d, -ad*	*-d, -ad*
Vocative	*-v, -o*	*-o*, -∅,

The following should also be noted in relation to Old Georgian (Babunashvili 1956; Vogt 1968; Shanidze 1976; Sarjveladze 1997 and others):

1. Absolutive case[9] is represented in the form of the nominal stem (70), and,
2. Suffixaufnahme is generated on the basis of the genitive. This was a frequent phenomenon in Old Georgian and is still used in some Georgian dialects today (Wier 2011a, 2011b). The rules for its occurrence are closely connected to the position of forms in the genitive case in relation to their nominal heads. While in Modern Georgian, the form in the genitive in the majority of cases precedes its head and does not vary according to the declension of its head, in Old Georgian the form in the genitive case repeats the ending of its head (Dondua 1956a, 1956b; Hewitt 1995 and others). In Old Georgian, this case stacking is encountered in the following cases:

   - Secondary ergative case, represented in the form of genitive and ergative case markers used together (71);
   - Secondary dative case, represented in the form of genitive and dative case markers used together (72);
   - Secondary genitive, represented by doubling of the genitive case marker (73);
   - Directional case, indicating direction and represented in the form of the genitive case with an extension vowel (74);
   - Secondary instrumental case, represented in the form of genitive and instrumental case markers used together (75);
   - Secondary adverbial case (the so-called 'purposive' (Shanidze 1976; Sarjveladze 1997 and others)), indicating purpose and created from the forms of the genitive and adverbial case markers used together (76).

[9] Opinions with regard to the differentiation of the absolutive and nominative cases differ. According to Danelia (1998), the absolutive was used from the fifth century until the ninth, following which it was replaced by the nominative. Other scholars, however, argue that the functions of the absolutive are similar to those of the nominative (Chikobava 1940, 1942; Topuria 1956; Uturgaidze 1986; Sarjveladze 1997 and others) and consider the absolutive to be simply the nominal root or an unmarked nominative, while others (Imnaishvili 1956; Shanidze 1976; Danelia 1998 and others) describe some functions of the absolutive as distinct from or shared with those of the nominative, and the absolutive as having had its markers replaced by nominative case markers (–i- with consonant-final and -y- with vowel-final nominals) in Old Georgian texts.

(70) a. *šurdul-∅*
catapult-SG.NOM
'catapult'
b. *šurdul-∅-i*
catapult-SG.NOM
'catapult'
c. *šurduleb-∅*
catapult-PL.NOM
'catapults'
d. *šurdul-eb-i*
catapult-PL.NOM
'catapults'

(71) *żel-∅-is-a-man*
made_of_wood-SG-GEN-EMPH-ERG
'made of wood'

(72) *saxl-∅-is-a-s-a*
house-SG-GEN-EMPH-DAT-EMPH
'to a house'

(73) *mk-∅-is-a-ys-a*
harvest-SG-GEN-EMPH-GEN-EMPH
'of the harvest'

(74) *kac'-∅-is-a*
man-SG-GEN-EMPH
'to the man'

(75) *abraham-is-it'=gan*
Abraham-GEN-INST=from.GEN
'from Abraham'

(76) *mep'-∅-is-ad*
man-SG-GEN-ADV
'for a king'

The secondary cases generated on the basis of the genitive are as follows (Table 2.9):

Table 2.9 Secondary case markers

Secondary cases	Doubling	Tripling
Nominative	*-is-a-y*	*-is-a-ys-a-y*
Ergative	*-is-a-man*	*-is-a-ys-a-man*
Dative	*-is-a-s-a*	*-is-a-ys-a-s-a*
Genitive	*-is-a-ys-a*	*-is-a-ys-a-ys-a*
Directional	*-is-a, -ys-a*	-
Instrumental	*-is-it', -is-yt'*	*-is-a-ys-a-yt'-a*
Purposive	*-is-a-d*	-
Vocative	*-is-a-o*	*-is-a-ys-a-o*

As it was mentioned above, opinions with regard to the absolutive case and Suffixaufnahme in the academic literature vary. Some (Chkhenkeli 1956; Imnaishvili 1956–1957; Shanidze 1976 and others) argue in their favour, while others (Uturgaidze 1986; Sarjveladze 1997; Danelia 1998 and others) exclude them on the basis that the forms of the absolute case are always interchangeable with the forms of the nominative case, leading them to view the absolutive instead as an 'unmarked' nominative, and that the forms of secondary cases are always interchangeable with forms of the genitive case reflecting direction, purpose, etc. The function of the genitive case in Old Georgian was to indicate an attributive relationship between nouns and required a doubling (77) or tripling (78) of case markers by means of the genitive and other cases with purpose.

(77)	*tażr-∅-is-a*	*żel-∅-is-a-ys-a*
	church-SG-GEN-EMPH	wood-SG-GEN-EMPH-GEN-EMPH
	'of a wooden church'	
(78)	sisxl-∅-is-a	*bral-∅-is-a-ys-a-s-a*
	blood-SG-GEN-EMPH	fault-SG-GEN-EMPH-GEN-EMPH-DAT-EMPH
	'because of blood'	

2.3.1.2 Number

Georgian has two number values: singular and plural. The genesis and use of number markers in Georgian are described in (Dondua 1956a, 1956b; Chikobava 1954, 1956; Sharashenidze 1956; Tuite 1998 and others). No special markers are used to denote singular number, so that a zero morph is attributed to the singular. By contrast, three markers are used for paradigm generation in the plural, namely: *-eb-*, which is used with all cases, *-n-*, which is used with the nominative and the vocative and *-t'-*, which is used with the ergative, dative and genitive cases. The dual, which refers to two objects or persons, is not attested in Georgian, although some scholars (Shanidze 1976–1967) believe the *-n-* and *-t-* suffixes to have originated from the marking of a dual number. The primary difference between the plural markers is that the *-n-* and *-t-* suffixes occur more frequently in Old Georgian than the *-eb-* suffix, while in Modern Georgian the *-eb-* suffix is more frequent than the other two. The markers also differ with respect to their concord: if a determinant requires the *-eb-* or *-t'-* markers, the modifier never takes them (79), while if a determinant takes the *-n-* marker, the modifier uses it as well (80).

(79)	*maġal-i*	*mt'-eb-i*
	high-NOM	mountain-PL-NOM
	'high mountains'	
(80)	*maġal-n-i*	*mt'a-n-i*
	high-PL-NOM	mountain-PL-NOM
	'high mountains'	

2.3.1.3 Postpositions and the Auxiliary Verb

Another feature which should be considered with regard to grammatical cases is their ability to reflect different syntactic behaviour and morphological structure by means of clitics. The main characteristic of clitics is that they behave like suffixes added to the host, but their behaviour is in some sense independent (Zwicky 1977–1985a, 1985b; Gerlach et al. 2000). In Georgian, contextual agreement can be shown in two ways: by means of particles, which form a closed class of items described additionally in Sect. 2.3.10, and by means of postpositions, which join to the nominal paradigm in the form of clitics and are usually distinct with respect to the case they assign to their complements. While the quantity of these items is not large, their use increases the generative possibilities of the nominal paradigm.

The final two slots of the nominal paradigm are occupied by two other types of clitics: the auxiliary verb *-a (aris)* 'is' in the third singular (81) and the indirect speech markers. While the first and the second indirect speech markers: *-met'k'i* 'I said' and *-t'k'o* 'tell smb. I said', require a hyphen and can be treated as independent words, the third indirect speech marker is placed without any punctuation marks at the end of nominal or verbal paradigms, forming an additional slot (82).

(81) *cign-∅-is-a=a*
book-SG-GEN-EMPH=be.3SG.AUX:PRS.IND
'is of a book'

(82) *val-∅-i=a=o*
debt-SG-NOM=be.3SG.AUX=3.QUOT:PRS.IND
'is a debt, as it was said'

2.3.1.4 The Extension Vowel

The academic literature (Dzotsenidze 1947; Zurabishvili 1972–1956; Shanidze 1973 and others) views the extension vowel as a morph without any morphological function which can be added to the stem in the dative, genitive and instrumental cases. Its frequent use is explained in phonological terms as being conditioned by the boundaries between affixes and by subsequent words in the sentence if a word is followed by the conjunctions *da* 'and' or *t'u* 'if'. Additional morphological constraints on the use of the extension vowel are as follows:

- Before the postposition *-vit'* 'like' (83)

(83) *cqaro-∅-s-a=vit'*
spring-SG-DAT-EMPH=like
'like a spring'

- Before the particle *-c'* 'and' (84)

(84) *k'alak'-∅-s-a=c'*
town-SG-DAT-EMPH=PTCL
'and the town'

- Before the auxiliary verb *-a (aris* 'is') (85)

(85) *saxl-∅=t'an-a=a*
house-SG-near-EMPH=be.3SG.AUX:PRS.IND
'is near the house'

2.3.1.5 Particles

Particles in Georgian, which include *-c'* 'too, and, even', *-c'a* 'too, and, even', *-ġa* 'only', *-ve* 'and' and others, may be added to any case except the vocative, but if a preceding slot ends in a consonant they require an extension vowel to be used preceding them (86–87).

(86) *xerx-∅-ma=c'*
method-SG-ERG=PTCL
'and method, technique'

(87) *mnišvneloba-∅-m-a=c'*
meaning-SG-ERG-EMPH=PTCL
'and meaning, importance'

The peculiarities of particles are described further in Sect. 2.3.5.3 (with reference to their use as clitics) and in Sect. 2.3.10 (with reference to their use as separate words).

2.3.1.6 Summary

As discussed above, different kinds of stems trigger different phonological processes. The rules for the formation of the declension types can be summarised as follows (Table 2.10):

Table 2.10 Declension types of nouns

Declension	Class	Features
1st Declension	Noun_1;	Consonant-final common nouns, non-syncopating
2nd Declension	Noun_2;	*-l, -r, -m, -n*-final common nouns, syncopating in the genitive, instrumental and adverbial cases in the singular and in all cases in the *-eb-* plural
3rd Declension	Noun_3;	*-r*-final common nouns, *o*→*v* alternation in the genitive, instrumental and adverbial cases in the singular and in all cases in the *-eb-* plural
4th Declension	Noun_4;	*-o* and *-u*-final common nouns, non-truncating
5th Declension	Noun_5;	*-a*-final common nouns, truncating in the genitive and instrumental cases in the singular and in all cases in the *-eb*-plural
6th Declension	Noun_6;	*-e*-final common nouns, truncating in the genitive and instrumental cases in the singular

(continued)

Table 2.10 (continued)

Declension	Class	Features
7th Declension	Noun_7;	*-e* and *-a*-final common nouns, syncopating in the genitive, instrumental and adverbial cases in the singular and truncating in the genitive and instrumental cases in the singular and syncopating and truncating in all cases in the *-eb*-plural
8th Declension	Noun_8;	Consonant-final proper nouns, non-syncopating
9th Declension	Noun_9;	*-l*, *-r*, *-m*, *-n*-final proper nouns, syncopating in the genitive, instrumental and adverbial cases in the singular and in all cases in the *-eb-* plural
10th Declension	Noun_10;	*-o* and *–u*-final proper nouns, non-truncating
11th Declension	Noun_11;	*-a*-final common nouns, truncating in the genitive and instrumental cases in the singular and in all cases in the *-eb-* plural
12th Declension	Noun_12;	*-e*-final common nouns, truncating in the genitive and instrumental cases in the singular

2.3.2 *Adjectival Inflection*

Like other parts of speech, adjectives can be defined at the morphosyntactic, semantic and syntactic levels (Vogel et al. 2000). Georgian adjectives are used to describe the qualities or states of nouns and constitute a structurally separate class of items. The syntactic function of adjectives is however shared between adjectives and noun forms in the genitive case, which can precede or follow the head depending on the context. Used attributively, consonant-final adjectives occur in structurally unmarked forms in the dative and adverbial cases and in partially marked forms in the genitive and instrumental cases, while vowel-final adjectives occur in their structurally unmarked forms in all cases. Used predicatively, both consonant-final and vowel-final adjectives follow rules of paradigm formation. While there are no restrictions on the use of adjectives preceding or following the noun, prepositive placement is more frequent in Modern Georgian.

Two types of adjective can be distinguished by their ability to produce the degree of comparison: adverbial and relative. Adverbial adjectives produce the degree of comparison, while relative adjectives do not. The distribution of adjectives between these two types is not associated with any special grammatical marker, but is strictly semantic, i.e. dependent on the lexicon. According to the opinions of some scholars (Sarjveladze 1997; Gogolashvili et al. 2011 and others) adverbial adjectives are also older than relative ones.

Adjectival inflection in Georgian follows the scheme: type → degree → number markers → case markers and/or clitics [postpositions] → extension vowel → clitics [auxiliary verb, markers of indirect speech]. The maximum possible number of slots is 11 (Hewitt 1995; Boeder 2005; Gogolashvili et al. 2011 and others); these comprise the following units (Table 2.11):

Table 2.11 Distribution of slots in the adjectival frame

−1	0	1	2	3	4	5	6	7	8	9
Degree marker (Degr)	R	Degr	Nbr	Case	Emph	Posp	Emph	Ptl	Aux	IS
mo		*o*	*eb*	*i*	*a*	*vit‘*	*a*	*c‘*	*a*	*met‘k‘i*
u		*es*	*n*	*ma, m*		*ze*		*c‘a*		*t‘k‘o*
			t‘	*s*		*t‘an*		*ġa*		*o*
				is		*ši*		*ġac‘*		
				it‘		*gan*		*ve*		
				d, ad		*t‘vis*		*me*		
				v, o		*ken*		*mc‘*		
						ebr				
						t‘anave				
						urt‘				
						dan				
						mde				

1. *Degree*, which is represented in the form of circumfixes occupying the first and the third slots in the adjectival paradigm;
2. *The nominal root*, which is subdivided depending on the final phoneme into different adjectival declension types, including those which undergo syncope and those which undergo truncation, and also dictates compatibility with degree markers;
3. *Degree*;
4. *Number*;
5. *Case*;
6. *Extension vowel*;
7. *Postposition*;
8. *Extension vowel*;
9. *Particle*;
10. *Auxiliary verb*; and
11. *Indirect speech markers*.

The aforementioned number of slots in combination with the number of possible markers enables the generation of approximately 5,544 inflected adjectival forms, without taking into consideration whether all of these are realized in the language.

2.3.2.1 Degree

There are four degrees of comparison: diminutive, positive, comparative and superlative, but the gradability expressed by these degrees differs slightly from the semantics of the majority of European languages. The diminutive degree (the so-called ‘-*ish* degree’) expresses a lesser degree, the positive degree is a neutral one, the comparative indicates that one item differs slightly from another, and the superlative represents higher levels of comparison (Shanidze 1973; Gogolashvili et al. 2011 and others).

Opinions with regard to the existence of the comparative degree in Old Georgian vary: Shanidze (1976) argues that only the positive and superlative degrees are present, while Sarjveladze (1997) distinguishes diminutive, positive and superlative degrees. As the purpose of the present project is to process not only Modern, but also Old and Middle Georgian, the approach taken by Sarjveladze has been adopted.

The degree of comparison is encoded in Georgian by two methods: synthetic and analytic. The synthetic method of forming the degree of comparison is closely connected to the use of special affixes, while the analytic method employs the adverbs *up’ro* ‘more’ (in the comparative degree) and *qvelaze* ‘most’, *qvelaze up‘ro* ‘most of all’ (in the superlative degree) before the adjective. While the synthetic method can be processed as a part of finite-state morphology, the analytic requires syntactic parsing.

The diminutive, comparative and superlative degrees are formed in the following way (Table 2.12):

Table 2.12 Formation of the diminutive, comparative and superlative degrees

	Synthetic method						Analytic method	
	Modern Georgian			Old Georgian			Modern Georgian	Old Georgian
Diminutive	*mo-*	R	*-o*	*mo-*	R	*-e*	*odnav*	
Comparative		-			-		*up‘ro*	*up‘ro*
Superlative	*u-*	R	*-es*	*xu-*	R	*-ēs/-es*	*qvelaze*	
				xu-	R	*-oys/-os*	*qvelaze up‘ro*	
				hu-	R	*-ēs/-es*		
				hu-	R	*-oys/-os*		
				u-	R	*-ēs/-es*		
				u-	R	*-oys/-os*		
				u-	R	*-e*		

Inflection then proceeds in accordance with the stem-final phoneme:

- Adjectives in the diminutive degree are inflected as *-o* final, non-truncating adjectives (88).

(88) *t‘et‘r-Ø-i* → *mo>t‘et‘r<o-Ø*, *mo>t‘et‘r<o-Ø-m* ‘white → whitish’, etc.

a. *t‘et‘r-Ø-i*
white-SG-NOM
‘white’

b. *mo>t‘et‘r<o-Ø*
DIM>white<DIM-SG.NOM
‘whitish’

c. *mo>t‘et‘r<o-Ø-m*
DIM>white<DIM-SG-ERG
‘whitish’

- Adjectives in the superlative degree are inflected as consonant-final, non-syncopating adjectives (89)

(89) *t'et'r-∅-i* → *u>t'et'r<es-∅-i, u>t'et'r<es-∅-ma* 'white → whitest', etc.

a. *t'et'r-∅-i*
white-SG-NOM
'white'

b. *u>t'et'r<es-∅-i*
SUP>white<SUP-SG-NOM
'whitest'

c. *u>t'et'r<es-∅-ma*
SUP>white<SUP-SG-ERG
'whitest'

In both cases, in constrast to *-l, -r, -m,* and *-n*-final one-syllable stems (90), sonant-final stems consisting of two or more syllables sometimes undergo syncopation before the beginning of inflection (91).

(90) *bnel-∅-i* → *mo>bnel<o-∅, mo>bnel<o-∅-m* 'dark → darkish', etc.

a. *bnel-∅-i*
dark-SG-NOM
'dark'

b. *mo>bnel<o-∅*
DIM>dark<DIM-SG.NOM
'darkish'

c. *mo>bnel<o-∅-m*
DIM>dark<DIM-SG-ERG
'darkish'

bnel-∅-i → *u>bnel<es-∅-i, u>bnel<es-∅-ma* 'dark → darkest', etc.

a. *bnel-∅-i*
dark-SG-NOM
'dark'

b. *u>bnel<es-∅-i*
SUP> dark <SUP-SG-NOM
'darkest'

c. *u*>dark<*es-∅-ma*
SUP>white<SUP-SG-ERG
'darkest'

(91) *maġ**al**-∅-i* → *mo>maġl<o-∅, mo>maġl<o-∅-m* 'high → less high', etc.

a. *maġ**al**-∅-i*
high-SG-NOM
'high'

b. *mo>maġl<o-∅*
DIM>high<DIM-SG.NOM
'less high'

c. *mo>maġl<o-∅-m*
DIM>high<DIM-SG-ERG
'less high'

*maġ**al**-∅-i* → *u>maġl<es-∅-i, u>maġl<es-∅-ma* 'high → highest', etc.

a. *maġ**al**-∅-i*
high-SG-NOM
'high'

b. *u>maġl<es-∅-i*
SUP>high<SUP-SG-NOM
'highest'

c. *u>maġl<es-∅-ma*
SUP>high<SUP-SG-ERG
'highest'

Adjectives can precede or follow the noun. The primary difference between Old and Modern Georgian with respect to the prepositive placement of adjectives relates to case-number agreement between words: in Old Georgian, the adjectival complement of a noun phrase agrees in case and number with its head (92), while in Modern Georgian it agrees in case and number with its head, but represents this agreement by means of a reduced form (93). Postpositive placement of adjectives in Modern Georgian is rare, while in Old Georgian this is frequently encountered (94).

(92)

a. *maġal-s* *saxl-s*
high-SG-DAT house-SG-DAT
'to a high house'

b. *maġl-eb-s-a* *saxl-eb-s-a*
high-PL-DAT-EMPH house-PL-DAT-EMPH
'to high houses'

c. *maġal-s-a* *saxl-eb-s-a*
high-SG.DAT-EMPH house-PL-DAT-EMPH
'to high houses'

d. *maġal-is* *saxl-is*
high-SG.GEN house-SG.GEN
'of a high house'

(93) a.

maġal	*saxl-s*
high	hous-SG.DAT

'to a high house'

b.

maġal	*saxl-eb-s*
high	house-PL-DAT

'to high houses'

c.

maġal-i	*saxl-is*
high-SG.GEN	house-SG-GEN

'of a high houses'

(94) a.

mocame-∅	*cmida-∅*
martyr-SG.NOM	saint-SG.NOM

'saint martyr'

b.

mocame-∅-m	*cmida-∅-m*
martyr-SG-ERG	house-SG-ERG

'saint martyr'

Sometimes adjectives are used as substantive nouns in a sentence (95–96), in which case they strictly follow the declension rules of the nominal paradigm.

(95) Modern Georgian:

qelqarqara	*lamaz-eb-o*
slender-necked	beautiful-PL-VOC

'slender beautiful women'

(96) Old Georgian:

vidre	*did-∅-ad=mde*
until	big- SG-ADV=till.ADV

'until the big'

2.3.2.2 Summary

Adjectival inflection is similar to nominal inflection in that it proceeds according to case and number and generally follows the same rules for consonant- and vowel-final stem declension types. To summarize, the adjectival declension types are as follows (Table 2.13):

Table 2.13 Declension types of adjectives

Declension	Class	Features
1st Declension	Adjective_1;	Consonant-final adjectives, non-syncopating
2nd Declension	Adjective_2;	*-l, -r, -m, -n*-final adjectives, syncopating in the genitive, instrumental and adverbial cases in the singular and in all cases in the *-eb-* plural
3rd Declension	Adjective_3;	*-a*-final adjectives, truncating in the genitive and instrumental cases in the singular and in all cases in the *-eb-* plural
4th Declension	Adjective_4;	*-e*-final adjectives, truncating in the genitive and instrumental cases in the singular
5th Declension	Adjective_5;	*-o* and *-u*-final adjectives, non-truncating

A special remark should be added for *-e*-final stem adjectives, which show parallel truncating (rarely) and non-truncating (frequently) forms in the plural (97).

(97) a. *mżim-eb-i* || *mżime-eb-i*
heavy-PL.NOM
'heavies'

The non-truncating forms strictly follow the rules of Modern Georgian and can be considered regular.

2.3.3 Numeral Inflection

As described by various authors (Aronson 1990; Hewitt 1995; Makharoblidze 2009 and others), Georgian numerals follow a base-20 or vigesimal system, whereby from 30 onward, the counting system follows '20 +' formation rules. Together with their written forms, which reveal quite complex morphosyntactic features, Georgian numerals can be represented in the following ways:

1. Numerals written in full (98)
   (98) *ert'i* 'one', *t'ert'meti* 'eleven', etc.
2. Arabic numerals (99)
   (99) *1* 'one', *11* 'eleven', etc.
3. Roman numerals (100)
   (100) *I* 'one', *XI* 'eleven', etc.
4. Acrophonic numerals[10] (101)
   (101) *a* 'one', *ia* 'eleven', etc.

While the first three forms of representations are used in Modern Georgian, the fourth was actively used in Old and Middle Georgian employing the *Asomtavruli* or *Mkhedruli* scripts.

The numerals can be of five types: cardinal, ordinal, fractional, approximative and multiple. The five types have different derivation rules which, while they do not form part of inflectional morphology, make it possible to distinguish them and to predict their associated declension types.

Numeral inflection is based on the following scheme: type markers → number markers → case markers and/or clitics [postpositions] → extension vowel → clitics [auxiliary verb, markers of indirect speech]. The maximum possible number of slots is 12 (Shanidze 1973; Hewitt 1995; Makharoblidze 2009 and others); these include (Table 2.14):

[10] For the full list of values attached to the letters of the Georgian alphabet see Table 2.1.

Table 2.14 Distribution of slots in the numeral frame

−1	0	1	2	3	4	5	6	7	8	9	10
Type marker (Type)	R	Type	Type	Nbr	Case	Emph	Posp	Emph	Ptl	Aux	IS
me		*e*	*d*	*eb*	*i*	*a*	*vit‘*	*a*	*c‘*	*a*	*met‘k‘i*
		ode[a]		*n*	*ma, m*		*ze*		*c‘a*		*t‘k‘o*
		jer		*t‘*	*s*		*t‘an*		*ġa*		*o*
					is		*ši*		*ġac‘*		
					it‘		*gan*		*ve*		
					d, ad		*t‘vis*		*me*		
					v, o		*ken*		*mc‘*		
							ebr				
							t‘anave				
							urt‘				
							dan				
							mde				

[a]In Old Georgian this particle was used as separate word *oden* ‘at the least’

1. *Type marker*, represented in the form of circumfixes occupying the first and the third slots in the case of ordinal numerals or the first, the third and the fourth slots in case of fractional numerals;
2. *The nominal root*, which depending on the final phoneme, subdivides adjectives into different declension types, including those which undergo syncope and those which undergo truncation, and determines compatibility with degree markers;
3. *Type marker*, occupied in the case of ordinal numerals;
4. *Type marker*, occupied in the case of fractional numerals;
5. *Number*;
6. *Case*;
7. *Extension vowel*;
8. *Postposition*;
9. *Extension vowel*;
10. *Particle*;
11. *Auxiliary verb*; and
12. *Indirect speech markers*.

The primary similarities between numerals and other nominals lie in the categories of number and case and in the attachment of clitics used to indicate spatial relations or which take the form of function morphemes (particles) or the auxiliary verb (to be). Numerals, like other nominals, are actively involved in number agreement depending on animacy, case assignment and case agreement. These syntactic relations should however be considered at the level of syntactic parsing with a focus on syntactic disambiguation, syntactic labeling, the determination of dependency relations and the assignment of clause boundaries.

2.3.3.1 Types of Numerals

The derivation of cardinal numerals is based on two types of stems: simple stems consisting of numerals from 1 to 10 and 20, and complex stems consisting of 10 or 20 + simple stems with or without the conjunction *da* 'and' (102–103).

(102) *t'+or+met-i*
ten+two+more-NOM
'twelve'

(103) *oc'+da+or-i*
twenty+and+two-NOM
'twenty two'

The principal differences between cardinal numerals in Old and Modern Georgian can be summarised as follows:

- from the ninth century onward, deletion of an initial *a*-vowel (104) resulting in the emergence of affricates in some numerals (105);

(104) *at'-'or-met-i* → *t'-or-met-i* 'twelve', etc.
at'+'or+met-i
ten+two+more-NOM
'twelve'

(105) *at'-sam-met-i* → *t'-sa-met-i* → *c'-a-met-i* 'thirteen', etc.
at'+sam+met-i
ten+three+more-NOM
'thirteen'

- From the 10th century, deletion of *-me-* 'yet' (106);

(106) *sam-me-oc'-i* → *sam-e-oc'-i* → *sam-oc'-i* 'sixty', etc.
sam+me+oc'-i
three+yet+twenty-NOM
'sixty'

- Changes in the meaning of individual words; for example, in Old Georgian *bevr-i* means 'ten thousand', while in Modern Georgian it means 'a lot';
- Disappearance of the word *ergasis-i* 'fifty'.

Accordingly, the cardinal numerals are inflected in the following way: the declension of *a*-final numerals is similar to *-a* final nominals, truncating in the genitive and instrumental cases in the singular, while the declension of consonant-final numerals is similar to that of consonant-final non-syncopating nominals.

The ordinal numerals are constructed by means of the *me- -e* circumfix, which in the case of simple-stem numerals removes the final vowel from *-a*-final stems (107) or the nominative case marker which follows consonant-final stems (108), while in the case of complex-stem numerals the circumfix is used only with the numeral placed after the conjunction *da* 'and' (109).

(107) *rva-∅* 'eight' → *me-rv-e* 'the eighth', etc.

a. *rva-∅*
eight-NOM
'eight'

b. *me-rv-e*
ORD>eight<ORD.NOM
'the eighth'

(108) *or-i* 'two' → *me-or-e* 'the second', etc.

a. *or-i*
two-NOM
'two'

b. *me-or-e*
ORD>two<ORD.NOM
'the second'

(109) *ot'x-m-oc'-da-sam-i* 'eighty three' → *ot'x-m-oc'-da-me-sam-e* 'the eighty third', etc.

a. *ot'x+m+oc'+da+sam-i*
four+yet+twenty+and+three-NOM
'eighty three'

b. *ot'x+m+oc'+da-me-sam-e*
four+yet+twenty+and-
ORD>three<ORD.NOM
'the eighty third'

'The first' is formed in two ways: (a) by means of the suppletive form *pirvel-i* and (b) by means of the *me- -e* circumfix: *me>ert'<e*. The first form is used separately, while the second form can be used only in complex-stem numerals after the conjunction *da* 'and' (110).

(110) *oc'+da-me-ert'-e*
twenty+and-ORD>one<ORD.NOM
'the twenty first'

The ordinal numerals are inflected like *-e*-final nominals, truncating in the genitive and instrumental cases in the singular. The suppletive form *pirvel-i* 'the first' is inflected like a consonant-final non-syncopating nominal.

Fractional numerals employ the following formation models: (1) by means of a *-d-* suffix added to ordinal numerals (111–112), (2) by means of an *-eul-* suffix added to cardinal numerals (113) and (3) by means of a *na- -al* circumfix added to cardinal numerals (114).

(111) *me-ot'x-e-d-i*
ORD>four<ORD-FRACT-NOM
'one quarter'

(112) Modern Georgian:

a. *meek‘vsedi*
ORD>six<ORD-FRACT-NOM
‘one sixth’

Old Georgian:

b. *me-ek‘us-e-d-i*
ORD>six<ORD-FRACT-NOM
‘one sixth’

(113) *ot‘x-eul-i* in Old Geogian, ‘one quarter’, in Modern Georgian, ‘quaternion’; *xut‘-eul-i* in Old Geogian, ‘one fifth’, in Modern Georgian, ‘unit/team of five’, etc.

a. *ot‘x-eul-i*
four-suff-NOM
‘one quarter, quaternion’

b. *xut‘-eul-i*
five-suff-NOM
‘one fifth, unit/team of five’

(114) a. *na-sam-al-i*
pref>three<suff-NOM
‘one third’

b. *na-zog-al-i*
pref>some<suff-NOM
‘one-half’

While the second and the third models are not active in Modern Georgian, the *-eul-* suffix is used to construct nouns from numerals indicating a quantity of something. In Old Georgian, *zogi* was a fractional numeral used in the sense of ‘a half’, while in Modern Georgian it is a pronoun meaning ‘some’. The fractional numerals are inflected like consonant final non-syncopating nominals.

Approximate and multiple numerals also exist. Approximate numerals are formed with the suffix *-ode (*115), while multiple numerals are formed using the suffix *-jer (*116) attached to the root of ordinal numerals. The numeral types do not have inflectional forms, however.

(115) *samiode* ‘about three’, *oc’iode* ‘about twenty’, etc.
(116) *samjer* ‘three times’, *oc’jer* ‘twenty times’, etc.

2.3.3.2 Summary

The regular numeral declension types are similar to those of the nominal paradigm, and are as follows (Table 2.15):

Table 2.15 Declension types of numerals

Declension	Class	Features
1st Declension	Numeral_1;	20-based numerals connected to the 3rd and 4th declensions
2nd Declension	Numeral_2;	100-based numerals connected to the 1st, 3rd and 4th declensions
3rd Declension	Numeral_3;	Consonant-based numerals, non-syncopating
4th Declension	Numeral_4;	*-a* and *-e*-final numerals, truncating in the genitive and instrumental cases

2.3.4 *Pronouns*

In the most traditional sense, pronouns are words used to substitute nouns, but they can be of different types and their classification is language-specific (Comrie 1989; Saxena 2006). Pronouns in Georgian are of the following types: personal, demonstrative, possessive, determinal/reflexive, indefinite, interrogative, relative, reciprocal and negative (Martirosov 1964; Gogolashvili et al. 2011 and others). In comparison with other nominals, the inflectional paradigms of the aforementioned pronoun types are very irregular; some of the them follow the rules of the nominal declensions and exhibit different forms based on agreement between person, case and number, while others do not.

Pronoun inflection follows the uniform scheme: type → number markers → case markers and/or clitics [postpositions] → extension vowel → clitics [auxiliary verb, markers of indirect speech]. The number of slots varies from type to type, but generally the maximum number is nine (Shanidze 1973; Gogolashvili et al. 2011 and others) in Modern Georgian and 10 in Old Georgian; these are as follows (Table 2.16):

Table 2.16 Distribution of slots in the pronominal frame

0	1	2	3	4	5	6	7[a]	8	9
R	Case	Nbr	Emph	Posp	Emph	Ptl	Ptl	Aux	IS
	eb	*i*	*a*	*vit‘*	*a*	*c‘*	*ese*	*a*	*met‘k‘i*
	n	*ma, m*		*ze*		*c‘a*	*ege*		*t‘k‘o*
	t‘	*s*		*t‘an*		*ġa*	*igi*		*o*
		is		*ši*		*ġac‘*			
		it‘		*gan*		*ve*			
		d, ad		*t‘vis*		*me*			
		v, o		*ken*		*mc‘*			
				ebr					
				t‘anave					
				urt‘					
				dan					
				mde					

[a]This slot is occupied only in Old Georgian

1. *The nominal root*, which, depending on the type of pronoun can be subdivided into vowel-final stems (117), consonant-final stems similar to nominal ones (118) and consonant-final stems which do not require a vowel in the nominative (119);
2. *Number*;
3. *Case*;
4. *Extension vowel*;
5. *Postposition*;
6. *Extension vowel*;
7. *Particle*;
8. *Auxiliary verb*;
9. *Indirect speech markers*.

117. *vinme-∅* ‘somebody’, *ege-∅* ‘this’, etc.
118. *romel-i* ‘which’, *zogiert‘-i* ‘certain’, etc.
119. *is-∅* ‘that’, *es-∅* ‘this’, etc.

2.3.4.1 Person

There are three persons of pronouns: the first person denotes the speaker (120), the second person, the person being addressed (121), and the third person, anybody else (122).

(120) *me* ‘I’, *č‘em-i* ‘my’, etc.
(121) *šen* ‘you’, *šen-i* ‘yours’, etc.
(122) *is* ‘he/she/it’, *mis-i* ‘his/her/its’, etc.

The formation of plural forms is not similar to that found in the nominal paradigm; each person has its own plural form (123).

(123) *č’ven* ‘we’, *č’ven-i* ‘ours’, etc.

The declension rules follow the declension principles of the nominal paradigm, with the difference that the stem for the nominal case depends on the type of pronoun and, in some instances, is different from the stems found in the other cases (124).

(124) a. *ese-n-i*
this-PL-NOM
‘these’

b. *ama-t‘*
this-PL-ERG
‘these’

2.3.4.2 Pronoun Types

The personal pronouns are used to represent people or things and can be subdivided into inflected and uninflected forms. The first and the second person pronouns belong to the uninflected forms, while the third person pronouns are inflected and, following (Martirosov 1964; Melikishvili 1980 and others), show the following peculiarities: (a) they use two separate suppletive forms for the formation of the nominative, ergative and other cases (125); (b) they form the ergative case by means of *-n (*125) in contrast to the nominal paradigm, which employs *-ma* for consonant-final stems and *-m* for vowel-final stems; (c) they do not use extension vowels, and; (d) they do not use the *-eb* marker for the formation of plural forms (126).

(125) a. *ege-∅*
this-3SG.NOM
'these'
b. *ama-n*
this-3SG.ERG
'these'

(126) a. *ege-n-i*
this-3PL-NOM
'these'
b. *ama-t'*
this-3PL.ERG
'these'

It should be noted that Georgian belongs to the so-called "pro-drop languages", which means that under certain circumstances pronouns can be omitted if they are understandable from the linguistic or situational points of view. Corpus data however reveal that under the impact of foreign languages, and especially English, the tendency to omit pronouns is in decline, and is no longer as strong as it was in Old or Middle Georgian. Another diachronic difference is the existence of the forms *isi* 'he/she/it' and *isini* 'they' in the nominative case in Modern Georgian.

The demonstrative pronouns grip the third personal pronouns, use them to point to something specific in a sentence (Chartolani 1985) and differ in meaning (127–128). The declension paradigms are similar to those of the nominal declension, particularly in the case of consonant-final stems.

(127) Modern Georgian *es* 'this', *eg* 'that (close to 2p)', *is* 'he, she, it', versus Old Georgian: *ese* 'this', *ege* 'this (that 2 person was talking of)', *isi* 'that', etc.

(128) Modern Georgian *amnairi* 'this sort of smth.', *eseti* 'this sort of smth.', versus Old Georgian *esemlevani* 'this sort of smth.', *esrēt'i* 'this sort of smth.', etc.

The possessive pronouns showing ownership form their declension paradigm like consonant-final non-syncopating nominals (129). The primary difference between Old and Modern Georgian in this respect is not a morphological, but rather a syntactic one: while possessive pronouns may be placed postpositively or prepositively in both Modern and Old Georgian, in Modern Georgian the former is very rare, whereas in Old Georgian this placement predominates (130).

(129) a. *č'em-i*
my-SG.NOM
'my'

b. *č'em-ma*
my-SG.ERG
'my'

c. *č'em-s*
my-SG.DAT
'my'

(130) *č'ant'a-∅* *č'em-i*
bag-SG.NOM my-SG.NOM
'my bag'

The interrogative pronouns, which are used to ask questions, have varying stem types and, accordingly, belong to varying declension types: (a) consonant-final non-syncopating pronouns (131); (b) consonant-final syncopating pronouns (132); (c) non-standard consonant final pronouns, which do not require the *-i* marker in the nominative (133); and (d) vowel-final truncating pronouns (134).

(131) a. *rogor-i*
what_type_of-SG.NOM
'what type of'

b. *rogor-ma*
what_type_of-SG.ERG
'what type of'

(132) a. *romel-i*
which-SG.NOM
'which'

b. *roml-is*
which-SG.ERG
'which'

(133) a. *vin*
who-SG.NOM
'who'

b. *vis*
who-SG.DAT
'who'

(134) a. *ra-∅*
what-SG.NOM
'what'

b. *r-is*
what-SG.GEN
'what'

The reflexive pronouns, which include *qoveli* ‘every’, *t‘vit‘on* ‘oneself’, etc., are used to refer back to a person or thing. Only *qvela* ‘all’ and *sxva* ‘other’ have plural forms: *qvela* ‘all’ → *qvela-n-i* ‘absolutely all’, *sxva* ‘other’ → *sxva-n-i* || *sxv-eb-i* ‘others’.

The declension paradigms are distinguished the stem-final phoneme of the pronoun and are as follows: (a) consonant-final syncopating pronouns; (b) consonant-final non-syncopating pronouns; (c) vowel-final non-truncating pronouns.

The indefinite pronouns, which refer to non-specific things, are formed in two general ways: (1) by borrowing forms of interrogative pronouns like *vin* ‘who’, *romeli* ‘which’, etc. in Old Georgian (Shanidze 1956a, 1956b); (2) by adding the particle *-me* in Old and Modern Georgian and the particle *-ġa-c* in Modern Georgian to the stem of theinterrogative pronoun (135). In the first case, the indefinite and the interrogative pronouns are differentiated by context (136).

(135) a. *vin=me-∅*
who=PTCL-SG.NOM
‘someone, somebody’

b. *vi=ġa=c‘*
who=PTCL=PTCL
‘someone, somebody’

(136) *kac‘-i* *vinme-∅*
man-SG.NOM someone-SG.NOM
‘someone’

The declension paradigm in the case of the *-me*-final stem is similar to that of *-e*-final nominals. The other cases can be considered to belong to a closed class of items which does not inflect.

The relative pronouns, which introduce relative clauses, are formed from the interrogative pronouns as follows: (1) by borrowing forms of interrogative pronouns like *ray* ‘that’ etc. in Old Georgian; (2) by adding the particles *-c’*, *-c’a* to the stem of the interrogative pronouns in Old and Modern Georgian (137); (3) by adding the pronouns: *-ese* ‘this’, *-ege* ‘that’, *-igi* ‘he/she/it’ to the stem of the interrogative pronouns (138).

(137) a. *vin=c‘*
who=PTCL
‘who’

b. *ra=c‘*
that=PTCL
‘that’

(138) a. *vin=c‘a=ese*
who=PTCL=SO
‘who’

b. *vin=c‘a=ege*
that=PTCL=this
‘who’

This group of pronouns do not alter in accordance with case or number.

The reciprocal pronouns, which refer to two subjects acting with respect to each other, are declined like *-e*-final nominals (139) or like consonant-final non-syncopating nominals (140). In Old Georgian, the reciprocal pronouns were used only in the dative and genitive cases (141) and underwent some lexical changes.

(139) a. *ert'imeore-∅*
each_other-SG.NOM
'each other'

b. *ert'imeor-is*
each_other-SG.GEN
'each other'

(140) a. *ert'manet'-i*
each_other-SG.NOM
'each other'

b. *ert'manet'-s*
each_other-SG.DAT
'each other'

(141) a. *urt'iert'a-s*
each_other-SG.DAT
'each other'

b. *ert'iert'-is-a*
each_other-SG.GEN-EMPH
'each other'

The negative pronouns (Imnaishvili 1952) indicating non-existence or forbidenness are formed by adding negative particles *ara-*, *ver-*, *vera-* and *nu-* 'no' to the interrogative pronouns *vin* 'who' and *ra* 'what' (142). The declension of the negative pronouns is similar to the declension of the interrogative pronouns.

(142) *aravin, nuravin* 'nobody', etc.

2.3.4.3 Summary

To summarize, pronominal stems in Georgian can be subdivided into: (a) consonant-final pronouns which require the *-i* marker in the nominative; (b) consonant-final pronouns which do not require the *-i* marker in the nominative; (c) vowel-final pronouns truncating in genitive and instrumental cases; (d) vowel-final pronouns which do not truncate. Leaving to one side a large number of irregular cases, the regular declension paradigms of pronouns are as follows (Table 2.17):

Table 2.17 Pronominal declension types

Declension	Class	Features
1st Declension	Pronoun_1;	Vowel-final personal pronouns, truncating in the genitive and instrumental cases in the singular
2nd Declension	Pronoun_2;	Consonant-final personal pronouns, non-syncopating
3rd Declension	Pronoun_3;	Consonant-final pronouns which do not require the *–i* marker in the nominative, non-syncopating
4th Declension	Pronoun_4;	Vowel-final pronouns, non-truncating

2.3.5 Clitics

A clitic is defined as a morpheme that is phonologically dependent on a word or phrase, but acts as a syntactically independent word (Marantz 1988; Miller 1992; Spencer et al. 2012 and others). Although a clitic behaves like an affix, syntactically it is independent of a host. There are three types of clitics in Georgian: postpositions, particles, and auxiliary verbs.

2.3.5.1 Postpositions and Case Marking

Georgian postpositions, which have been described at length by various scholars (Chikobava 1934, 1937, 1961; Shanidze 1973 and others), can be represented by a suffix attached to an inflected nominal, or by an independent word which follows it. The case of nouns or other nominals is determined by the postposition. Each postposition is associated with a specific case, and some with two cases, such as the postposition *-vit* 'like', which can be used with either the nominative or the dative case (Sharashenidze 1939). There are no postpositions that govern the ergative or vocative cases (Table 2.18).

Table 2.18 Postpositions

Case markers	Modern Georgian	Old Georgian (clitics)	Old Georgian (separate words)
Absolutive	-	*-ebr, -ebriv* 'like'	
Nominative	*-vit'* 'like'	*-vit'*	
Ergative	-	-	
Dative	*-vit'*, *-ze* 'on', *-t'an* 'with', *-ši* 'in', *-k'veš* 'under'	*mi-*'till', *mo-*'till', *-vit'*, *-ze, -t'an, -ši*	*t'ana* 'with', *zeda* 'on', *šina* 'in', *šoris* 'between', *cinaše* 'in front of', *k'ueše* 'under', *gare* 'outside', *gareše* 'without'

(continued)

Table 2.18 (continued)

Case markers	Modern Georgian	Old Georgian (clitics)	Old Georgian (separate words)
Genitive	*-gan* 'from', *-t'vis* 'for', *-ken* 'to', *-ebr* 'like', *-ebriv* 'like', *-t'anave* 'just as', *-vit'*	*-gan, -t'ws* || *t'wn* || *-t'vis, -da* 'for', *-ken, -ebr, -ebriv, -t'anave, -vit'*	*t'ana, zeda, šoris, cinaše, k'ueše*[a], *mier* 'by', *gamo* 'because of', *t'wnier* 'besides'
Directional	-	*-mde, -mdis*	*momart'* 'towards', *mimart'* 'towards regarding (sb/smth)'
Instrumental	*-urt'* 'with', *-gan* 'from', *-dan*[b] 'from'	*-urt', -gan*	*gamo, gardamo* 'from heaven', *keržo* 'from or to'
Adverbial	*-mde* || *-mdis* 'up to'	*-mde* || *-mdi* || *-mdis*	
Vocative	-	-	

[a]In Old Georgian *t'ana* 'with', *zeda* 'on', *šoris* 'between', *cinaše* 'in front of' and *k'ueše* 'under' can be used in dative and genitive cases. The main difference is that in dative case these postpositions can be used only with inanimate, while in genitive - with animate nouns

The phonological process started in the tenth century caused generation of this form from instrumental case marker *-it* and postposition *-gan*, i.e. *-it+gan* → *id+gan* → *idan*

In Modern Georgian, postpositions which appear as separate words are derived from initial stems of adverbs indicating time, place, etc. if they follow a noun, adjective, etc. in the genitive case (143).

(143) a. *mank'an-is* *cin*
car-SG.GEN front
'in front of the car'

b. *mank'an-is* *k'veš*
car-SG.GEN under
'under the car'

There are no reasons from a morphological perspective to consider these separately appearing postpositions clitics. In Old Georgian, postpositions can appear either as clitics or as separate words, and can also be found prepositively as well as postpositively (144–145).

(144) *glaxak-t'a* *zeda*
beggar-PL.DAT on
'on beggars' (Doborjginidze et al. 2014)

(145) *cinaše* *beržen-t'*
in_front greek-PL.GEN
mep'-is-a
king-SG.GEN-EMPH
'in front of the King of Greece' (Doborjginidze et al. 2014)

This sequence can be observed in Modern Georgian as well (146).

(146) *zed* *magida-∅=ze*
on table-SG=on.DAT
'on the table' (Doborjginidze et al. 2014)

2.3.5.2 Auxiliary Verbs

Auxiliary verbs, which add functional and grammatical meaning to the sentence, expressing tense, aspect, mood, etc., can be of two types: (a) those which accompany the nominal paradigm and (b) those which accompany the verbal paradigm (Chumburidze 1984). In both cases, auxiliaries can act either as clitics or as separate words.

Verb forms that can be syntactically independent of a host while attaching to its stem include the first, second and third-person forms of the auxiliary verb 'to be'. While the first and the second persons appear as clitics only with the verbal paradigm (147–148), a contracted form of the third person singular *-a* can also cliticize to the nominal paradigm (149).

(147) *da-v-xt-i=var*
PV-1SGSBJ-jump-TS=be.3SG.AUX:PRS.IND
'I am jumping'

(148) *da-xt-i=xar*
PV-jump-TS=be.2SG.AUX:PRS.IND
'you are jumping'

(149) *saxl=ši=a*
home=in.DAT=be.3SG.AUX:PRS.IND
'he/she/it is at home'

All three forms increase the generative possibilities of the nominal and verbal paradigms.

2.3.5.3 Particles

Particles in Georgian may be subdivided into those which are stated separately in a closed class of items described in Sect. 2.3.10 and those which act as part of the nominal paradigm and increase the number of inflected forms (Topuria 1956a, 1956b). Depending on the PoS, these particles occupy slots 6–9 of the nominal paradigm and are subdivided into lexical types like the following (Table 2.19):

Table 2.19 Types of particles

	Modern Georgian	Old Georgian
Exclusive	*-ġa*	*-ġa, -ġac'a, -da*
Interrogative	-	*-a, -me*
Relative	*-c'a*	*-c'a, -ese, -ege, -igi, -c'a-ese, -c'a-ege, -c'a-igi*
Infinitive	*-me*	*-me*
Inclusive	*-c', -c'a, -ve*	*-ve*
Optative	*-mc'*	*-mc'a*

Mention should also be made of the particle *-qe* described by Tuite (1998) and the particle *-a* described by Shanidze (1973), which do not exist in literary Georgian, but are preserved in Georgian dialects. Particles may appear together one after the another (150) and cliticize generally to nominal (151) and sometimes to verbal (152) paradigms, only in Old Georgian.

(150) *-ġa* → *-ġa-c'* → *-ġa-c'a* etc.

(151) Modern Georgian:

a. *vi=ġa=c'a*
who=PTCL=PTCL
'someone'

b. *ima=ve*
same=PTCL
'the same'

Old Georgian:

c. *vit'ar=mc'a*
as=PTCL
'like'

d. *mc'ire-d=ġa=c'a*
small-ADV=PTCL=PTCL
'with a small one'

(152) Old Georgian:

a. *h-xedvi-d-a=c'a*
3SGOBJ-ask-EM-IMPF.3SGSBJ=PTCL
'as s/he/it could see'

b. *itq-od-es=c'a*
say-EM-IMPF.3SGSBJ=PTCL
as s/he/it said'

There is no consensus in the literature as to which specific class a given particle belongs to; for instance, Shanidze (1973) considers *-c'a* a relative particle, while Gabunia (2016) considers it an intensive particle.

2.3.5.4 Quotation Particles

As described in (Kvachadze 1996; Boeder 2002; Ramat and Topadze 2007 and others) Georgian uses forms derived from the verb *t'k'ma* 'to say' to indicate sources of information:

- The first indirect speech marker *-met'k'i* 'I said', derived from the form *me vt'k'vi* 'I said', is used to denote words spoken by a first-person singular speaker
- The second indirect speech marker *-t'k'va* or *-t'k'o* 's/he/it said', derived from the form *t'k'va* 's/he/it said', denotes words spoken by a third person of which the

first-person speaker is already aware (154). In Old Georgian, an independent form *t'k'ua* 's/he/it said' was used to denote the same

- The third indirect speech marker *-o* 'as it is said, as smb. said', which appears to be a truncated form of the second indirect speech marker, is used to denote words spoken by a third person (155).

(153) a. *še-i-c'val-a=met'k'i*
PV-PRV-change-3SGSBJ=1.QUOT:AOR.IND
'it was changed as I said'

b. *saxl-i-a=met'k'i*
house-SG.NOM-3SG.AUX=1.QUOT
'it is a house as I said'

(154) a. *da-brun-d-a=t'k'o*
PV-return-EM-3SGSBJ=2.QUOT:AOR.IND
'he is back as he said'

b. *cign-i-a=t'k'o*
book-SG.NOM-3SG.AUX=2.QUOT
'it is a book as he said'

(155) a. *ga-a-ket'-a=o*
PV-PRV-do-3SGSBJ=3.QUOT:AOR.IND
'he has done as smb. said'

b. *kac'-s-a=o*
man-SG.DAT-EMPH=3.QUOT
'to the man as smb. said'

Quotation particles can cliticize either to nominal or to verbal paradigms, occupying the final slot in either case. While the first and the second speech markers may appear either written separately or attached to their host with a hyphen, the third speech marker may appear only in an orthographically continuous form with its host; the hyphenated as well as the unhyphenated forms are clitics.

2.3.6 Verbal Inflection

The verb is the fundamental item of the sentence and expresses relationships between one or more participants or events. These relations, which may refer to various arguments, are fundamental to understanding the inflection of the Georgian verb, which shows person and number agreement with its subject and direct and indirect objects. A traditional approach (Chikobava 1968; Imnaishvili and Imnaishvili 1996; Shanidze 1973; Apridonidze 1986; Boeder 1989; Aronson 1984, 1990 and others) explains the morphosyntactic constituents of verbal forms and predicts the properties in accordance with which the ordering of affixes with their stems produces a verbal form. Regular verbs are inflected in accordance with TAM series, which brings together so-called 'inflectional classes', while irregular verbs follow the main inflectional classes, but contain suppletive forms or have paradigms with missing forms.

Verbal inflection in Georgian involves the participation of a variety morphemes which, from one point of view, are typical of agglutinating structures, and from another are typical of fusional structures, so that the morphological structure of Georgian can be characterized as both agglutinative and fusional. The Georgian verb generally uses bound morphemes to indicate its grammatical attributes. Morphemes are added to the root in the form of affixes and may in some cases change the root itself. The following formation types can be distinguished:

- Affixation, for instance *cancal-eb-s* 'walks about endlessly' → *i-cancal-eb-d-a* 'would walk about endlessly'
  Lexical Level: `Ipfv+წანწალებ-ს+Verb+Main+IDt+#9+RelStat+Intr +AutAct+FutCond+<NomSubj>+Subj3Sg`
  Surface Level: იწანწალებდა
- Root vowel alternation, for instance *drek-s* 'bends smth.' → *mo-drik-a* 'bent smth.'
  Lexical Level: `Ipfv+დრეკ-ს+Verb+Main+IDt+#20+Din+Trans+Act +Pres+<NomSubj>+<DatObj>+Subj3Sg+Obj3`
  Surface Level: დრეკს
  Lexical Level: `Pfv+დრეკ-ს+Verb+Main+IDt+#20+Din+Trans+Act +Aor+<ErgSubj>+<NomObj>+Subj3Sg+Obj3`
  Surface Level: მოდრიკა
- Root alternation, for instance *eubn-eb-a* 'says smth. to smb.' → *e-tqv-i-s* 'will say smth. to smb.'
  Lexical Level: `Ipfv+ეუბნებ-ა+Verb+Main+Trans+Act+Fut +<NomSubj>+<DatObjRec>+<DatObj>+Subj3Sg+ObjRec3+Obj3`
  Surface Level: ეტყვის

The maximum possible number of slots in the verbal template varies from nine to 12, as described in Hewitt (1995), Cherchi (1997), Boeder (2005) and others and, generally, consists of the following units: (1) preverbs, (2) prefixal pronominal markers, (3) version markers, (4) root, (5) passive markers, (6) thematic suffixes, (7) causative markers, (8) screeve markers, (9) suffixal person markers. Additional slots are posited for tmesis and object markers in Old Georgian and for extension markers, auxiliary verbs, and number and indirect speech markers in both Old and Modern Georgian (Table 2.20).

Table 2.20 Distribution of verb frame slots in Modern Georgian

−4	−3	−2	−1	0	1	2	3	4	5	6	7
Preverb (Prev)	Prev	Person marker (Pers)	Version marker (Vers)	R	Passive marker (Pass)	Thematic suffix (TS)	Causative marker (Caus)	Extension marker (EM)	Tense marker (Tns)	Pers, Nmbr, Aux	IS
mi		*v*	*u*		*d*	*i*[a]	*in*	*d*	*i*	*s*	*met‘k‘i*
mo		*x*	*a*			*av*	*evin*	*od*	*e*	*a*	*t‘k‘o*
a	*mo*	*h*	*e*			*am*			*o*	*o*	*o*
da		*s*	*i*			*em*				*en*	
č‘a	*mo*	*m*				*eb*				*an*	
še	*mo*	*gv*				*ob*				*nen*	
ga	*mo*	*g*				*op‘*				*n*	
ca	*mo*									*es*	
gada	*mo*									*t‘*	
										var	
										xar	
										a	
										vart‘	
										xart‘	
										arian	
										viqav	
										iqav	
										iqo	
										iqos	
										viqavit‘	
										iqavit‘	
										iqvnen	
										iqon	

[a]The inclusion of *-i-* suffix into the list of thematic suffixes is made conventionally and it should be mentioned that neither Shanidze (1973), nor Melikishvili (2014) do not consider it as an equal to other suffixes in a list

1. *Preverb 1*;
2. *Preverb 2* filled only by the preverb *mo-* indicating motion towards the speaker or addressee;
3. *Prefixal person marker,* sometimes referred to as the 'prefixal pronominal marker' (Makharoblidze 2018) or the 'prefixal nominal marker' (Gurevich 2006a, 2006b);
4. *Version marker*[11], referred to hereafter as the 'object correlation marker';
5. *Root,* which can be represented by a consonant (156) or a sequence of six consonants (157) with or without vowels. While the root does not provide a basis for the subdivision of verbs into inflectional classes, its position in the sequence of slots causes the so-called 'lemmatization problem' for Georgian dictionaries;
6. *Passive marker*;
7. *Thematic suffix*;
8. *Causative marker*;
9. *Extension marker,* which is sometimes referred to as an 'imperfective marker' (Makharoblidze 2018);
10. *Tense marker*;
11. *Person marker, number marker, auxiliary verb*[12];
12. *Indirect speech marker.*

(156) *a-b-am-s*
PRV-tie_up-3SGSBJ:PRS.IND
'ties up smth.'

(157) *gv-brdġvn-i-s*
1PLOBJ-tie_up-TS-3SGSBJ:PRS.IND
'smb. is plucking us'

The total number of slots is 13. Without imposing constraints on generational possibilities, by adding the aforementioned markers to a single verbal root, approximately, 15×7×4×1×7×2×2×3×9(excluding auxiliaries)×3 = 952,560 inflected word forms can be generated, including the possibility of overgeneration (Table 2.21).

---

[11] Opinions with regard to the grammatical category of version differ. Shanidze (1973) argues that version expresses a goal-possession relationship between the subject and object or objects, while Melikishvili (2014) describe the version as a category used to present an object in general and a version vowel as a marker used to indicate the orientation of the subject towards the object or objects.

[12] The suffixes like *-var, –xar* etc. occupying the sixth slot originated as clitic auxiliaries, but become grammaticalized to the verb as agreement affixes.

Table 2.21 Distribution of slots of verb frame in Old Georgian

−7	−6	−5	−4	−3	−2	−1	1	2	3	4	5	6
Prev	Prev	Tmesis (TM)	Pers	Pers	Pers	Vers	Pass	TS	Caus	EM	Tns	Pers, Nmbr, Aux
mi		*aray*	*x*	*v*	*h*	*u*	*d*	*i*	*en*	*d*	*i*	*s*
mo		*ve*	*h*	*û*	*s*	*a*		*av*	*in*	*od*	*e*	*a*
a	*mo*	*viet'me*		*xû*		*e*		*am*			*o*	*o*
da		*vinme*		*hû*		*i*		*em*			*a*	*d*
č'a	*mo*	*t'u vinme*		*x*				*eb*				*en*
še	*mo*	*me*		*h*				*ob*				*an*
ga	*mo*	*mc'a*		*s*				*op'*				*ed*
ca	*mo*	*nu*		*š*				*ev*				*n*
gada	*mo*	*nu vin*		*m*				*ov*				*es*
		ray		*g*								*t'*
		re		*gu*								
		ukue										
		ġa										
		ġat'u										
		c'a										
		xolme										
		xolo										

1. *Preverb 1*;
2. *Preverb 2* filled only by the preverb *mo-* indicating motion towards the speaker or addressee;
3. *Tmesis*, which does not exist in Modern Georgian;
4. *Prefixal person marker,* which is occupied by the third object marker *x-* in front of the first subject marker *û* only (158);
5. *Prefixal person marker*;
6. *Version marker*;
7. *Root*;
8. *Passive marker*;
9. *Thematic suffix*;
10. *Causative marker,* which can occupy a slot before and/or after a thematic suffix (159);
11. *Extension marker*;
12. *Tense marker*;
13. *-Person and number markers, auxiliary verb.*

(158) *x-u-es-av*
3SGDOBJ-1SGSBJ-hope-TS:PRS.IND
'I have hope'

(159) *č'amo-a-gd-eb-in-eb-s*
PV.PFV-PRV.3OBJ-throw-TS-CAUS-TS-3SGSBJ:FUT.IND
's/he/it will have smb./smth. thrown down'

2.3.6.1 Types of Verb

There are two types of verb: main verbs and auxiliary verbs. Lexical verbs, which have their own lexical meaning, indicate semantic relationship between participangs in the clause, while auxiliary verbs (*aris* 'be'), which contribute only grammatical meaning, can be attached to main verbs or nouns in the form of a clitic (160) or appear independently depending on the type of clause (161).

(160) a. *cign-∅-i=a*
book-SG-NOM=3SG.AUX
'it is a book'

b. *da-v-u-cer-i=var*
PV.PFV-1SGSBJ-PRV-write-PF.IND=1SG.AUX
'I have been written somewhere'

(161) *šexeduleb-eb=ši* *aris* *saert'o-∅*
point_of_view- PL=in.DAT 3sg.aux similar-NOM
nišn-eb-i
mark-PL-NOM
'there are similarities in point of views' (Doborjginidze et al. 2012)

Main verbs are subdivided into stative verbs, which represent a state of being (162), and dynamic verbs, which describe an action or change (163). While dynamic verbs in Georgian are considered a regular group with well-developed symmetric inflection, stative verbs are considered irregular, and follow the formation of TAM series in an asymmetric way by analogy with dynamic verbs.

(162) a. *qvir-i-s*
cry-TS-3SGSBJ:PRS.IND
'cries'

b. *cev-s*
lie-3SGSBJ:PRS.IND
'lies'

(163) a. *xat-av-s*
paint-TS-3SGSBJ:PRS.IND
'paints'

b. *šl-i-s*
spread-TS-3SGSBJ:PRS.IND
'spreads'

Both of these groups are subdivided into absolute and relative. Absolute verbs are unipersonal, while relative verbs – bipersonal or tripersonal. At the same time stative verbs can agree one or two persons (164), while dynamic – one, two, three (165) and very rarely four persons (166).

(164) a. *cux-s*
worry-3SGSBJ:PRS.IND
's/he/it is sad'

b. *u-cux-s*
PRV-worry-3SGSBJ:PRS.IND
'smb. feels week'

(165) a. *cux-d-eb-a*
worry-PASS-TS-3SGSBJ:PRS.IND
's/he/it feels sad'

b. *a-cux-eb-s*
PRV-worry-TS-3SGSBJ:PRS.IND
's/he/it disturbs smb.'

c. *a-cux-eb-in-eb-s*
PRV-worry-TS-CAUS-TS--
3SGSBJ:PRS.IND
's/he/it lets smb. to bother smb.'

(166) *m-i-čm-i-a*
1SGOBJ-PRV-RFL-eat-PF.IND-3SGSBJ
's/he/it made me feed smth. to smb.'

The principal morphological categories which affect verbal inflection are as follows: the TAM (tense-aspect-mood) series, which specifies case-marking and relationships between participants such as agent and patient by means of preverbs, version markers and thematic suffixes; diathesis/voice, which can be subdivided into the active, autoactive, inactive, passive and mediopassive voices; personality, which covers unipersonal, bipersonal and tripersonal verbs; and number.

2.3.6.2 Preverbs

Preverbs are defined by (Booij et al. 2003 and others) as special prefixes that appear in front of a verb. Georgian preverbs, which have been widely discussed in the literature (Gigashvili 2004a, b; Asatiani 2009; Melikishvili et al. 2010; Gogolashvili et al. 2011; Makharoblidze 2018 and others), appear in the form of prefixes and have the following key functions:

- to indicate spatiality, orientation and direction (167)

(167) a. *mi-d-i-s*
away.PV-go-PRS.IND-3SGSBJ
'goes away'

b. *mo-d-i-s*
from.PV-go-PRS.IND-3SGSBJ
'comes from somewhere'

- to change the lexical meaning of a word (168)

(168) a. *a-sxma-Ø*
up.PV-bearing-SG.NOM
'splashing up'

b. *gada-sxma-Ø*
over.PV-bearing-SG.NOM
'pouring out'

- to represent aspectual features of a verb (169)

(169) a. *xat-a*
draw-3SGSBJ:AOR.IND
'he was drawing'

b. *da-xat-a*
PV.PFV-draw-3SGSBJ:AOR.IND
'he has drawn'

- to distinguish between present and future tenses (170)

(170) a. *a-ket'-eb-s*
up.PV-do-TS-3SGSBJ:PRS.IND
's/he/it is doing smth.'

b. *ga-a-ket'-eb-s*
from_inside_to_outside.PV-do-TS-3SGSBJ:FUT.IND
's/he/it will do smth.'

While the first two functions are strictly lexical, the last two are morphosyntactic, and therefore of greater significance from a generation perspective.

Structurally, there are two types of preverbs: (1) simple, (2) complex. Simple preverbs consist predominantly of a single-syllable prefix which attaches to the beginning of a verbal root. Complex preverbs, which are formed by adding the preverb *mo-* after other simple preverbs, denote spatiality represented by the first preverbal constituent and direction towards the speaker and sometimes listener/addressee represented by the second. Complex preverbs likewise attach to the beginning of the verbal root. Taking into consideration the formation principles of complex preverbs, it can be observed that preverbs occupy not only the first, but the second verbal slot as well (Table 2.22).

Table 2.22 Preverbs

Modern Georgian		Old Georgian	
Simple	Complex	Simple	Complex
mi- 'from speaker'	-	*mi-*	*mimo-* 'around the speaker or the addressee'
mo- 'to speaker'	-	*mo-*	*mimoda-* 'around the speaker or thing that is below'
a- 'up'	*amo-*'up to speaker'	*aġ-* 'up'	*aġmo-* 'up to speaker'
da- 'down'	-	*da-*	*damo-* 'down hither'
č'a- 'down/into'	*č'amo-* 'down to speaker'	*št'a-* 'down/into'	*št'amo-*'down to speaker'
še- 'into'	*šemo-* 'from outside to inside, around'	*še-*	*šemo-*
ga- 'away'	*gamo-* 'away, but hither, towards speaker or 1 and 2p, not thither, away from speaker or to 3p'	*gan-* 'away'	*gamo-*
ca-'away'	*camo-* 'away from speaker'	*car-* 'away'	*carmo-* 'away from speaker'
gada- 'across, through'	*gadmo-* 'across towards speaker'	*garda-*'across, through'	*gardamo-*'across towards speaker'
		uku/ukun- 'behind, back'	*ukumo-* 'from outside to inside'
		ciaġ- 'across'	*ciaġmo-* 'from outside to speaker'

The Old Georgian preverbs *aġ-*, *aġmo-*, *št'a-*, *gan-*, *garda-*, *car-*, and *carmo-* still occur occasionally in Modern Georgian as well (171).

(171) a. *aġ-zrd-i-s*
up.PV-grow-3SGSBJ:FUT.IND
's/he/it will grow smb./smth.'

b. *aġmo-a-č'en-s*
up_hither.PV-PRV.3OBJ-find-3SGSBJ:FUT.IND
's/he/it will find smb./smth.'

c. *gan-i-xil-av-s*
out.PV-PRV.RFL-discuss-TS-3SGSBJ:FUT.IND
's/he/it will discuss smth.'

d. *št'a-a-gon-eb-s*
down.PV-PRV.3OBJ-instil-TS-3SGSBJ:FUT.IND
's/he/it will instil smth. in smb.'

Preverbs in Old Georgian are also involved in instances of tmesis, a phenomenon which occurs at the boundaries between slots supposing to form a continuous word. Tmesis can be observed in Old Georgian at the boundaries between preverbs and personal pronouns, where the former are separated from the latter by pronouns, conjunctions or particles, which in these cases occupy an additional slot between the preverb and prefixal person markers (172).

(172) a. *aġ-ray-dg-a*
up.PV-as.TM-rise-3SGSBJ:AOR.IND
'he has risen'

b. *aġ-nu vin-ant'-i-s*
up.PV-no_one.TM-enflame-TS-3SGSBJ:FUT.IND
'no one will enflame'

Aspect, which has been examined in Georgian by Holisky (1981a, 1981b), Harris (2003), Melikishvili et al. (2010) and others, indicates how an action expressed by a verb extends over time. Aspect can be imperfective (173) or perfective (174). Imperfective aspect refers to an incomplete action, while perfective aspect refers to a complete action. There are also some preverbs in Georgian which are so-called 'empty' or 'neutral' perfectivizers, forms generated on the basis of which are neither perfective, nor imperfective (175).

(173) *∅-cer-s*
IPFV-write-3SGSBJ:PRS.IND
's/he/it writes'

(174) *da-cer-s*
PV.PFV-write-3SGSBJ:FUT.IND
's/he/it will finish writing'

(175) *mi-c'oc'-av-s*
PV-crawl-TS-3SGSBJ:PRS.IND
'*s/he/it crawls along*'

While aspect as a grammatical category is considered to form part of the TAM (Tense-Aspect-Mood) series system in Georgian, it is not indicated by any special markers in the language other than preverbs, and examination of the development of the verbal system in Georgian also reveals that preverbs cannot be considered markers used solely to denote aspectual features of verbs.

While in Modern Georgian, perfective aspect forms occur in the past and future tenses and imperfective aspect forms in the past, present and future tenses, aspect cannot be associated with the presence or absence of preverbs in verbal paradigm in every case (176).

(176) a. *∅-h-kit'x-a*
PFV-3SGIOBJ-ask-3SGSBJ:AOR.IND
's/he/it has asked'
b. *∅-u-pasux-a*
PFV-PRV.3IOBJ-answer-3SGSBJ:AOR.IND
's/he/it has answered'

In Old and Middle Georgian (Shanidze 1976; Sarjveladze 1997; Gigashvili 2004 and others), the distinction between the perfective and imperfective aspects aligns with divisions within the TAM series system; specifically, all verbal forms of the first series are imperfective (177), while all forms of the second and the third series are perfective (178).

(177) a. *∅-gan-v-a-g-eb*
PV.IPFV-1SGSBJ-PRV.3OBJ-manage-TS:PRS.IND
'I manage smth.'
b. *∅-v-a-kurt'x-ev*
IPFV-1SGSBJ-PRV.3OBJ-bless-TS:PRS.IND
'I bless smb./smth.'

(178) a. *gan-v-a-g-e*
PV.PFV-1SGSBJ-PRV.3OBJ-manage-AOR.IND
'I have managed smth.'
b. *∅-v-a-kurt'x-e*
PFV-1SGSBJ-PRV.3OBJ-bless-AOR.IND
'I have blessed smb./smth'
c. *m-i-t'k'u-am-s*
PFV-1SGSBJ-PRV.3OBJ-bless-TS-3SGSBJ:PF.IND
'I said smth. to smb.'

An opposition can also be observed between the presence and absence of thematic suffixes, which has recently given rise to a discussion as to the possible existence of additional aspect markers in Old Georgian represented by the thematic suffix vowels *-i-* and *-e-*. According to Chikobava (2013) and Melikishvili (2014), these markers can serve to indicate the aspectal features of a verb (179–180).

(179) a. *i-scav-eb*
PRV.RFL -study-TS:IPFV.PRS.IND
'you study'
b. *i-scav-i*
PRV.RFL-study-IPFV:AOR.COND
'you studied'
c. *i-scav-e*
PRV.RFL-study-PFV:AOR.IND
'you studied to completion'

(180) a. *da-i-mal-v-i*
PV-PRV.RFL-hide-TS-IPFV:PRS.IND
'you hide'
b. *da-i-mal-i*
PV-PRV.RFL-hide-IPFV:AOR.COND
'you hided'
c. *da-i-mal-e*
PV-PRV.RFL-hide-PFV:AOR.IND
'you hid to completion'

This evidence may provide grounds for the aformentioned strict opposition between series with regard to aspectual forms in Old Georgian to be reconsidered.

2.3.6.3 Person and Number

Georgian verbal morphology includes agreement between the verb and its arguments in terms of person, case and number. While in Indo-European languages, the verb generally agrees with the subject of the sentence, in Georgian the verb agrees not only with the subject, but with its objects as well, both direct and/or indirect. The verb in Georgian has core and peripheral arguments. A core argument agrees morphologically with the verb by means of person and number markers, while a peripheral argument does not. The number of core arguments affects the conjugation system as a whole, subdividing it into subject and object paradigms (these are the conventionally used terms).

The category of person is closely connected to the category of number. Person markers can be of prefixal and suffixal formation. Prefixal person markers occupy the fourth slot in Modern and the fifth slot in Old Georgian. Suffixal person markers share the twelfth slot with number markers and auxiliaries, establishing so-called 'long-dependencies' on their prefixal counterparts. These long dependencies form the subject and object agreement paradigms of the Georgian verb, which vary according to TAM series (Table 2.23).

Table 2.23 Person and number in the subject paradigm

	Modern Georgian		Old Georgian		Modern Georgian		Old Georgian	
	Singular		Singular		Plural		Plural	
1	*v-*	-	*v-, û-, xû-, hû-, ∅-*	-	*v-*	*-t‘*	*v-, û-, xû-, hû,-∅-*	*-t‘*
2	*∅-, x-, *h-, *s-*	-	*∅-, x-, h-, s-, š-*	-	*∅-, x-, *h-, *s-*	*-t‘*	*∅-, x-, h-, s-, š-*	*-t‘*
3	-	*-s, -a, -o*		*-s, -a, -o, -n*		*-en, -an, -n, -nen, -es*		*-en, -an, -n, -es, -ed*

The person markers of the second person singular subject are not active in Modern Georgian; the marker *x-* appears only in verb forms such as *x-ar* 'you are', *(mi)-x-val* 'you will go (to)', *(mi)-x-ved* 'you went (to)' and other forms generated from the root *val* 'go', while the second person subject prefixes *h-* and *s-* appear in texts at the end of nineteenth and at the beginning of twentieth centuries and very rarely today.

Old Georgian texts can be classified according to the use in them of alternate agreement markers for the first person singular subject: *xû-*, *hû-* and for the second person singular subject: *x-*, *h-*, *s-* and *š-* into *Xanmeti* (V–VIII cc.), *Haemeti* (VII–VIII cc.) and *Sannarevi (*starting from IXth c.) texts. *Xanmeti* texts employ *v-*, *û-*, *xû-* as first-person subject markers and Ø-, *x-* as second-person subject markers, while *Haemeti* texts employ *v-*, *û-*, *hû-* as first-person subject markers and Ø-, *h-* as second-person subject markers. *Sannarevi* texts follow strict phonological rules with regards to the use of the second-person subject markers *h-*, *s-* and *š-*; specifically:

- *h-* is used before *b, p‘, p, g, k‘, k, x̣, q, v, z, s, š, q, x, l, m, n* and *r*;
- *s-* is used before *d, t‘, t, ż, c‘* and *c*;
- *š-* is used before *j, č‘, č*.

The operation of this rule is likewise observed in the object paradigm with regard to the representation of the third-person singular object markers. Another marker which depends on the object paradigm is the first-person singular subject marker *û-*, which appears only if it is preceeded by the third-person singular object marker *x-* (Table 2.24).

Table 2.24 Person and number in the object paradigm

	Modern Georgian		Old Georgian		Modern Georgian		Old Georgian	
	Singular		Singular		Plural		Plural	
1	*m-*	-	*m-*	-	*gv-*	-	*m-*, *gu-*	-
2	*g-*	-	*g-*	-	*g-*	*-t‘*	*g-*	-
3	Ø-, *h-*, *s-*	-	Ø-, *x-*, *h-*, *s-*, *š-*		*h-*, *s-*, Ø-	*-t‘*	Ø-, *x-*, *h-*, *s-*, *š-*	-

According to Sarjveladze (1997), Gurgenidze (2009), Melikishvili (2009a, 2009b) and others, in the case of first-person plural objects, while historically the marker *m-* was used to indicate exclusivity, whereby the addressee is excluded, whereas the marker *gu-* was used to indicate inclusivity, whereby the addressee is included in the meaning of 'we', from the eighth century onward Old Georgian texts do not demonstrate a strict opposition between *m-* and *gu-* with regard to the inclusion of the addressee, so that these can be considered parallel forms.

A comparison of of the subject and object agreement paradgims makes it clear that the subject paradigm can be considered agglutinative, while the object paradigm is fusional because it includes morphemes used to mark two grammatical categories simultaneously, such as the marker *gv-* which combines features of first person and plural number.

As stated in Aronson (1990), Melikishvili et al. (2010), Wier (2011a, 2011b) and others, the main constraints on the use of the above-mentioned markers are as follows:

- The first-person subject marker cannot be used together with a first-person object marker either in the singular or in the plural;
- The second-person subject marker cannot be used together with a second-person object marker either in the singular or in the plural;
- The combination of the first-person subject with the second-person object at the root-initial position results in the appearance of the object marker rather than the subject marker;
- The combination of the second-person subject with the first-person object at the root-initial position results in the appearance of the object marker rather than the subject marker;
- The combination of a third person subject with the first, the second or a third-person object at the root-initial position results in the appearance of the object marker rather than the subject marker;
- First-person singular or plural subjects used in combination with the second-person object in the plural require the marker *-t‘* only (181);
- A third-person plural subject used in combination with the second-person plural object removes *-t‘* plural marker (182);
- In aorist, the third singular subject marker *-s* is substituted with *-a* (183) and the third plural subject marker *-en* is often substituted with *-es* (184).

(181) *g-kr-av-t‘*
2PLOBJ-strike-TS-3PLSBJ:PRS.IND
‘I strike you’ or ‘you strike them’

(182) *g-kr-av-en*
2PLOBJ-strike-TS-3PLSBJ:PRS.IND
‘they strike you’

(183) a. *g-kr-av-s*
2PLOBJ-strike-TS-3PLSBJ:PRS.IND
‘s/he/it strikes you’

b. *g-kr-a*
2PLOBJ-strike-3SGSBJ:AOR.IND
‘s/he/it striked you’

(184) a. *g-kr-av-en*
2PLOBJ-strike-TS-3PLSBJ:PRS.IND
‘they struck you’

b. *g-kr-es*
2PLOBJ-strike-3PLSBJ:AOR.IND
‘they struck you’

Thorough analyses of number agreement in Old and Modern Georgian carried out by Imnaishvili (1957), Sarjveladze (1997), and Tuite (1998) have revealed that the principle difference between Old and Modern Georgian with respect to the representation of number lies in the differences between the subject and object sets. The subject set reflects agreement between two or three persons in two numbers (singular or plural), while the object set makes a distinction between persons in its assignment of number (singular or plural) to them. After the Old Georgian period clausal subjects assigned nominative or ergative case control number agreement, initially with the *-n-* or *-t'-* plural markers (185) and only after the tenth century with the *-eb-* plural marker (186–187), while clausal subjects assigned dative case do not.

(185)	car-a-vlin-n-a		*moc'ik'ul-n-i*
	PV-PRV-send-PL-3SGSBJ:PFV.AOR.IND		apostle-PL-NOM

'he sent apostles' (H-2080, Doborjginidze et al. 2012)

(186)	*kac'-eb-man*	*man*	*vit'ar=c'a*
	man-PL-ERG	this:ERG	as=PTCL
	i-xil-a	*sascaul-i*	*igi*
	PRV-see- 3SGSBJ:PFV.AOR.IND	miracle-SG.NOM	this:NOM

'when the people saw the miracle' (Adishi Lives of Saints', Doborjginidze et al. 2012)

(187)	huria-t'a	*k'mr-eb-man*	*vit'ar=c'a*
	Jew-PL.GEN	servant-PL-ERG	as=PTCL
	i-smin-es	*cinayscarmetqwēleba-y*	
	PRV-hear-3PLSBJ:PFV.AOR.IND	prophecy-NOM	

'when the servants of the Jews heard the prophesy' (P'arxali Lives of Saints, Doborjginidze et al. 2012)

The basic rules for the combination of number markers can be summarised as follows: a verb always agrees with first and second-person subjects in number, while third-person inanimate subjects require singular number agreement regardless of their logical number.

After the Old Georgian period, the animacy of participants has gradually come to play a crucial role with regard to person, number and case agreement. In Modern Georgian, as described in Kiziria (1982), Kvachadze (1996) and others, while number agreement strictly occurs in the case of animate NP-s with the *-eb-*, *−n-* and *-t'-* plural markers (188), it very rarely occurs in the case of inanimate NP-s with the *-eb-* plural marker (189–190).

(188)	*t'avadaznaur-eb-i*	*da*
	noble-PL-NOM	and
	vačr-eb-i=c'	*at'asob-it'*
	merchant-PL-NOM=PTCL	thousand-INST
	mi-di-od-nen	*ruset'=ši*
	PV-visit-EM-3PLSBJ:IMPF.IND	Russia=in.DAT

'A lot of nobles and merchants visited Russia' (Doborjginidze et al. 2012)

(189) *dġe-eb-i* *mi-di-od-a*
day-PL-NOM PV-pass-EM-3PLSBJ:IMPF.IND
'The days were passing' (Doborjginidze et al. 2012)

(190) cl-eb-i *ki* *mi-di-od-nen*
year-PL-NOM however PV-pass-EM-3PLSBJ:IMPF.IND
'However, the years were passing' (Doborjginidze et al. 2012)

It should be noted that the category of animacy does not have any special morphological markers, and can instead be considered a semantic feature of a nominal which affects its agreement with the verb at the syntactic level. The principal rule followed by verbs with regard to number agreement can however be described as follows: an animate agent is prevails over an inanimate, and accordingly, the first person always prevails, the second prevails unless it conflicts with the first one, and both of them prevail over the third one.

2.3.6.4 Valency and Transitivity

The aforementioned person markers are used to represent relationships between subject and object persons in the conjugation system. The Georgian verb reflects relations between two, three or four arguments and distinguishes the recipient, causer, causee, beneficiary and location of an action by means of prefixal and suffixal agreement markers which interact with inflectional class within the TAM series system and provide a mapping between morphology and syntactic features such as the roles of participants (Shanidze 1942; Sukhishvili 1986; Beridze 1998 and others). While these person markers are not enough to indicate their roles in the clause, the ability of the Georgian verb to represent relations between the predicate and its arguments serves as a base for defining the valency of a verb, which counts all arguments including the subject. This category can subcategorize verbs into:

- Impersonal verbs, which do not have a subject (191);

(191) a. *cvim-s*
rain-3SG:PRS.IND
'it is raining'

b. *k'ux-s*
thunder-3SG:PRS.IND
'it is thunder'

- Intransitive verbs, which take a subject only (192);

(192) a. *cux-s*
sad-3SGSBJ:PRS.IND
'she/he/it is sad'

b. *tir-i-s*
cry-TS-3SGSBJ:PRS.IND
'she/he/it is crying'

- Indirect transitive verbs, which take two arguments: a subject and an indirect object (193);

(193) a. *da-v-e-mal-e*
PV.PFV-1SGSBJ-PRV-hide-AOR.IND
'I have hidden from smb./smth.'
b. *še-xed-a*
PV.PFV-look-3SGSBJ:AOR.IND
's/he/it looked at smb./smth.'

- Transitive verbs, which take two arguments: a subject and a direct object (194);

(194) a. *v-xat-av*
1SGSBJ-draw-TS:PRS.IND
'I draw smb.'
b. *m-xat-av-s*
1SGDOBJ-draw-TS:PRS.IND
's/he/it draws me'

- Ditransitive verbs, which take three arguments: a subject and a direct and indirect object (195).[13]

(195) a. *v-u-xat-av*
1SGSBJ-PRV.3IOBJ-draw-TS:PRS.IND
'I draw smth. for smb.'
b. *m-i-xat-av-s*
1SGIOBJ-PRV.RFL-draw-TS-3SGSBJ:PRS.IND
's/he/it draws smth. for me'

The agent, i.e. subject, which possesses its own markers and patients, i.e. objects (both direct and indirect), which possess their own markers, have similar generative possibilities; for instance, a transitive bipersonal verb can generate up to 18 different forms – three times more than an intransitive monopersonal verb, which generates only six forms for singular and plural, as is also the case in the majority of Indo-European languages.

There are three ways to increase the valency of a verb: (a) using the marker *a-* with the thematic suffix *-eb* (196); (b) using the marker *a-* with the causative suffix *-in* (197), and (c) using the marker *a-* (or very rarely the object correlation marke *e-*) with the causative and thematic suffixes *-in-eb* (198–199).

(196) *a-kiv-eb-s*
PRV.3IOBJ-cry-TS-3SGSBJ:PRS.IND
's/he/it makes smb. cry'

[13] Taking into account that only one verb – namely, the verb *mičmia* 's/he made me feed smth. to smb.' – can be described as a tritransitive verb with four arguments, we have not allowed for the generation of verbs of this kind in the Georgian verbal system.

(197) *da-a-cqeb-in-a*
PV.PRF-PRV.3IOBJ-start-CAUS-3SGSBJ:AOR.IND
's/he/it made smb. start smth.'

(198) *a-cqeb-ineb-s*
PRV.3IOBJ-start-CAUS-3SGSBJ:PRS.IND
's/he/it makes smb. start smth.'

(199) *e-t'lev-in-eb-a*
PRV.3IOBJ-count-CAUS-TS-3SGSBJ:PRS.IND
's/he/it makes smb. count smth.'

Causativity introduces a new argument – namely, the causer – into the arguments of a transitive verb (Asatiani 1989). Causitivity, which is sometimes referred to as the category of contact (Hewitt 1995; Makharoblidze 2009; Baratashvili 2019 and others) denotes the action of a causer (so-called 'direct contact') or the action of a cause carried out under the influence of a causer (so-called 'indirect contact'). The principal semantic feature of causativity is the relation between the causer and the causee.

The difference between types of object and their agreement with the verb in a clause is bound to the transitivity of the Georgian verb and, accordingly, to case agreement between the predicate and its arguments; specifically, the subject can be marked by the nominative (200), ergative (201) or dative (202) case, while the object is marked by the nominative (201–202) or dative case (203–204) with or without a postposition.

(200) *kac'-i* *lek's-s* *cer-s*
man-SG.NOM poem-SG.DAT write-3SGSBJ:PRS.IND
'a man writes a poem'

(201) *kac'-ma* *lek's-i*
man-SG.ERG poem-SG.NOM
da-cer-a
PV.PFV-write- 3SGSBJ:AOR.IND
'a man wrote a poem'

(202) *kac'-s* *lek's-i* *t'urme*
man-SG.DAT poem- SG.NOM apparently
da-u-cer-i-a
PV.PFV-PRV.3IOBJ-write-PF.IND-3SGSBJ
'apparently, a man has written a poem'

(203) *kac'-i* *k'al-s* *lek's-s*
man-SG.NOM woman-SG.DAT poem-SG.DAT
u-cer-s
PRV.3IOBJ-write-3SGSBJ:PRS.IND
'a man writes a poem to a woman'

(204) *kac'-s* *lek's-i*
man-SG.DAT poem- SG.NOM
k'al-is=t'vis *da-u-cer-i-a*
woman-SG.GEN =for.GEN PV.PFV-PRV.3IOBJ-write-PF.IND-3SGSBJ
'a man has apparently written a poem to a woman'

While differing approaches reveal mismatches between verbal agreement, valency and case marking in Georgian (Tuite 1998; Gurevich 2004; Wier 2011a, 2011b and others), briefly put, the correlation between person, case and number markers with regard to the conjugation system in Old and Modern Georgian shows the following regularities:

1. If an agent, i.e. an active subject of a verb, is in the ergative case, it requires the *v*-type inflectional class with appropriate markers from the so-called '*v*-set';
2. If an agent is in the dative case, it requires the *m*-type inflectional class with appropriate markers from the so-called '*m*-set';
3. An actant in the nominative case can be used with both types of conjugation: if an actant in the nominative case is an agent of a clause, it requires the *v*-type inflectional class and a patient in the nominative case, while if it is a patient of a clause, it requires the *m*-type inflectional class and an agent in the ergative.

Harris (1981), Gurevich (2006b), Wier (2011a, 2011b), Tuite (2019) and others discuss the so-called '*s*–/*h*-set' with regard to the marking of the third-person indirect object in the verb by means of phonologically conditioned allomorphs of the third-person object marker. According to traditional approaches, this set is derived on the basis of the *m*-type inflectional class, which splits into an *m*-set and an *h*-set. The main constraint with regard to this set is that while the *m*-set can be used together with version markers (205), the *h*-set occupies the same slot as the version markers and can never be used in combination with them (206).

(205) a. *m-i-cer-s*
1SGDOBJ-PRV.RFL-write-3SGSBJ:PRS.IND
's/he/it is writing me smth.'

b. *m-a-cer-s*
1SGDOBJ-PRV-write-3SGSBJ:PRS.IND
's/he/it is levying from me'

(206) a. *mi-s-cer-a*
PV-3SGIOBJ-write-3SGSBJ:AOR.IND
's/he/it wrote smth. to smb.'

b. *mi-u-cer-a*
PV-PRV.3IOBJ-write-3SGSBJ:AOR.IND
's/he/it wrote smth. for smb.'

c. *mi-i-cer-a*
PV-PRV.RFL-write-3SGSBJ:AOR.IND
's/he/it 'scribed something to themself'

As such, the h-set cannot be considered a person marker which indicates an indirect object in a verb. It can instead be defined as an object correlation marker, or version marker possessing certain attributes similar to that of an indirect object marker, as proposed by Boeder (1968) and Shanidze (1973). Accordingly, these markers should be considered to occupy not the third, but the fourth slot in the verbal paradigm. In addition to the *h*-set of markers, there are four version markers: *u-*, *a-*, *e-*, and *i-*, which can be placed between the person markers and the root or directly between preverbs and the root if the person marker slot is not occupied to indicate the relationship between the subject, direct and indirect object.

2.3.6.5 Inversion and Object Correlation Markers

The Georgian verb's reflection of agent and patient, which can be compared to logical subject and logical object in Lexical Functional Syntax (Bresnan 2016) and the differentiation of thematic roles and syntactic arguments is crucial to understanding the process of inversion and the functionality of the categories of voice and version, the markers of which are referred to as 'person correlation markers' (Melikishvili et al. 2010).

The inversion process can be considered: (a) a strictly morphological switch in the valency of a verb by means of special morphological markers (207) according to Shanidze (1961, 1973) and others, who discuss inversion in perfect series forms from a synchronic perspective; (b) a morphosyntactic change caused by the relationship between valency and personal markers with regard to the presentation of the logical subject and logical object of a clause (208) according to Chikobava (1936, 1946), who describes inversion in the third series from a diachronic perspective, or (c) a process that allows the personal markers of the v-set and m-set to indicate each other's features according to Uturgaidze (2001) and Datukishvili (1992, 1997a, 1997b).

(207) a. *v-cer*
1SGSBJ-write:PRS.IND
'I write him/her/it'

b. *da-m-ı-cer-ı-a*
PV.PFV-1SGOBJ-PRV.RFL-write-PF-3SGSBJ:PERF.IND
'I have written smth.'

(208) a. *v-u-qvar = var*
1SGSBJ-PRV-love-be.1SG.AUX:PRS.IND or
1SGDOBJ-PRV-love-be.1SG.AUX:PRS.IND
(*v-* used to indicate direct object)
's/he/it loves me'

b. *m-i-qvar-s*
1SGDOBJ-PRV-love-3SGSBJ:PRS.IND or
1SGSBJ-PRV-love-3SGOBJ:PRS.IND (*m-* used to indicate subject)
'I love him/her/it'

Generally speaking, all discussions of the inversion process (Harris 1981; Gurevich 2006b; Wier 2011a, 2011b; Gogolashvili et al. 2011 and others) describing perfect series forms and the forms of the fourth conjugation[14] as inversion of the functions of the person markers are based on the aforementioned synchronic or diachronic perspectives. From a diachronic perspective, inversion is triggered by a passive, non-active subject in stative verbs and by analogy in dynamic verbs, whereas for dynamic verbs with a very strong active subject, this process is impossible. A correspondence between case agreement with regard to conjugation types as described by Melikishvili (2001a, 2001b, 2009b) can be summarized as follows (Table 2.25):

Table 2.25 Correlation between case and conjugation system

v-type inflectional class		*m*-type inflectional class	
NOM	NOM (*v*-set)		
NOM	NOM (*v*-set) + DAT	DAT (*m*-set)	
NOM	ERG (*v*-set) + DAT	NOM (*m*-set)	
NOM	ERG (*v*-set) + DAT	NOM (*m*-set) + DAT	DAT (∅ *-a*)
NOM	ERG (*v*-set) + DAT	NOM (∅ set) + DAT	DAT (*m*- *-a*)

From our perspective, the most important conclusion is that the markers used in the *v*-type and *m*-type inflectional classes can be interchanged to indicate the real subject and the real object of a clause; while this process is not complete in Modern Georgian, its influence is expanding in comparison with Old (209).

(209) a. *m-a-natr-eb-s*
1SGIOBJ-PRV-miss-TS-3SGSBJ:PRS.IND
's/he/it makes me miss smb./smth.'

b. *m-e-natr-eb-a*
1SGOBJ-PRV-miss-TS-3SGSBJ:PRS.IND or
1SGSBJ-PRV-miss-TS-3SGDOBJ:PRS.IND
'I miss smb./smth.'

A distinction between types of object can be made at the syntactic level by observing the cases used by nominals, or at the morphological level by means of special correlation markers known as version markers, which enable us to distinguish the roles of objects from one point of view, and from another to change the meaning of a verb as a whole. For example, a transitive verb can govern an indirect

[14] Scholars discussing mismatches in Georgian verbal paradigms always appeal to the inconsistencies of marking and agreement between four types of conjugation scheme proposed by Shanidze (1973) . Specifically, they argue against the idea that the perfect series should be considered an example of syntactic inversion from a synchronic point of view; Gurevich (2004), for example, argues that the perfect series should not be considered as synchronous inversion from a constructional point of view, while Wier (2011a, 2011b) considers inversion a morphological, but not a syntactic process.

object without special marking of its features at the syntactic level; in other words, an argument can be omitted from an utterance, but be understood from the discourse. As such, a distinction between the roles of objects can additionally be indicated by agreement markers (210).

(210) a. *a-šen-eb-s*
PRV.3OBJ-build-TS-3SGSBJ:PRS.IND
' s/he/it builds smth.'

b. *a-a-šen-a*
PV.PFV-PRV.3OBJ-build-3SGSBJ:AOR.IND
'ss/he/it built smth.'

c. *a-u-šen-eb-i-a*
PV.PFV-PRV.3OBJ-build-PF.IND-3SGSBJ
's/he/it has built smth.'

d. *u-šen-eb-s*
PRV.3IOBJ-build-TS-3SGSBJ:PRS.IND
's/he/it builds smth. for smb.'

e. *a-u-šen-a*
PV.PFV-PRV.3IOBJ-build-3SGSBJ:AOR.IND
's/he/it built smth. for smb.'

f. *a-u-šen-eb-i-a*
PV.PFV-PRV.3IOBJ-build-PF.IND-3SGSBJ
's/he/it has build smth.'

g. *i-šen-eb-s*
PRV.RFL-build-TS-3SGSBJ:PRS.IND
's/he builds for himself/herself'

h. *a-i-šen-a*
PV.PFV-PRV.RFL-build-3SGSBJ:AOR.IND
's/he/it built for himself/herself'

Version can be compared to applicative constructions, which involve a participant that would not normally be instantiated in a core object relation but rather as an oblique of one sort or another, in a core (usually direct object) instantiation, as described by Alsina et al. (1990) and Peterson (1999, 2007); at the same time, however, as described by Gurevich (2006b), they can be compared to applicatives only partially. It is important to note with respect to this category that the use of these correlation markers is connected to the the difference between transitive and intransitive verbs. While transitive verbs posess all of the forms associated with version, intransitive verbs possess only limited possibilities in this regard. The principal constraint is that intransitive verbs, which do not govern direct objects, never use subjective version, but only the remaining two types: objective and locative.

Objective version, which is associated with the markers *i-* and *u-*, marks an indirect object in the verbal argument structure and underlines the belonging of the direct object to the indirect object. The two markers are used in differing conditions:

the marker *i-* is used with the first and the second-person markers of the object marker paradigm (211), while the marker *u-* is used in combination with all of the person markers in the *v*-type paradigm (212) and with the third-person markers in the *m*-type paradigm (213).

(211) a. *m-i-cer-s*
1SGIOBJ-PRV.3OBJ-write-3SGSBJ:PRS.IND
'S/he/it writes for me'
b. *g-i-cer-s*
2SGIOBJ-PRV.3OBJ-write-3SGSBJ:PRS.IND
'S/he/it writes for you'
(212) a. *v-u-cer*
1SGSBJ-PRV.3OBJ-write:PRS.IND
'I write to him'
b. *u-cer*
PRV.3OBJ-write:2SGSBJ.PRS.IND
'you write to him'
c. *u-cer-s*
PRV.3OBJ-write-3SGSBJ:PRS.IND
'S/he/it writes to him'
(213) *u-cer-s*
PRV.3OBJ-write-3SGSBJ:3SGIObj.PRS.IND
'S/he/it writes to him'

These features of objective version are strictly represented in transitive verbs which govern direct objects. On the other hand, the peculiarities of intransitive verbs, in which an opposition can be observed between the use of *i-* and *e-* agreement markers (214), gives rise to the question of whether these markers represent version or voice.

(214) a. *šeš-d-eb-a*
stop-PASS-TS-3SGSBJ:PRS.IND
'S/he/it becomes numb'
b. *u-šeš-d-eb-a*
PRV.3OBJ-stop-PASS-TS-3SGSBJ:PRS.IND
'smb's smth. goes numb'
c. *i-k'ač'-eb-a*
PRV-pull-PASS-TS-3SGSBJ:PRS.IND
'S/he/it is conceited'
d. *e-k'ač'-eb-a*
PRV.3OBJ-pull-PASS-TS-3SGSBJ:PRS.IND
'S/he/it tugs hard at smth.'

These different approaches are concerned with the functions of objective version in the case of conversion – a process described in the Georgian academic literature (Shanidze 1973; Gogolashvili et al. 2011 and others) as a mechanism of relation between the active and passive voices - in which objective version reflects that the subject belongs to the indirect object. The markers of objective version are always oriented towards indicating the benefactive of an action or possession by the indirect object and, following Gurevich (2006b), if there is a choice between using a construction with or without a version marker, the general deciding factor is the degree to which a participant is affected by the action.

Subjective version, which is reflected by the marker *i-*, participates syntactically in the formation of subject and object agreement by adding a notion of reflexivity or meaning of directionality to the subject (215), as stated by Shanidze (1973). Taking into account that subjective version shares the marker *i-* with objective version, some scholars suggest a differentiation between them on the basis of semantic analysis (Machavariani 1987), while others propose a treatment of subjective version as a subtype of objective version (Boeder 1968); all of them, however, agree that subjective version features a subject of a bipersonal transitive verb represented as a benificiary of an action within a construction which follows regular subject/direct object agreement principles.

(215) a. *i-ker-av-s*
PRV.RFL-sew-TS-3SGSBJ:PRS.IND
'S/he/it is sewing for themself'

b. *i-loc'-av-s*
PRV.RFL-pray-TS-3SGSBJ:PRS.IND
'S/he/it is praying'

While subjective version can be considered a sub-type of objective version, its distinct functions reveal similarities between subjective version and middle voice as described in Shanidze (1973), Tuite (2019) and others, to the extent that version is in some cases treated as an extension of the category of voice.

Locative (neutral) version, which is associated with the markers *a-* or ∅-, adds an additional argument to the verb which is not necessary an indirect object (216). In the majority of cases, this means that the argument cannot be considered a beneficiary of an action, or to belong to anybody. The *a-* marker is also used to indicate location 'downward' (217) and, together with the thematic suffix *-eb*, is used as circumfix that generates so-called 'morphological causatives' from nominal or adjectival roots (218), as described by Aronson (1990), Hewitt (1995), Gurevich (2006b) and others. In this case, the *a-* marker can be easily substituted with other markers to reflect the beneficiaries of action.

(216) a. *a-t'b-ob-s*
PRV.3OBJ-warm-TS-3SGSBJ:PRS.IND
'S/he/it warms smb./smth.'

b. *a-gor-eb-s*
PRV.3OBJ-roll-TS-3SGSBJ:PRS.IND
'S/he/it rolls smth. along'

(217) a. *a-cer-s*
downward.PRV.3OBJ-write-3SGSBJ:PRS.IND
'*s*/he/it signs smth.'

b. *a-a-sp'alt-eb-s*
PV-downward.PRV.OBJ-asphalt-3SGSBJ:PRS.IND
's/he/it asphalts smth.'

(218) a. *brial-i* 'rotation' → *a-brial-eb-s* 's/he/it is flashing her/his/its eyes', *lamaz-i* 'beautiful' → *a-lamaz-eb-s* 's/he/it adorns smb./smth.', etc.
brial-i
rotation-SG.NOM
'rotation'
a-brial-eb-s
PRV.3OBJ-rotate-TS-3SGSBJ:PRS.IND
's/he/it is flashing her/his eyes'

b. *lamaz-i*
beautiful-SG.NOM
'beautiful'
a-lamaz-eb-s
PRV.3OBJ-adorn-TS-3SGSBJ:PRS.IND
's/he/it adorns smb./smth.'

As can be observed, the most productive are forms generated by the markers of objective version; less productive are those generated by the markers of subjective and locative version. On the other hand, the distribution of the *i-* marker is quite extensive, in that it is shared by the objective and subjective versions and appears with active (219), passive (220) and so-called mediopassive (221) verb forms, as discussed in great detail in Gurevich (2006a, 2006b), Gogolashvili et al. (2011) and others.

(219) a. *v-i-xat-av*
1SGSBJ-PRV.RFL-draw-TS:PRS.IND
'I paint smth. for smb.'

b. *m-i-xat-av*
1SGIOBJ-PRV.RFL-draw-TS:PRS.IND
'you paint smth. for me'

(220) a. *v-i-čr-eb-i*
1SGSBJ-PV-cut-TS-PRS.IND
'I cut into smb.'s territory'

b. *v-i-msxvr-ev-i*
1SGSBJ-PV-shatter-TS-PRS.IND
'I am shattered'

(221) a. *v-i-cval-eb*
1SGSBJ-PV-suffer-TS-PRS.IND
'I am suffering tornment'

b. *v-i-cv-eb-i*
1SGSBJ-PV-hot-TS-PRS.IND
'I am getting hot'

The views of Ertelishvili (1965) should also be noted with regard to locative version, who did not consider it in opposition to objective and subjective version, chiefly on the grounds that the prefix *a-* does not express participant afectedness or any other version-like meanings. Accordingly, there is only an opposition between subjective and objective versions, and no opposition involving a locative version.

To summarize, the distribution of object correlation markers is separated into five sets, which can be used both in singular and in plural forms and which occupy the fourth slot in Modern Georgian and the sixth slot in Old Georgian (Table 2.26):

Table 2.26 Sets of object correlation markers

	-i-/-u- set	*-i-* set	*-e-* set	*-a-* set	*h-/s-* set
1	*-i-*	*-i-*	*-e-*	*-a-*	∅-
2	*-i-*	*-i-*	*-e-*	*-a-*	∅-
3	*-u-*	*-i-*	*-e-*	*-a-*	*h-/s-*

The differing functions attributed to version markers appear to be closely connected to the differeing understandings of the grammatical category of voice discussed in great detail in Datukishvili (1996), Gurevich (2006b), Melikishvili et al. (2010), Gogolashvili et al. (2011), Tuite (2019) and others, and to its representation in the inflectional system of the verb. It is clear from scholarly discussions of this topic that, in the case of Georgian, the category of voice can be considered not only from a morphological, but also from a morphosyntactic point of view, and is associated with different issues such as the problem of inversion, the distinction between the functions of the passive and middle voices (222), or the forms of the active and middle voices (223) as understood from traditional approaches (Imnaishvili 1968; Shanidze 1973; Makharoblidze 2009; Gogolashvili et al. 2011 and others).

(222) a. *mačankl-ob-s*
act_as_a_matchmaker-TS-3SGSBJ:PRS.IND
'➝s/he/it acts as a matchmaker'

b. *e-mačankl-eb-a*
PRV.3OBJ-act_as_a_matchmaker-TS-3SGSBJ:PRS.IND
's/he/it acts as a matchmaker'

(223) a. *a-kanob-eb-s*
PRV.3OBJ-legalize-TS-3SGSBJ:PRS.IND
's/he/it legalizes smth.'

b. *a-kanon-eb-s*
PRV-legalize-TS-3SGSBJ:PRS.IND
's/he/it legalizes smth.'

The grammatical category of voice describes the relationship between an action and the participants of an action. If the subject is the agent of the action, the verb is in the active voice, and if the subject is the patient of the action, the verb is in the passive voice. If the category of voice is understood in this way, it becomes clear that a lot of verbs in Georgian language do not match this definition; the agent of an action is often not only its agent, but its patient as well (224).

(224) a. *duġ-s*
boil-3SGSBJ:PRS.IND
'boils'
b. *č'k'ep'-s*
roar-3SGSBJ:PRS.IND
'roars'

Traditional approaches consider verbs of this type to be medial passives, which form only present screeves and borrow their other screeves from active forms by means of subjective version, but they do not consider a group of medial passives which form their present indicative with the *i-* marker (225) as well.

(225) a. *xvneš-i-s*
sigh-TS-3SGSBJ:PRS.IND
'sighs'
b. *i-xvneš-i-s*
PRV.RFL-sigh-TS-3SGSBJ:PRS.IND
'sighs'

Traditional approaches also generally consider the *e-* prefix to be a marker of passive voice, without taking into consideration that the expression of the passive should have an active opposition formed by means of the *i-* marker, whereas the opposition to these "passives" is in fact created by the autoactive forms of monopersonal verbs (226).

(226) a. *lak'lak'-eb-s*
chatter-TS-3SGSBJ:PRS.IND
's/he/it chatters endlessly'
b. *e-lak'lak'-eb-a*
PRV.3OBJ-chatter-TS-3SGSBJ:PRS.IND
's/he/it chatters endlessly with smb.'
c. **i-lak'lak'-eb-a*, etc.

This means that the *e-* prefix, just like the *u-* prefix, is used to create bipersonal verbs from monopersonal verbs and indicates a relationship with an indirect object, while the *a-* prefix is used to indicate a direct object relation.

2.3.6.6 Diathesis and Voice

Following the discussions in Gurevich (2006b), Tuite (2019) and others, it can be concluded that traditional approaches do not always make clear whether or not there is a synchronic category of middle voice in Georgian and whether there is a clear distinction in Georgian between this category and reflexivity. The standard understanding of passive voice is not always viable, even if active forms are obtained by means of the *i-* and *u-* objective markers from the so-called 'medial passives', as discussed in detail by Melikishvili (1979, 2010). Following a more recent approach (Melikishvili et al. 2010), Georgian verbs can be classified according to the category of diathesis, which is based on the notion of reflexivity and voice categories.

There are two morphological types of verbs in Georgian: (1) R-∅ (*glej-∅* 'you tear smth. up', *t'xleš-∅* 'you beat smb.', etc.) and (2) R-*i* (*krt'eb-i* 'you tremble', *skdeb-i* 'you crack', etc.) and three syntactic constructions: (1) Nominative (*kvnes-i-s* 's/he/it moans', *qviris* 's/he/it shouts', etc.), (2) Ergative (*i-kvnes-a* 's/he/it moaned', *iqvira* 's/he/it shouted', etc.) and, (3) Dative (*u-kvnes-i-a* 'apparently smb moaned', *uqviria* 'apparently smb. shouted', etc). These morphological and syntactic constructions are assigned to three diatheses and three series.

The first diathesis consists of relative stative autoactive and dynamic active verbs and is represented by three different morphological structures: (a) root (227), (b) root with thematic suffix (228), (c) root with *e/i* vowel alternation (229).

(227) *č'k'ep'-s*
roar-3SGSBJ:PRS.IND
's/he/it roar'

(228) *kaškašeb-s*
shine-3SGSBJ:PRS.IND
'you shine brightly'

(229) *zel-s*
knead-3SGSBJ:PRS.IND
'you knead smth.'

This diathesis follows the principles of the changeable Nominative-Ergative-Dative-type construction, meaning that the subject of the first series is in the nominative case, the subject of the second series is in the ergative case and the subject of the third series is in the dative case.

The second diathesis consists of absolute stative and dynamic passive verbs, and is represented in morphological structure in two ways: (a) root with *-i-* suffix (230), (b) root with thematic suffixes and the *-i-* suffix in the case of the first and the second persons (231); while the first is extremely rare, the second is very frequent.

(230) *cer-i-a*
write-PRS.IND-be.3SG.AUX:PRS.IND
'it is written'

(231) a. *i-par-eb-a*
PRV.RFL-move_with_stealth-TS-3SGSBJ:PRS.IND
's/he/it moves with stealth'

b. *e-jajġan-eb-a*
PRV.3IOBJ-try_to_shift-TS-3SGSBJ:PRS.IND
's/he/it tries to shift smth. heavy'

The syntactic structure associated with this diathesis is nominative, which means that the subject in all three series appears in the nominative case.

The third diathesis consists of stative inactive and relative stative and relative dynamic verbs, and is represented in three types of morphological structure: (a) root (232); (b) root with thematic suffix (233); (c) root with *-i/–a* or root followed by thematic suffix with *-i/–a* (234). The syntactic structure associated with the third diathesis is invariably dative for all three series.

(232) *m-žul-s*
1SGIOBJ-hate-3SGSBJ:PRS.IND
'I hate smb.'

(233) *m-a-p'ik'r-eb-s*
1SGIOBJ-PRV-think-TS-3SGSBJ:PRS.IND
'smb. or smth. makes me to think about'

(234) *m-e-č'ven-eb-a*
1SGIOBJ-PRV.RFL-appar-TS-3SGSBJ:PRS.IND
's/he/it is appearing to me'

To summarize, the main principles of the classification proposed by Melikishvili (2010) depend not only on the correlation between tense, aspect and mood, but also on the syntactic construction associated with the verb. The first diathesis follow the rules of the nominative construction: the subject is in the nominative case and direct and indirect objects are in the dative case; the second diathesis follows the rules of the ergative construction: the subject is in the ergative case, the direct object is in the nominative case and the indirect object is in the dative case; and the third diathesis follows the rules of the dative: the subject is in the dative case, the direct object is in the nominative case, and the indirect object is represented by a postpositional phrase.

The differences between classes proposed by Melikishvili (2010) are based on different uses of preverbs, different screeve endings, loss of thematic suffixes in different screeves, root vowel alternations and other non-standard behaviours. Accordingly, the classification itself consists of 66 inflectional classes and one additional class for irregular verbs. The regular inflectional classes are split in accordance with valence conjugation between the three diatheses and are associated with the following patterns (Table 2.27):

Table 2.27 Classes of verbs as used in the morphological analyser of Georgian

Type	Class	Features
1st paradigm	Verb_1;	∅-*R*-∅ verbs forming future forms with the *i*- and *-eb* affixes and aorist – with the *i*- an *-e* affixes.
2nd paradigm	Verb_2;	∅-*a-/u-R*-∅ verbs with *e/i* root vowel alternation: monopersonal verbs form future and aorist with the *i*- prefix, bipersonal verbs with the *a*- and *u*- prefixes.
3rd paradigm	Verb_3;	∅-*R-i* verbs forming future and aorist with the *i*- and *-eb* affixes and aorist with the *i*- an *-e* affixes.

(continued)

Table 2.27 (continued)

Type	Class	Features
4th paradigm	Verb_4;	*∅-R-i* monopersonal and bipersonal verbs which form parallel forms with auxiliaries for the first and the second persons in the present.
5th paradigm	Verb_5;	*R-∅* monopersonal verbs forming present with the preverbs *da-, ga-, mo-, še-* and auxiliaries for the first and the second persons.
6th paradigm	Verb_6;	*R-av* monopersonal verbs, which drop the *-av* suffix and use the *i-* and *-eb* affixes to form future and *i-* or *-e* to form aorist.
7th paradigm	Verb_7;	*R-av* monopersonal verbs which use the *i-* and *-av* affixes to form future and the *i-* an *-e* affixes to form aorist.
8th paradigm	Verb_8;	*R-av* monopersonal verbs which form the present with the preverbs *da-, mi-, mo-, še-*.
9th paradigm	Verb_9;	*i-R-eb* verbs formed by means of stem reduplication which form future and aorist with the *i-* an *-e* affixes.
10th paradigm	Verb_10;	*i-R-eb* verbs which form the future and aorist with preverbs and drop the suffix *-eb* in aorist.
11th paradigm	Verb_11;	*a-R-eb* verbs which form future and aorist with preverbs and drop *-eb* in aorist.
12th paradigm	Verb_12;	*u-R-eb* verbs which form future and aorist with preverbs and drop *-eb* in aorist.
13th paradigm	Verb_13;	*R-eb* verbs which form the present with the preverbs *da-, mi-, č'a*.
14th paradigm	Verb_14;	*∅-R-ob* verbs which drop the suffix *-ob* in aorist.
15th paradigm	Verb_15;	*∅-R-ob* verbs which drop the suffix *-ob* in the aorist and form future and aorist be means of the *i-* and *u-* prefixes.
16th paradigm	Verb_16;	*R-il/ul-ob* verbs which drop *-il/ul-ob* in aorist and form future and aorist be means of the *i-* and *u-* prefixes.
17th paradigm	Verb_17;	*R-ob* verbs which form the present with the preverbs *da-, mi-, mo-*.
18th paradigm	Verb_18;	*∅-R-∅* verbs which use similar forms for the future and aorist and add preverbs in the aorist.
19th paradigm	Verb_19;	*∅-R-av* verbs, which have parallel forms with/without *-av* in future and drop *-av* to form aorist.
20th paradigm	Verb_20;	*∅-R-∅* verbs with *e/i* root vowel alternation and preverbs in the aorist.
21st paradigm	Verb_21;	*∅-R-en* verbs with *e/i* root vowel alternation which add preverbs and drop *-en* in the aorist.
22th paradigm	Verb_22;	*∅-R-ev* verbs with *e/i* root vowel which add preverbs and drop *-ev* in the aorist.
23th paradigm	Verb_23;	*∅-R-i* verbs with *∅/e* root vowel alternation in the aorist.
24th paradigm	Verb_24;	*∅-R-i* verbs with *∅/a* root vowel alternation in the aorist.
25th paradigm	Verb_25;	*∅-R-i* verbs which have parallel forms with/without the *a-* prefix.
26th paradigm	Verb_26;	*∅-R-av* verbs which drop *-av* in the aorist.

(continued)

Table 2.27 (continued)

Type	Class	Features
27th paradigm	Verb_27;	*∅-R-av* verbs with *∅/a* root vowel alternation which drop *-av* in the aorist.
28th paradigm	Verb_28;	*a-R-eb* verbs which drop *-eb* in the aorist and use *-e* to form the aorist and *-o* to form the aorist subjunctive; *a-R-eb* verbs which drop *-eb* in the aorist, insert *–i* after the root and use *-e* to form the aorist and *-o* to form the aorist subjunctive.
29th paradigm	Verb_29;	*a-R-eb* verbs which drop *-eb* in the aorist and use *-o* to form the third person of the aorist.
30th paradigm	Verb_30;	*a-R-eb* verbs with *∅/e* root vowel alternation in the aorist which use *-i* to form the aorist.
31st paradigm	Verb_31;	*a-R-ob* verbs which use *-e* to form the first and the second person and *-o* to form the third person of the aorist.
32th paradigm	Verb_32;	*∅-R-ob* verbs which replace *-ob* with *-eb* in the future, drop *-ob* in the aorist and use *-e* to form the first and the second person and *-a* to form the third person of the aorist. *∅-R-il/ul-ob* verbs which drop *-il/ul* and replace *-ob* with *-eb* in the future, drop *–ob* in the aorist and form the future and aorist by means of the *i-* and *u-* prefixes.
33th paradigm	Verb_33;	*∅-R-eb* verbs with *∅/a* root vowel alternation in the aorist which use *-i* to form the aorist.
34th paradigm	Verb_34;	*∅-R-am/av* verbs which drop *-am/av* in the aorist and use *-i* to form the first and the second person and *-a* to form the third person of the aorist.
35th paradigm	Verb_35;	*i-/e-R-eb* verbs which drop *-eb* in the aorist and use *-e* to form the first and the second person and *-a* to form the third person of the aorist.
36th paradigm	Verb_36;	*i-/e-R-i-eb* verbs which drop *-eb* in the aorist.
37th paradigm	Verb_37;	*i-/e-R-ev* verbs with *∅/e* root vowel alternation in the aorist which drop *-ev* in the aorist.
38th paradigm	Verb_38;	*i-/e-R-ev* verbs which substitute *-ev* with *-v* or drop *-ev* in the aorist.
39th paradigm	Verb_39;	*i-/e-R-n/r-eb* verbs with *∅/e* root vowel alternation in the aorist which drop *-eb* in the aorist.
40th paradigm	Verb_40;	*i-/e-R-n/r-eb* verbs with *∅/a* root vowel alternation in the aorist which drop *-eb* in the aorist.
41st paradigm	Verb_41;	*i-/e-R-n/r-eb* verbs which drop *-eb* in the aorist.
42th paradigm	Verb_42;	*i-/e-R-eb* verbs which drop *-eb* in the aorist.
43th paradigm	Verb_43;	*i-/e-R-eb* verbs with *∅/a* root vowel alternation which drop *-eb* in the aorist.
44th paradigm	Verb_44;	*R-d-eb* verbs, which drop *-eb* in the aorist.
45th paradigm	Verb_45;	*e-R-eb* verbs which drop *-eb* in the aorist.
46th paradigm	Verb_46;	*i-R-eb* verbs which have first-series forms only.

Table 2.27 (continued)

Type	Class	Features
47th paradigm	Verb_47;	*i-R-eb* verbs which drop *-eb* in the aorist.
48th paradigm	Verb_48;	*R-eb* verbs which drop *-eb* in the aorist.
49th paradigm	Verb_49;	*i-/e-R-ob* verbs with *∅/e* root vowel alternation which drop *-eb* in the aorist.
50th paradigm	Verb_50;	*a-R-ob* and *∅-R-ob* verbs which drop *-ob* in the aorist and use *-e* to form the first and the second person and *-o* to form the third person of the aorist.
51st paradigm	Verb_51;	*R-m-eb* or *R-m-ev* verbs, which drop *-eb* or *-ev* in the aorist and use *-i* to form the first and the second person and *-a* to form the third person of the aorist.
52th paradigm	Verb_52;	*R-i-AUX* or *a-R-i-AUX* verbs which have irregular paradigms without the imperfect indicative, present subjunctive, future conditional or future subjunctive.
53th paradigm	Verb_53;	*a-/u-R-i-AUX* verbs with irregular paradigms without the imperfect indicative or present subjunctive.
54th paradigm	Verb_54;	*a-/u-R-i-AUX* verbs with irregular paradigms without the imperfect indicative, present subjunctive and imperative, which use *-o* suffix to form the third persion of the aorist
55th paradigm	Verb_55;	Verbs with *prev-R-AUX* in opposition to the *h-/s-R-∅* of inversive constructions.
56th paradigm	Verb_56;	Verbs with *R-i-AUX* in opposition to the *h-/s-R-i/∅* or *h-/s-R-av* of inversive constructions.
57th paradigm	Verb_57;	*∅-/i-/u-R* or *h-/s-R* inversive verbs.
58th paradigm	Verb_58;	*m-/g-/s-R-a* verbs with irregular inversive constructions.
59th paradigm	Verb_59;	*a-R-eb* verbs with irregular inversive constructions.
60th paradigm	Verb_60;	*a-R-eb* or *a-R-ebineb* verbs with irregular inversive constructions.
61st paradigm	Verb_61;	*a-R-ineb* verbs with irregular inversive constructions.
62th paradigm	Verb_62;	*e-R-eb* verbs with irregular inversive constructions which have only the present forms.
63th paradigm	Verb_63;	*e-R-eb* verbs with irregular inversive constructions which drop *-eb* in aorist and which do not have third-series forms.
64th paradigm	Verb_64;	*e-R-eb* verbs with irregular inversive constructionswhich drop *-eb* in the aorist.
65th paradigm	Verb_65;	*a-/u-/s-R-eb* verbs with irregular inversive constructions which drop *-eb* in the aorist.
66th paradigm	Verb_66;	*e-R-eb* or *e-R-ev* verbs which can be used only with negative particles.
67th paradigm	Verb_67;	Irregular verbs

The above-listed verbal conjugation classes generally follow the paradigmatic structure proposed by Melikishvili (2010) with regard to Modern Georgian. Although we have also adopted this structure for the annotation of Old Georgian, this module has to be improved in order to take into account all of the morphosyntactic variations encountered in this case. The preliminary results of this module are given in Sect. 4.4.3.

2.3.6.7 Tense Aspect Mood (TAM) Series

The verbal inflectional paradigm in Modern Georgian consists of 12 screeves grouped within three TAM series which indicate tense, aspect and mood based on similar morphological formation and case-marking and agreement between subjects and objects; as such, the Georgian inflectional paradigm is not strictly morphological, but also takes syntactic and semantic features into account. While time and aspect are notionally quite straightforward categories, mood differences are more difficult to distinguish between semantically. The most recent research in this area tends to distinguish the category of evidentiality as a form of mood within the TAM series system which is encountered as a secondary meaning of the perfect tense (Boeder 2000; Ramat and Topadze 2007; Topadze 2011 and others) (Table 2.28).

Table 2.28 Distribution of screeves in Georgian

I series subdivided into Present and Future groups in Modern Georgian		II series representing Aorist	III series representing Perfect
Modern Georgian			
Present indicative	Future indicative	Aorist indicative	Perfect indicative
Imperfect indicative	Future conditional	Aorist subjunctive	Pluperfect
Present subjunctive	Future subjunctive	Aorist imperative	Perfect subjunctive
Old Georgian			
Present indicative		Aorist indicative	Perfect indicative
Iterative present		Future imperative	Pluperfect
Imperfect indicative		Iterative aorist	Iterative perfect
Present imperative		Future subjunctive	Perfect subjunctive
Iterative imperfect			
Present subjunctive			

The formation of screeves is based on the stem in addition to thematic suffixes, or ‘complex stem’, or on the stem minus thematic suffixes, or so-called ‘simple stem’. The first series comprises verbs with thematic suffixes and the *-e-* root vowel, and is associated with the nominative construction. The second series is characterized by the dropping of thematic suffixes and the replacement of root vowel *-e-* with *-i-* as a result of the so-called ‘root vowel alternation process’. The associated construction in this case is ergative. The third series brings comprises transitive verbs of the first and the second series in the dative construction formed as a result of the inversion process (Arabuli 1984 and others) discussed in Sect. 2.3.6.5. From a historical point of view, the simple stem of the aorist indicative can be considered the basis for the present indicative, in which thematic suffixes appear (235).

(235) a. *kap‘-av-s*
skim-TS-3SGSBJ:PRS.IND
‘s/he/it skims smth.’
b. *ga-kap‘-a*
PV.PFV-skim-3SGSBJ:AOR.IND
‘s/he/it skimmed smth.’

In Old Georgian, 14 screeves are grouped within three series. The first series comprises the following screeves: present indicative, iterative present, imperfect indicative, present imperative, iterative imperfect and present subjunctive. The second series comprises four screeves: aorist indicative, aorist imperative, iterative aorist and future subjunctive. The third series contains four screeves: perfect indicative, pluperfect, iterative perfect and perfect subjunctive. The main differences here concern those screeves which are not represented in Modern Georgian, namely:

(a) The iterative present, which is used to express repeated action in the present tense and formed in the third person with -∅- for active forms (236) and the *-i-* marker for passive (237) forms.

(236) a. *a-kurt‘x-ev-n*
prv-bless-3sgSbj:ipfv.prs.cond
‘s/he/it blesses smb. repeatedly’
b. *cer-n*
write-3SGSBJ:IPFV.PRS.COND
‘s/he/it writes smth. repeatedly’
(237) a. *i-qop‘-i-n*
PRV.RFL-divide-TS-PRS.COND-3SGSBJ:IPFV
‘s/he/it divides smth. repeatedly’
b. *i-qop‘-i-en*
PRV.RFL-divide-TS-PRS.COND-3PLSBJ:IPFV
‘they divide smth. repeatedly’

(b) The present imperative, which is used to expres an imperfective form in imperative mood of the future tense and represented by the -∅- marker with the *-d-* extension marker (238) or by the *-e-* marker with the *-od-* extension marker (239).

(238) a. *mo-s-drek-d-i-n*
PV-3SGIOBJ-bow-EM-3SGSBJ:IPFV.PRS.IMP
‘s/he/it has to bow before smb.’
b. *mo-s-drek-d-ed*
PV-3SGIOBJ-bow-EM-3SGSBJ:IPFV.PRS.IMP
‘they have to bow before smb.’

(239) a. *i-qop'-od-e-n*
PRV.RFL-divide-EM-PRS.IMP-3SGSBJ:IPFV
's/he/it has to divide smth.'
b. *i-qop'-od-e-d*
PRV.RFL-divide- EM-PRS.IMP-3PLSBJ:IPFV
'they have to divide smth.'

The *-i-* marker is encountered in the present imperative and imperfect conditional of the first series and the aorist conditional of the second series, and is replaced by the *-e-* marker in the present subjunctive of the first series. In the present imperative, it is controversially sometimes treated as an additional extension marker used between consonants (Sarjveladze 1997).

(c) The iterative aorist, which is used to express a repeated perfective action in the past tense and sometimes to represent forms without specifying their tense, as described by (Sarjveladze 1997), and uses the *-i-* marker (240).

(240) a. *mo-drik-i-s*
PV-bow-AOR.COND-3SGSBJ:PFV
'if s/he/it had bowed before smb.'
b. *mo-drik-i-an*
PV-bow-AOR.COND-3SGSBJ:PFV
'if they had bowed before smb.'

(d) The second imperative, which is used to express a perfective future action in the imperative mood. It shares its screeve markers with the aorist: *-∅-* and *-e-* (241).

(241) a. *i-y-av-∅*
PRV.RFL-be-TS-FUT.IMP:PFV
'you should be'
b. *mo-drik-e*
PV-bow-FUT.IMP:PFV
'you should bow'

It should be noted that our inclusion of the second imperative in the screeves of the second series in Modern Georgian diverges from traditional approaches, which identify only two screeves in the second series: the aorist indicative and aorist subjunctive (Shanidze 1973; Gogolashvili et al. 2011 and others).

(e) The iterative perfect, which is used to express a repeated perfective action in the past tense and is represented by the *-i-* marker (242).

(242) a. *e-cer-i-s*
PRV-write-PF.CON:PFV
's/he/it would have written'

b. *gan-e-g-i-s*
PV-PRV-write-PF.CON:PFV
's/he/it woul have governed'

Some special remarks should be made concerning the existence of the perfect subjunctive in Modern Georgian. While some scholars (Hewitt 1995; Gurevich 2006b and others) consider it to be represented in Modern Georgian only in poetry or archaic expressions, and it is true that forms of the perfect subjunctive do not occur very frequently, their existence in conversation and in informal speech is unquestionable (243).

(243)

am	*simart'l-it'*
this	truth-SG.INS
e-c'xovro-s	*maginebel-s*
PRV.3OBJ-live-3SGSBJ:PF.SUBJ	swearing_person-PL.DAT

'let the swearing person live with this truth' (Doborjginidze et al. 2012)

Finally, each series subdivided into inflectional classes serves as a pattern for the representation of a verb and its arguments. The inflectional classes provide a linking between participants and specify their own TAM properties.

2.3.6.8 Participle and Verbal Noun

Opinions in the Georgian academic literature with regard to the status of verbal nouns and participles in Georgian differ; some consider them to be separate PoS-es (Davitiani 1973), some consider them to be verbal forms (Shanidze 1973), and some to be nominal forms (Chikobava 1953). These differing approaches to the nature of verbal nouns and participles in Georgian can be explained in their exhibiting both verbal and nominal grammatical features: verbal nouns and participles have categories of case with appropriate case markers, which are not characteristic of the verbal paradigm, while simultaneously being associated with categories of aspect, causativity, voice, etc. which are not characteristic of the nominal paradigm.

The participle or verbal adjective is a non-finite form of the verb which plays a role similar to that of the adjective but lacks the category of degree. Its formation follows the scheme: preverbs → person markers → thematic suffixes → number markers → case markers and/or clitics [postpositions] → extension vowel → clitics [auxiliary verb, markers of indirect speech]. The maximum number of slots is 15 and includes the following units (Table 2.29):

Table 2.29 Distribution of slots in the participial frame

−3	−2	−1	0	1	2	3	4	5	6	7	8	9	10	11
Prev	Prev	Pers	R	TS	Caus	Der. Suffix (DS)	Nbr	Case	Emph	Posp	Emph	Ptl	Aux	IS
mi		*m*		*av*	*in*	*e*	*eb*	*i*	*a*	*vit‘*	*a*	*c‘*	*a*	*met‘k‘i*
mo		*ma*		*am*	*evin*	*el*	*n*	*ma, m*		*t‘an*		*c‘a*		*t‘k‘o*
a	*mo*	*mo*		*em*		*ul*	*t‘*	*s*		*ši*		*ġa*		*o*
da		*me*		*eb*		*il*		*is*		*gan*		*ġac‘*		
č‘a	*mo*			*ob*		*ar, are*		*it‘*		*t‘vis*		*ve*		
še	*mo*			*op‘*				*d, ad*		*ken*		*me*		
ga	*mo*							*v, o*		*ebr*		*mc‘*		
ca	*mo*									*t‘anave*				
gada	*mo*									*urt‘*				
										dan				
										mde				

1. *Preverbs*, which occupy the first or the second slots of the participial paradigm and represent aspectual differences;
2. *Person markers*, which establish long dependencies on their suffixal derivational counterparts;
3. *Verbal root*;
4. *Thematic suffix;*
5. *Causative marker;*
6. *Derivational suffix,* which is dependent on the second slot associated with person markers and triggers the subdivision of participles into different declension types in accordance with the stem-final phoneme, whereby some stems undergo syncope and some truncation;
7. *Number*;
8. *Case*;
9. *Extension vowel*;
10. *Postposition*;
11. *Extension vowel*;
12. *Particle*;
13. *Auxiliary verb*; *and*
14. *Indirect speech markers.*

It should be noted that the formation principles of participles depend not only on inflectional affixes indicating grammatical categories, but on derivational affixes as well. Subjective participles are formed by means of an *m-* marker (244) which may occur with different vowels (*mo-*, *ma-*, *me-*) and derivational suffixes in the following combinations: *m-, m- -e, m- -el, ma- -el, mo- -e, mo- -ul, m- -ar/–are, me- (da-m-glov-i* 'mourner', *ga-m-c'il-eb-el-i* 'guide', *m-č'k'ep'-are* 'burbling', etc.). Objective participles are formed by means of the derivational suffixes *-ul*, which occurs in the case of the thematic suffixes *-av, –am, –ev, –eb, –em* (*da-m-tvre-ul-i* 'broken', *da-bne-ul-i* 'scattered', etc.), and *-il*, which is used in all other cases (*ga-t'l-il-i* 'peeled', etc.) (245).

(244) a. *m-k'ux-are-∅*
SBJ-thunder-SG.NOM
'thundering'

b. *ga-m-t'b-ar-∅-i*
PV.PFV-SBJ-warm-SG-NOM
'warmed'

(245) a. *ga-k'c'e-ul-∅-i*
PV.PFV-escape-SG-NOM
'escaped'

b. *ga-t'l-il-∅-i*
PV.PFV-peel-SG-NOM
'peeled'

To summarize, although participles share certain features with both nominals and verbs, in comparison with the shared nominal features, the features shared with verbs are derivational rather than inflectional. The prevailing categories to be determined are number, case and clitics peculiar to nominals and, accordingly, the declension of participles is as follows (Table 2.30):

Table 2.30 Declension types of participles

Declension	Class	Features
1st Declension	Participle_1;	Consonant-final participles, non-syncopating
2nd Declension	Participle_2;	*-l, -r, -m, -n*-final participles, syncopating in the genitive, instrumental and adverbial cases in the singular and in all cases in the *-eb-* plural
3rd Declension	Participle_3;	*-a*-final participles, truncating in the genitive and instrumental cases in the singular and in all cases in the *-eb-* pural
4th Declension	Participle_4;	*-e*-final participles, truncating in the genitive and instrumental cases in the singular
5th Declension	Participle_5;	*-o* final participles, non-truncating

Following Shanidze (1973), Tskhadadze (1984), Hewitt (2005), Tuskia (2010), Gogolashvili et al. (2011) and others, the verbal noun, or so-called 'masdar', is a non-finite verbal form which shares morphological features of both nouns and verbs, but which syntactically acts like a noun. Its inflection scheme is as follows: preverbs → thematic suffixes → causative markers → derivational suffixes → number markers → case markers and/or clitics [postpositions] → extension vowel → clitics [auxiliary verb, markers of indirect speech]. In Modern Georgian the maximum possible number of slots is 14; these consist of the following (Table 2.31):

Table 2.31 Distribution of slots in the verbal noun frame

−3	−2	0	1	2	3	4	5	6	7	8	9	10	11
Prev	Prev	R	TS	Caus	DS	Case	Nbr	Emph	Posp	Emph	Ptl	Aux	IS
mi			*av*	*in*	*a*	*eb*	*i*	*a*	*vit‘*	*a*	*c‘*	*a*	*met‘k‘i*
mo			*am*	*evin*	*ul*	*n*	*ma, m*		*t‘an*		*c‘a*		*t‘k‘o*
a	*mo*		*em*		*il*	*t‘*	*s*		*ši*		*ġa*		*o*
da			*eb*				*is*		*gan*		*ġac‘*		
č‘a	*mo*		*ob*				*it‘*		*t‘vis*		*ve*		
še	*mo*		*op‘*				*d, ad*		*ken*		*me*		
ga	*mo*						*v, o*		*ebr*		*mc‘*		
ca	*mo*								*t‘anave*				
gada	*mo*								*urt‘*				
									dan				
									mde				

1. *Preverbs*, which occupy the first or the second slots of the verbal noun paradigm and represent aspectual differences;
2. *Verbal root*;
3. *Thematic suffix*;
4. *Causative marker*;
5. *Derivational suffix,* which, depending on the final phoneme, triggers a subdivision of verbal nouns into different declension types, including those which undergo syncope and those which undergo truncation;
6. *Number*;
7. *Case*;
8. *Extension vowel*;
9. *Postposition*;
10. *Extension vowel*;
11. *Particle*;
12. *Auxiliary verb*; and
13. *Indirect speech markers.*

The verbal noun can be produced by adding derivational suffixes to the root of a verb and retaining a slot for preverbs while removing all other markers, including the markers of version, voice and subject or object, in the present or future indicative. With regard to thematic suffixes, there are three possibilities: (a) the verbal noun retains them (246.c); (b) the verbal noun drops them (246.b); (c) the verbal noun retains the consonant of the thematic suffix but drops its vowel (247).

(246) a. *rakrak-eb-s*
burble-TS-3SGSBJ:PRS.IND
'it burbles'

b. *č̣a-rakrak-eb-a-∅*
PV.PFV-burble-TS-DS-SG.NOM
'burbling down'

c. *rakrak-i*
burble-SG.NOM
'burbling'

(247) a. *sunt'k'-av-s*
breath-TS-3SGSBJ:PRS.IND
's/he/it breathes'

b. *sunt'k'-v-a-∅*
breath-TS-DS-SG.NOM
'breathing'

c. *amo-sunt'k'-v-a-∅*
PV.PFV-breath-TS-DS-SG.NOM
'breathing out'

Sometimes the stem-final vowel *-a* is complemented by the suffixes *-n* (*i-xvec-s* 'implores', *xvec-n-a* 'imploring', etc.), *–ol* (*żrc-i-s* 's/he/it trembles', *żrc-ol-a* ‘trembling’, etc.), or *-om* (*jd-eb-a* ‘s/he/it sits down’, *jdoma* ‘sitting down’, etc.). Medial and the indirect verbs, which, regardless of series, require the logical subject to be in the dative case and the logical object in the nominative, do not follow clear rules with respect to verbal noun formation, and some verbs do not have associated verbal nouns at all.

While it is clear that verbal nouns, like participles, share features of both nominals and verbs, in comparison with nominal features, the majority of verbal features are lost or concealed. The prevailing categories to be determined are number, case and clitics peculiar to nominals and, accordingly, the regular declension paradigm of verbal nouns is as follows (Table 2.32):

Table 2.32 Declension types of verbal nouns

Declension	Class	Features
1st Declension	Masdar_1;	Consonant-final common verbal nouns, non-syncopating
2nd Declension	Masdar_2;	*-l, -r, -m, -n*-final common verbal nouns, syncopating in the genitive, instrumental and adverbial cases in the singular and in all cases in the *-eb-* plural
3rd Declension	Masdar_3;	*-a*-final common verbal nouns, non-truncating
4th Declension	Masdar_4;	*-a*-final common verbal nouns, truncating in the genitive and instrumental cases in the singular and in all cases in the *-eb-* plural

Neither participles nor verbal nouns have syntactic functions different from those of nouns and adjectives. Although they are related to verbs, their generation is strictly nominal.

2.3.7 Adverbs

Adverbs, which are discussed in Georgian by Shanidze (1973), Gogolashvili et al. (2011) and others, are words that provide additional information about a verb, an adjective or other PoS-es. The majority of adverbs are derived from consonant-final or vowel final adjectival stems by the addition of the adverbial case markers[15] *-ad* for consonant-final stems (248) and *-d* for vowel-final stems (249). In dialects of Georgian, *−d* often undergoes devoicing to *-t*‘ (248–249).

[15] For additional information regarding adverbial case markers see Sect. 2.3.1.1.

(248) *karg-i* 'good' → *karg-ad* (dial. *karg-it*') 'well', *t'bil-i* 'warm' → *t'bil-ad* (dial. *t'bil-at'*) 'warmly', etc.
(249) *mc'ire-∅* 'short' → *mc'ire-d* (dial. *mc'iret'*) 'shortly', *mżime-∅* 'heavy' → *mżime-d* (dial. *mżime-t'*) 'heavily', etc.

Semantically, there are eight different types of adverbs in Georgian: local, temporal, modifier, quantitative, causal, specifier, interrogative and relative. Generally speaking, adverbs can be considered a closed class of items which can be expanded with two slots, namely a slot for postpositions and for indirect speech markers.

The formation of adverbs follows the scheme: type → clitics [postpositions] → clitics [indirect speech markers]. The number of slots varies by adverb type, but is generally 5; these include the following units (Table 2.33):

Table 2.33 Distribution of slots in the Georgian adverb

0	1	2	3	4
R	Posp	Emph	Ptl	IS
	ze	*a*	*c'*	*met'k'i*
	t'an		*c'a*	*t'k'o*
	ši		*ġa*	*o*
	gan		*ve*	
	t'vis			
	ken			
	ebr			
	t'anave			
	urt'			
	dan			
	mde			

1. *Root*;
2. *Postposition*;
3. *Extension vowel*;
4. *Particle*; and
5. *Indirect speech markers.*

The subdivision of adverbs into types can be considered a lexical one, in that there are no special morphological markers which ascribe type features to the root. There are two types of formation: (1) initial stems, which are not generated from other PoS-es (250); (2) secondary stems generated from nouns, adverbs or other parts of speech. As discussed in the Georgian academic literature (Peikrishvili 2010; Shanidze 1973 and others) the secondary stems are formed as follows: (a) from a nominal stem without case or other markers (251), (b) from a nominal stem with the adverbial case markers *-ad* or *-d* (252), (c) from a nominal stem with the instrumental case marker *-t'* (253), or (d) from a nominal stem with the dative case marker *-s* (254).

(250) *gušin*
yesterday
adv
'yesterday'

(251) a. *żlier-i* 'strong' → *żlier* 'extremely'
żlier-i
strong-SG.NOM
'strong'

b. *żlier*
extremely
adv
'extremely'

(252) a. *karg-i* 'good' → *karg-ad* 'well'
karg-i
good-SG.NOM
'good'

b. *karg-ad*
good-SG.ADV || good.ADV
'well'

(253) a. *ġame-∅* 'night' → *ġam-it'* 'at night'
ġame-∅
night-SG.NOM
'night'

b. *ġam-it'*
night-SG.INS || at_night.ADV
'at night'

(254) a. *kvira-∅* 'Sunday' → *kvira-s* 'on Sunday'
kvira-∅
Sunday-SG.NOM
'Sunday'

b. *kvira-s*
Sunday-SG.DAT || on_Sunday.ADV
'on Sunday'

It should be noted that the reasoning for the traditional inclusion of nouns, adjectives and other PoS-es in the dative, instrumental and adverbial cases within the class of adverbs is strictly syntactic. Only in these cases do nouns, adjectives, etc. behave like syntactic adjuncts and participate in the formation of adverbial phrases indicating time, place, manner, etc. In any case, the traditional treatment of the aforementioned second formation of adverbs, i.e. the ones generated from other PoS-es is doubtful. It was difficult for the annotators working on the evaluation of the analyser's output to delimit the morphological features of a concrete PoS from its syntactic function, and mutually exclusive decisions affected the analyzer's output and revealed a significant problem with regard to these forms.

At the time of writing, from a morphosyntactic point of view there are two options with regards to the description of adverbs in Georgian: (a) to revise the morphosyntactic functions of the adverbial case with regards to its position in the case system; (b) to revise the derivational mechanism of adverbs from other PoS-es with the purpose of delimiting the morphological structure of a concrete PoS and its syntactic functions.

2.3.8 Conjunctions

There are two types of conjunctions in Georgian: coordinating (254) and subordinating (255). Coordinating conjunctions connect words, phrases and clauses, while subordinating conjunctions connect a dependent clause to an independent one. Conjunctions are considered a closed class of items which do not undergo any changes.

(255) *da* 'and', *t'u* 'or', etc.

(256) *vinc'* 'who', *rac'* 'that', *romelic'* 'which', *sadac'* 'where', etc.

2.3.9 Particles

In Georgian, the particle is considered to be an independent PoS which adds meaning to a word or a sentence. As described by (Shanidze 1973), particles belong to a so-called 'uninflected closed class' of items which is subdivided into the following lexical classes: interrogative, negative, infinitive, intensive, relative, prohibitive, word-by-word and positive. Some authors (Gabunia 2016) additionally identify the classes approximate, inclusive, desirable and optative. The principal issue with these classifications is discrepancies in the number of classes defined on the basis of their semantics rather than their structure.

Some particles belong to clitics described additionally in Sect. 2.3.5 and occupy concrete slots in the nominal paradigm (*−ġa, c'a* etc.), while others behave as independent words and precede (*ar* 'not', *ver* 'not' etc.) or follow (*xolme* 'regularly', *t'k'va* 'as s/he/it said' etc.) other words. It should be noted that those particles which behave as independent words frequently have morphological structures which overlap with those of adverbs and auxiliary verbs (257), and in the majority of cases the classification of these forms as particles is dubious.

(257) *mere* 'after', *mxolod* 'only', *ik'neb* 'may be', etc.

2.3.10 Interjections

An interjection is an independent part of speech that describes the emotion or feelings. Interjections in Georgian can stand alone or be placed before or after a sentence (258).

(258) *č'u* 'shush', *eh* 'oh, dear', *vai* 'alas', etc.

Some authors (Gogolashvili et al. 2011, and others) also describe verbs and other parts of speech as interjections where they are used in this way (259).

(259) *gagimarjos* 'how do you do?', *get'aqva* 'my dear', *ġmert'mani* 'God be my witness', etc.

2.4 Summary

In this chapter we have described the main features of Georgian phonology, morphotactics and inflectional morphology used to develop the morphological analyzer for the Georgian language.

References

Abesadze, Nino. 1956. piris (adamianis) saxelt'a bruneba žvelsa da axal k'art'ulši (Declension of proper nouns in Old and Modern Georgian). *saxelis brunebis istoriisat'vis k'art'velur enebši (To the history of declension in Kartvelian languages)*, 129–137.

Akhvlediani, George. 1949. *Zogadi p'onetikis sap'užvlebi (foundations of general phonetics)*. Tbilisi: t'bilisis saxelmcip'o universiteti (Tbilisi State University).

Alsina, Alex, and Sam Mchombo. 1990. The syntax of applicatives in Chichewa: Problems for a theta theoretic asymmetry. *Natural Language and Linguistic Theory* 8: 493–506.

Amiridze, Nino. 2006. *Reflexivization Strategies in Georgian*. LOT: PhD Dissertation, University of Utrecht.

———. 2018. Accommodating loan verbs in Georgian: Observations and questions. *Journal of Pragmatics* 133: 150–165.

Amiridze, Nino, R. Asatiani, and Z. Baratashvili. 2019. Compounds or phrases? Pattern borrowing from English into Georgian. *Lecture Notes in Computer Science (LNCS)* 11456: 1–20.

Anderson, Stephen. 1976. On the notion of subject in ergative. In *Subject and topic*, ed. C.N. Li, 1–23. New York: Academic Press.

———. 1992. *A-morphous morphology*. Cambridge: Cambridge University Press.

Apridonidze, Shukia, and Chkhaidze, Levan. 2004. *From Georgian and into Georgian*. Transliteration of Georgian Alphabet. https://transliteration.eki.ee/pdf/Georgian.pdf. Accessed 19 Dec 2021.

Apridonidze, Shukia. 1986. *Sitqvat'ganlageba axal k'art'ulši (Word order in modern Georgian)*. Tbilisi: mec'niereba (Science).

Arabuli, Avtandil. 1984. *Mesame seriis nakvt'eult'a carmoeba da mnišvneloba žvel k'art'ulši (The form and meaning of series III screeves in Old Georgian)*. Tbilisi: mec'niereba (Science).

Aronoff, Mark. 1994. *Morphology by itself: Stems and inflectional classes*. Cambridge, MA: MIT Press.

Aronson, Howard. 1969. Towards a formal analysis of the Georgian declension. *General Linguistics* 9: 173–184.

———. 1984. On homonymy in the Georgian verbal system. *Folia Slavica* 7: 21–37.

———. 1989. Inflection vs. derivation in Georgian conjugation. In *Non-Slavic languages of the USSR: linguistic studies*, ed. H. Aronson, 1–19. Chicago: Chicago Linguistic Society.

———. 1990. *Georgian: A reading grammar*. Bloomington: Slavica Publishers, Inc.

———. 1997. Georgian phonology. *Phonologies of Asia and Africa* 2: 929–939.

Asatiani, Rusudan. 1989. kauzac'ia da kontak'ti k'art'velur enebši (Causativity and contact in Kartvelian languages). *mac'ne (Bulletin)* 1: 119–129.

———. 2009. A dynamic conceptual model for the linguistic structuring of space: Georgian Preverbs. In *The 7th International Symposium on LLC*, 38–47. Tbilisi: Springer.

Babunashvili, Elene. 1956. mic'emit'i da vit'arebit'i brunvebis urt'iert'obisat'vis žvel k'art'ulši (To the relation between Dative and Instrumental cases in Old Georgian). *saxelis brunebis istoriisat'vis k'art'velur enebši (To the history of declension in Kartvelian languages)*, 393–403.

Baker, Mark, and Jonathan Bobaljik. 2017. On inherent and dependent theories of ergative case. In *The oxford handbook of ergativity*, ed. J. Coon et al., 111–134. Oxford: Oxford University Press.

Bakker, Dik, König, Ekkehard, Dahl, Östen, Haspelmath, Martin, Koptjevskaja-Tamm, Maria, Lehmann, Christian, and Siewierska, Anna. 1993. Eurotyp Guidelines. European Science Foundation in Language Typology.

Baratashvili, Zurab. 2019. The types of the causative construction in Georgian. *Bulleting of the Georgian National Academy of Sciences* 13: 126–136.

Bauer, Laurence. 2006. Compound. In K. A. Brown, Encyclopedia of language & linguistics *(Second Edition)*, 719–726. Boston: Elsevier.

Beridze, Marine. 1998. Statikur zmnat'a ert'i jgup'isa da gardamaval zmnat'a I t'urmeobit'is carmoebis sakit'xisat'vis (To the formation of Perfect Indicative of transitive verbs and one group of static verbs). *saenat'mec'niero žiebani (Linguistic issues)*, 68–74.

———. 2006. *sak'art'velos lingvisturi portreti (Linguistic portrait of Georgia)*. http://www.corpora.co/. Accessed 7 Nov 2019.

Boeder, Winfried. 1968. Über die Versionen des georgischen Verbs. *Folia Linguistica* 2: 82–152.

———. 1979. Ergative syntax and morphology in language change: the South Caucasian languages. In *Ergativity: towards a theory of grammatical relations*, ed. F. Plank, 435–480. Orlando: Academic Press.

———. 1989. Verbal person marking, noun phrase and word order in Georgian. In *Configurationality: the typology of asymmetries*, ed. L. Marácz and P. Muysken, 159–184. Dordrecht: Foris.

———. 2000. Evidentiality in Georgian. In *Evidentials: Turkic, Iranian and neighbouring languages*, ed. L.U. Johanson, 275–328. Berlin, New York: Mouton de Gruyter.

———. 2002. Speech and thought representation in the Kartvelian (South Caucasian) languages. *Reported Discourse. A Meeting-Ground of Different Linguistic Domains. Typological Studies in Language*, 3–48.

———. 2005. The South Caucasian languages. *Lingua* 115: 5–89.

Booij, Geert. 2006. Inflection and derivation. In K. A. Brown, Encyclopedia of language & linguistics *(Second Edition)*, 654–661. Boston: Elsevier.

Booij, Geert, Van Kemenade, and Ans. 2003. Preverbs: An introduction. *Yearbook of Morphology* 2003: 1–11.

Booij, Geert. 2010. *Construction morphology*. Oxford: Oxford University Press.

Bresnan, Joan. 2016. *Lexical-functional syntax*. Chichester: Wiley Blackwell.

Broselow, Elen. 1982. On predicting the interaction of stress and epenthesis. *Glossa* 16: 115–132.

Butskhrikidze, Marika. 2002. *The consonant phonotactics of Georgian*. Utrecht: LOT.

———. 2001. On v-metathesis in modern Georgian. *Surface syllable structure and segment sequencing*: 91–101.

Chartolani, Natia. 1985. *č'venebit' nac'valsaxelt'a sistemebi k'art'ulši sxva k'art'velur enebt'an šedarebit' (the demonstrative pronoun system of Georgian compared to other Kartvelian languages)*. Tbilisi: mec'niereba (Science).

Cherchi, Marcello. 1997. *Modern Georgian morphosyntax*. Wiesbaden: Harrasowitz Verlag.

Chikobava, Arnold. 1934. gan t'andebulis xmarebisat'vis nat'esaobit't'an da mok'medebit't'an (To the use of postposition 'from' in genitive and instrumental cases). *k'art'velur enat'a struk'turis sakit'xebi (ssues of the Structure of Kartvelian Languages)*, 13–17.

———. 1936. *čanuris gramatikuli analizi tek'stebit'urt' (Grammatical analysis of Chan language with texts)*. Tbilisi: ssrk mec'nierebat'a akademia-sak'art'velos p'iliali (Branch of the Academy of Sciences of the USSR).

———. 1937. ert'i uc'nobi t'andebuli axal k'art'ulši (To one unknown postposition in Modern Georgian). *enimkis moambe (Bulletin of the Institute of language, history and material culture)* 1: 55–65.

———. 1940. Mesame piris subiek'tis uẓvelesi nišani k'art'velur enebši (the oldest 3rd-person subject marker in the Kartvelian languages). *Enimki-s moambe* V–VI: 13–46.

———. 1942. *Saxelis p'užis užvelesi agebuleba k'art'velur enebši (the earliest structure of nominal)*. Tbilisi: mec'niereba (science).

———. 1946. *Inversiuli zmnebi da saxelt'a klasip'ikac'ia (inverted verbs and nominal classification)*. Tbilisi: Saxalxo ganat'leba (national education).

———. 1950–1964. *k'art'uli enis ganmartebit'i lek'sikoni (Georgian Explanatory Dictionary)*. Tbilisi: Academy of Sciences.

———. 1953. masdarisa da mimġeobis istoriuli urt'iert'obisat'vis k'art'ulši (To the historic relationship between verbal noun and participle). *iberiul-kavkasiuri enat'mec'niereba V (Iberian-Caucasian Linguistics)*, 33–49.

———. 1954. mravlobit'is sup'ik'st'a genezisat'vis k'art'ulši (On the genesis of the Georgian plural suffixes). *iberiul-kavkasiuri enat'mec'niereba (Iberian-Caucasian Linguistics)*, 67–76.

———. 1956. mravlobit'obis sup'ik'st'a genezisat'vis k'art'ulši (To the genesis of plural suffixes in Georgian). *saxelis brunebis istoriisat'vis k'art'velur enebši (To the history of declension in Kartvelian languages)*, 313–325.

———. 1961. t'andebulian brunvat'a sakit'xisat'vis k'art'ulši (On the question of adpositional cases in Georgian). *k'art'uli enis struk'turis sakit'xebi II (Issues on the structure of Georgian language)*, 197–208.

———. 1968. *martivi cinadadebis problema k'art'ulši (the problem of the simple sentence in Georgian)*. Tbilisi: mec'niereba (Science).

———. 2008 [1952]. *enat'mec'nierebis šesavali (Introduction to linguistics)*. Tbilisi: t'bilisis saxelmcip'o universiteti (Tbilisi State University).

———. 2013 [1945]. gramatikuli klas-kategoria da zmnis uġvlilebis zogi sakit'xi žvel-k'art'ulši (Grammatical class-category and some issues on verbal conjugation in Old Georgian). *iberiul-kavkasiuri enat'mec'niereba (Iberian-Caucasian Linguistics)*, 397–410.

Chikobava, Arnold, and Juansher Vateishvili. 1983. *pirveli k'art'uli nabečdi cignebi (First printed books in Georgian)*. Tbilisi: xelovneba (Art).

Chkhenkeli, Thomas. 1956. sakut'ar saxelt'a bruneba oškuri xelnaceris mep'et'a cignebši (To the declension of proper nouns in the Book of Kings of Oshki manuscript). *saxelis brunebis istoriisat'vis k'art'velur enebši (To the history of declension in Kartvelian languages)*, 76–129.

———. 1977. asomt'avrulis geometriuli struk'tura (Geometrical structure of Asomtavruli). *sabčot'a xelovneba (Soviet Art)*, 67–81.

Chubinashvili, David. 1855. *Kratkaja gramatika gruzinskogo jazyka (A brief Grammar of Georgian, in Russian)*. The Emperor Academy of Sciences (Imperatorskaya Akademia Nauk): Saint Petersburg.

Chumburidze, Zurab. 1984. mešveli zmnis šekvec'ili p'ormis istoriisat'vis (To the history of auxiliary verb). *žveli k'art'uli enis kat'edris šromebi (Proceedings of the department of Old Georgian language)* 25: 39–43.

Comrie, Bernard. 1989. *Language universals and linguistic typology: Syntax and morphology*. Oxford: Blackwell Publisher.

Comrie, Bernard, Martin Haspelmath, and Balthasar Bickel. 2008. *The Leipzig glossing rules: conventions for interlinear morpheme-by-morphene glosses*. Leipzig: Max Planck Institute for Evolutionary Anthropology.

Danelia, Korneli. 1975. uc'xo enat'a gavlenis kvali žveli k'art'uli cerilobit'i žeglebis enaši (Traces of influence of foreign languages on the language of Old Georgian documents). *mac'ne*, 79–90.

———. 1998. crp'elobit'is adgilisat'vis žveli k'art'ulis brunebis sistemaši (To the place of absolute case in the declension system of Old Georgian). *k'art'uli istoriuli gramatikis sakit'xebi (Issues of Georgian historical grammar)*, 525–533.

Danelia, Korneli, and Zurab Sarjveladze. 1997. *k'art'uli paleograp'ia (Georgian paleography)*. Tbilisi: Nekeri.

Datukishvili, Ketevan. 1992. zmnuri kategoriebis klasip'ikac'ia uġlebis sistemast'an mimart'ebit' (Classification of verbal categories with regards to conjugation system)). *saenat'mec'niero žiebani (Linguistic issues)*, 52–61.

———. 1996. vnebit'is qalibis mk'one statikuri p'ormebi k'art'ulši. *saenat'mec'niero žiebani (Linguistic issues)*, 73–77.
———. 1997a. piris nišant'a sistema k'art'ulši (Person markers in Georgian). *zurab čumburižes (dabadebis 70 clist'avisadmi mižġvnili krebuli) (Proceedings dedicated to the 70th anniversary of Zurab Chumburidze)*, 66–76.
———. 1997b. Some questions of computer synthesis of verb in Georgian. In *The Second Tbilisi Symposium on Language, Logic and Computation*, 83–85. Tbilisi: t'bilisis saxelmcip'o universiteti (Tbilisi State University).
Davitiani, Akaki. 1973. *k'art'uli enis sintak'si (syntax of Georgian language)*. Tbilisi: ganat'leba (Science).
DeLancey, Scott. 1981. An interpretation of split ergativity and related patterns. *Language* 57: 626–657.
Dixon, Robert. 1994. *Ergativity*. Cambridge: Cambridge University Press.
Doborjginidze, Nino, Lobzhanidze, Irina, Gunia, Irakli. 2012. *Georgian language corpus*. http://corpora.iliauni.edu.ge/. Accessed 30 Oct 2019.
Doborjginidze, Nino, Lobzhanidze, Irina, Mirianashvili, George. 2014. *Corpus of Georgian Chronicles*. http://corpora.iliauni.edu.ge/. Accessed 30 Oct 2019.
Dondua, Karpez. 1956a. K voprosu o roditelnom emfaticheskom v drevneliteraturnom gruzinskom jazike (To the issue of genitive marker with extension vowel in Old Georgian language. *saxelis brunebis istoriisat'vis k'art'velur enebši (To the history of declension in Kartvelian languages)*, 204–218.
———. 1956b. O dvux suffiksax množestvennosti v gruzinskom (On two suffixes of plurality in Georgian). *saxelis brunebis istoriisat'vis k'art'velur enebši (To the history of declension in Kartvelian languages)*, 290–313.
Dzotsenidze, Ketevan. 1947. emp'atikuri xmovani żvel k'art'ulši. *t'bilisis saxelmcip'o universitetis šromebi (Works of Tbilisi State University)* 30–31: 345–350.
Eberhard, David M., Gary F. Simons, and Charles D. Fennig. 2019. *Ethnologue: languages of the world*. Dallas, TX: SIL International. Online version: http://www.ethnologue.com. Accessed 15 Nov 2019.
Ertelishvili, Parnaoz. 1965. *k'c'evis sakit'xisat'vis k'art'ulši, t'bilisis saxelmcip'o universitetis šromebi (Proceedings of the Tbilisi State University)*. Vol. 14, 177–198. Tbilisi: t'bilisis saxelmcip'o universiteti (Tbilisi State University).
———. 1970. *Phonemic structure and historical aspects of verbal stems in Georgian [in Georgian]*. Tbilisi: TSU.
———. 1980. *saxelur p'użet'a p'onematuri struk'turisa da istoriis sakit'xebi k'art'ulši (Phonemic structure and historical aspects of nominal stems in Georgian)*. Tbilisi: t'bilisis saxelmcip'o universiteti (Tbilisi State University).
Everson, Michael. 1991–2019. *Georgian Supplement, Range: 2D00-2D2F*. from https://unicode.org/charts/PDF/U2D00.pdf. Accessed 16 Jul 2019.
———. 1991–2019. *Georgian, Range: 10A0-10FF*. https://unicode.org/charts/PDF/U10A0.pdf. Accessed 16 Jul 2019.
Everson, Michael, Gujejiani, Nika, Razmadze, Akaki. 2016, *Proposal for the addition of Georgian characters to the UCS*. https://unicode.org/L2/L2016/16034-n4707-georgian.pdf. Accessed 16 Jul 2019.
Gabunia, Kakha. 2016. *k'art'uli enis gramatikis zogadi kursi (Breif course of Georgian Grammar)*. Tbilisi: sak'art'velos ganat'lebisa da mec'nierebis saministro (Ministry of Education and Science of Georgia).
Gamkrelidze, Thomas. 2006. Europe, Christian: alphabets. In K. A. Brown, Encyclopedia of language & linguistics *(Second Edition)*, 295–305. Boston: Elsevier.
———. 2011. *żveli k'art'uli asomt'avruli damcerloba (Old Georgian Asomtavruli Script)*. Tbilisi: sak'. et'nograp'. memkvidreobis dac'vis p'ondi (Foundation for Preservation of Georgia's Ethnographic Heritage).
Gamkrelidze, Thomas, and Gudava, Todo. 1998. Kartvelian (South Caucasian) languages. *Encyclopedia Britannica*, https://www.britannica.com/topic/Caucasian-languages#ref75090. Accessed 22 Jul 2019.

Gamkrelidze, Thomas, and Grigol Machavariani. 1965. *sonantt'a sistema da ablauti k'art'velur enebši: saert'o k'art'veluri struk'turis tipologia (the system of sonants and ablaut in the Kartvelian languages)*. Tbilisi: mec'niereba (Science).

Gerlach, Birgit, and Janet Grijzenhout. 2000. *Clitics in phonology, morphology and syntax*. Amsterdam: John Benjamins.

Giacalone Ramat, Anna, and Manana Topadze. 2007. The coding of evidentiality: a comparative look at Georgian and Italian. *Italian Journal of Linguistics* 19: 7–38.

Gigashvili, Ketevan. 2004a. aspek'tis gamoxatvast'an dakavširebuli sakit'xebi sašual k'art'ulši (Aspect features in Middle Georgian). *saenat'mec'niero žiebani (Linguistic issues)*, 60–72.

———. 2004b. t'emis nišant'a da zmniscint'a istoriuli urt'iert'mimart'ebisat'vis k'art'ulši (To the interrelationship between thematic affixes and preverbs in Georgian). *saenat'mec'niero žiebani (Linguistic issues)* 17:50–60.

Glonti, Alexander. 1964. *k'art'uli lek'sikologia (Georgian Lexicology)*. Tbilisi: c'odna (Knowledge).

Gogolashvili, George. 2004. k'art'uli enis periodizac'iis sakit'xisat'vis (to the periodization of Georgian language). *Issues in linguistics*, 32–38.

Gogolashvili, George, Avtandil Arabuli, Murman Sukhishvili, Mariam Manjgaladze, Nino Chumburidze, and Nino Jorbenadze. 2011. *t'anamedrove k'art'uli enis morp'ologia (morphology of modern Georgian language)*. Tbilisi: Meridiani.

Gurevich, Olga. 2004. On mismathces between syntax and morphology in Georgian. In *International Symposium on the Typology of Argument Structure and Grammatical Relations in Languages Spoken in Europe and North and Central Asia (LENCA-2)*, 61–64. Kazan: Kazan State University.

———. 2006a. *A finite-state model of Georgian verbal morphology. Proceedings of the human language technology conference of the north American chapter of the ACL*, 45–48. New York: Association for Computational Linguistics.

———. 2006b. *Constructional morphology: The Georgian version*. Berkeley: PhD Dissertation, University of California.

Gurgenidze, Tariel. 2009. inkluziv-ek'skluzivis kategoria k'art'velur enebši (To the inclusivity-exclusivity category in Kartvelian languages). *iberiul-kavkasiuri enat'mec'niereba (Iberian-Caucasian linguistics)* 37:88–101.

Harley, Heidi, and Rolf Noyer. 2000. Formal versus encyclopedic properties of vocabulary: evidence from nominalizations. *The Lexicon-Encyclopedia Interface*: 349–374.

Harris, Alice. 1981. *Georgian syntax: a study in relational grammar*. Cambridge: Cambridge University Press.

Harris, Alice C. 1982. Georgian and the Unaccusative hypothesis. *Language* 58 (2): 290–306.

———. 1985. *Diachronic syntax: The Kartvelian case*. New York: Academic.

———. 2003. Preverbs and their origin in Georgian and Udi. In *Yearbook of morphology 2003*, ed. G.J. Booij, 61–87. Dordrecht: Kluwer Academic Publishers.

Harris, Alice, Xu, Z. 2006. Diachronic morphological typology. In K. A. Brown, Encyclopedia of language & linguistics *(Second Edition)*, 509–515. Boston: Elsevier.

Hewitt, George. 1983. Review of Alice C. Harris, Georgian syntax: a study in relational grammar. *Lingua* 59: 247–274.

———. 1987. Georgian: Ergative or active? *Lingua* 71: 319–340.

———. 1995. *Georgian: A structural reference grammar*. Amsterdam: John Benjamins.

———. 2005. *Georgian: A Learner's grammar*. New York: Routledge.

Holisky, Dee Ann. 1981a. *Aspect and Georgian medial verbs*. New York: Caravan Books.

———. 1981b. Aspect theory and Georgian aspect. In *Tense and aspect (syntax and semantics)*, ed. P.Z. Tedeschi, 127–144. New York: Academic.

Iacobini, Claudio. 2006. Morphological typology. In K. A. Brown, Encyclopedia of language & linguistics *(Second Edition)*, 278–282. Boston: Elsevier.

Imnaishvili, David. 1952. uarqop'it'i nac'valsaxelebi da uarqop'it'i zmnisart'ebi iberiul-kavkasiur enebši (Negative pronouns and negative adverbs in Iberian-Caucasian langauges). *iberiul-kavkasiuri enat'mec'niereba (Iberian-Caucasian linguistics)* 4:53–71.

Imnaishvili, Ivane. 1956. crp'elobit'i brunvis sakit'xi sakut'ar saxelebši (to the issue of absolute case in proper nouns). *Saxelis brunebis istoriisat'vis k'art'velur enebši (to the history of declension in Kartvelian languages)*, 59–76.

———. 1957. *saxelt'a bruneba da brunvt'a p'unk'c'iebi żvel k'art'ulši (Noun declension and case function in Old Georgian)*. Tbilisi: t'bilisis saxelmcip'o universiteti (Tbilisi State University).

———. 1968. vnebit'i gvaris zmnat'a t'aviseburebani żvel k'art'ulši (Characteristics of the passive voice in Old Georgian). *żveli k'art'uli enis kat'edris šromebi II (Proceedings of the Department of Old Georgian Language)*, 27–54.

Imnaishvili, Ivane, Imnaishvili, Vakhtang. 1996. *Zmna żvel k'art'ulši (verb in old Georgian)*, 2 vols. Frankfurt-am-Main.

International Phonetic Association. 1999. https://www.internationalphoneticassociation.org/. Accessed 16 Jul 2019.

Javakhishvili, Ivane. 1949. *k'art'uli damcerlobat'amc'odneoba anu paleograp'ia (Georgian script-study or paleography)*. Tbilisi: t'bilisis saxelmcip'o universiteti (Tbilisi State University).

Johnson, Bruce. 2011. *ALA-LC Romanization Table: Georgian*. https://www.loc.gov/catdir/cpso/romanization/georgian.pdf. Accessed 16 Jul 2019.

Jorbenadze, Besarion. 1998. *k'art'uli dialek'tologia (Georgian dialectology)*. Tbilisi: mec'niereba (Science).

Kapanadze, Oleg. 2009. Describing Georgian morphology with a finite-state system. In *Proceedings of the 8th international conference on finite-state methods and natural language processing*, 114–122. Pretoria: Springer.

Kay, Paul. 2002. An informal sketch of a formal architecture for construction grammar. *Grammars* 5 (1): 1–19.

Kay, Paul, and Charles Fillmore. 1999. Grammatical constructions and linguistic generalizations: The What's X doing Y? Construction. *Language* 75 (1): 1–33.

Kehrein, Wolfgang. 2002. *Phonological representation and phonetic phasing: Affricates and laryngeals*. Tubingen: Max Niemeyer Verlag.

Kiziria, Anton. 1982. *Martivi cinadadebis šedgeniloba k'art'velur enebši (the structure of the simple sentence in the Kartvelia languages)*. Tbilisi: mec'niereba (science).

Kurdiani, Mikheil. 2008. *k'art'uli ena da damcerloba (Georgian language and writing system)*. Tbilisi: Artanuji.

Kvachadze, Leo. 1996. *t'anamedrove k'art'uli enis sintak'si (syntax of modern Georgian language)*. Tbilisi: Rubikoni.

Lakoff, George. 1987. *Women, fire, and dangerous things: what categories reveal about the mind*. Chicago: University of Chicago Press.

Lopez Rua, Paula. 2006. Nonmorphological word formation. In K. A. Brown, Encyclopedia of language & linguistics *(Second Edition)*, 675–678. Boston: Elsevier.

Machavariani, Elene. 1982. *k'art'uli anbanis grap'ikuli sap'użvlebi (graphical basis of Georgian alphabet)*. Tbilisi: Nakaduli.

———. 2015. *mcignobrobay k'art'uli (The Old Georgian script)*. Tbilisi: xelnacert'a erovnuli c'entri (National Centre of Manuscripts).

Machavariani, Mukhran. 1987. *k'c'evis gramatikuli kategoriis semantika (semantics of the grammatical category of version)*. Tbilisi: mec'niereba (science).

Makharoblidze, Tamar. 2009. *A short grammar of Georgian*. Munich: Lincom Europe.

———. 2018. On Georgian Preverbs. *Open Linguistics*: 163–183.

Manjgaladze, Al. 1963. saxelt'a prep'ik'suli carmoebisat'vis żvel k'art'ulši (On the prefixal formation of nominals in Old Georgian). *goris pedagogiuri institutis šromebi (Proceedings of Gori Teaching Institute)* VIII:85–88.

Marantz, Alec. 1982. Re reduplication. *Linguistic Inquiry*: 483–545.

———. 1988. Clitics, morphological merger, and the mapping to phonological structure. In *Theoretical morphology*, ed. M.A. Hammond, 253–270. New York: Academic.

Margvelani, Lamara. 1999–2001. A subsystem analyzing Georgian word-forms and its application to spellchecking. In *Proceedings of the 3rd and 4th International Symposium on language, logic and Computation*, 1–7. Borjomi: ILLC Scientific Publications.

Martirosov, Aram. 1958. abstrak'tul saxelt'a carmoeba da sacarmoebel ap'ik'st'a šedgeniloba żvel k'art'ulši (For formation of abstract nominals and composition of affixes in Old Georgian). *Iberian-Caucasian Linguistics (ICL)*, 121–127.

———. 1964. *nac'valsaxeli k'art'velur enebši (the pronoun in the Kartvelian languages)*. Tbilisi: mec'niereba (science).

McCarthy, John, and Alan Prince. 1986/1996. *Prosodic morphology 1986*. New Brunswick, NJ: Rutgers University Center for Cognitive Science.

McCoy, Priscilla. 1999. Harmony and sonority in consonant clusters in Georgian. In *Proceedings of the International Congress of Phonetic Sciences*, 447–450. Berkley: University of California.

Melikishvili, Damana. 1979. mok'medebit'i gvaris zmnis uġlebis sistema t'anamedrove k'art'ulši (Active voice conjugation of a verb in Modern Georgian). *mac'ne (Bulletin)* 1: 84–87.

———. 1980. Piris nac'valsaxelt'a p'użis agebulebast'an dakavširebuli zogiert'i sakit'xi (some issues with regards to the stem structure of personal pronouns). *Narkvevebi iberiul-kavkasiur enat'a morp'ologiidan (essays on the morphology of Iberian-Caucasian languages)*, 48–58.

———. 2001a. *k'art'uli zmnis uġlebis sistema (system of Georgian verbal paradigm)*. Tbilisi: Logos Press.

———. 2001b. Zmnis struk'tura da konstruk'c'ia k'art'ul enaši diat'ezisa da gvarebis t'eoriis kontek'stši (structure of a verb in Georgian language with regards to the theoro of diathesis and voice). *Varlam t'op'uria* 100: 135–142.

———. 2009a. inkluziv-ek'skluzivis kategoriis gamoxatvis istoriisat'vis k'art'ul zmnaši (To the category of inclusivity-exclusivity of Georgian verb). *p'ilologiuri żiebani (Philological issues)*, 116–123.

———. 2009b. inversia k'art'ul zmnaši diak'roniuli da sink'roniuli aspek'tit' (Inverstion of Georgian verb from diachronic and synchronic points of view). *p'ilologiuri żiebani (Philological issues)*, 589–592.

Melikishvili, Damana, John Humphries, and Maia Kupunia. 2010. *The Georgian verb: A Morphosyntactic analysis*. Hyattsville, MD: Dunwoody Press.

Melikisvhili, Damana. 2014. *k'art'uli zmnis sistemuri morp'o-sintak'suri analizi (Morphosyntactic analysis of Georgian verbal system)*. Tbilisi: t'bilisis saxelmcip'o universiteti (Tbilisi State University).

Mester, Armin. 1990. Patterns of truncation. *Linguistic Science* 21: 478–485.

Meurer, Paul. 2007. A computational grammar for Georgian. In *Lecture notes in computer science*, 1–15. Berlin: Springer.

Miller, Philip. 1992. *Clitics and constituents in phrase structure grammar*. New York: Garland.

Moravcsik, Edith. 1978. Reduplicative constructions. *Universals of human language, volume 3, word Structure*, 297–334.

Nash, Léa. 2017. The structural source of split ergativity and ergative case. In *The Oxford handbook of Ergativity*, ed. J. Coon et al., 175–204. Oxford: Oxford University Press.

Nebieridze, Givi. 1974. *saliteraturo k'art'uli enis generatoriul-p'onologiuri modeli da misi agebis princ'ipebi (A generative phonology model of the Georgian literary language and the principles of its construction)*. Tbilisi: t'bilisis saxelmcip'o universiteti (Tbilisi State University).

Pataridze, Ramaz. 1980. *k'art'uli asomt'avruli (Georgian Asomtavruli)*. Tbilisi: Nakaduli.

Peikrishvili, Jujuna. 2010. *k'art'uli enis morp'ologia (Morphology of Georgian language)*. Kutaisi: k'ut'aisis saxelmcip'o universitetis gamomc'emloba (Kutaisi State University).

Peterson, David. 1999. *Discourse-functional, historical, and typological aspects of applicative constructions*. Berkeley: ProQuest Dissertations Publishing.

———. 2007. *Applicative constructions*. Oxford: Oxford University Press.

Plank, Frans. 1995. *Double case: Agreement by Suffixaufnahme*. New York: Oxford University Press.

Pochkhua, Bidzina. 1974. *k'art'uli enis lek'sikologia (Lexicology of Georgian Language)*. Tbilisi: t'bilisis saxelmcip'o universiteti (Tbilisi State University).

Sarjveladze, Zurab. 1997. *żveli k'art'uli ena (Old Georgian Language)*. Tbilisi: Tbilisi State Pedagogical University Press.

Saxena, Anju. 2006. Pronouns. In K. A. Brown, Encyclopedia of language & linguistics *(Second Edition)*, 131–133. Boston: Elsevier.

Shanidze, Akaki. 1942. zmnat'a gardamavlobis sakit'xisat'vis k'art'velur enebši (to the transitivity of verbs in Kartvelian languages). *Bulletin of the Georgian Academy of Sciences* 3: 182–189.

———. 1956a. codebit'i p'ormis adgilisat'vis gramatikaši (to the place of vocative case in grammar). *Saxelis brunebis istoriisat'vis k'art'velur enebši (to the history of declension in Kartvelian languages)*, 48–56.

———. 1961. gramatikuli subiek'ti zogiert' gardauval zmnast'an k'art'ulši (Grammatical subject of some intransitive verb in Georgian). *Proceedings of the Department of Old Georgian Language*, 207–238.

———. 1967. orobit'i ric'xvis sakit'xisat'vis xevsurulši (On the issue of the dual number in Xevsurian). *t'bilisis saxelmcip'o universitetis šromebi (Proceedings of Tbilisi State University)*, 23–27.

———. 1973. *k'art'uli gramatikis sap'užvlebi, morp'ologia (Foundations of Georgian Grammar, Morphology), I.* Tbilisi: t'bilisis saxelmcip'o universiteti (Tbilisi State University).

———. 1976. *žveli k'art'uli ena (old Georgian language)*. Tbilisi: Tbilisi State University.

———. 1984. *k'art'uli kiloebi mt'aši (Georgian dialects in mountains) I.* Tbilisi: mec'niereba (Science).

Shanidze, Mzekala. 1956b. romel nac'valsaxelis p'unk'c'iisa da adgilisat'vis žvel k'art'ulši (To the function and place of which pronoun in Old Georgian). *saxelis brunebis istoriisat'vis k'art'velur enebši (To the history of declension in Kartvelian languages)*, 140–143.

Sharadzenidze, Tinatin. 1939. 'vit'' t'andebuli k'art'ulši ('Like' postposition in Georgian). *t'bilisis saxelmcip'o universitetis šromebi (Proceedings of Tbilisi State University)* 10: 145–159.

Sharashenidze, Tinatin. 1956. -t'a sup'ik'siani mravlobit'i mok'medebit'sa da vit'arebit's brunvebši (–t plural marker in instrumental and adverbial cases). In V. Topuria, *saxelis brunebis istoriisat'vis k'art'velur enebši (to the history of nominal declensions in Kartvelian languages)*, 1, 271-285. Tbilisi: t'bilisis saxelmcip'o universiteti (Tbilisi State University).

Shinjiashvili, Meri. 1984. ganqenebuli šinaarsis saxelt'a carmoebast'an dakavširebuli zogi sakit'xisat'vis t'anamedrove k'art'ulši (Some issues on the formation of abstract nominals in Modern Georgian). *Questions of Georgian Word Culture*, 195–226.

Shosted, Ryan. 2006. Standard Georgian. *Journal of the International Phonetic Association*, 255–264.

Spencer, Andrew, and Ana Luis. 2012. *Clitics: an introduction*. New York: Cambridge University Press.

Sproat, Richard. 1992. *Morphology and computation*. Cambridge: MIT.

Standardization, ISO. 1996. *Information and documentation — Transliteration of Georgian characters into Latin characters, No 9984.* https://www.iso.org/standard/17892.html. Accessed 16 Jul 2019.

———. 2017. Information technology — Universal Coded Character Set (UCS), No 10646. https://www.iso.org/standard/69119.html. Accessed 16 Jul 2019.

Stump, Gregory. 2001. *Inflectional morphology: a theory of paradigm structure*. Cambridge: Cambridge University Press.

———. 2002. Morphological and syntactic paradigms: arguments for a theory of paradigm linkage. In *Yearbook of morphology 2001*, ed. G.V. Booij, 147–180. Dordrecht: Kluwer.

Sukhishvili, Murman. 1986. *Gardamavali zmnebi k'art'ulši, sistemisa da istoriis zogi sakit'xi (transitive verbs in Georgian: Issues on system and history)*. Tbilisi: Georgian Academy of Sciences.

Topadze, Manana. 2011. The expression of evidentiality between lexicon and grammar: A case study from Georgian. *Linguistic Discovery* 9: 122–138.

Topuria, Varlam. 1956a. codebit'i brunvisat'vis (To Vocative case). *saxelis brunebis istoriisat'vis k'art'velur enebši (To the history of declension in Kartvelian languages)*, 36–48.

———. 1956b. -me, -ve, -ġa, -ġac'(a) nacilakian saxelt'a bruneba (To the declension of nouns ending in -me, -ve, -ġa, -ġac'(a) particles). *saxelis brunebis istoriisat'vis k'art'velur enebši (To the history of declension in Kartvelian languages)*, 131–139.

Tskhadadze, Badri. 1984. *masdaris carmoeba žvel k'art'ulši: (acmqos p'užis istoriast'an dakavširebit') (On the formation of Masdar in Old Georgian: with regards to the history of present stem)*. Tbilisi: mec'niereba (Science).

Tuite, Kevin. 1984. *Case attraction and case agreement*, Eastern States Conference on Linguistics. Vol. 1, 110–121. Ohio: Ohio State University.

———. 1998. *Kartvelian morphosyntax: number agreement and morphosyntactic orientation in the South Caucasian Languages*. Munich: LINCOM.
———. 2017. Alignment and orientation in Kartvelian. In *The Oxford Handbook of Ergativity*, ed. J. Coon et al., 1114–1138. Oxford: Oxford University Press.
———. 2019. On the origin of Kartvelian "version". 1–50. https://www.academia.edu/40077656/On_the_origin_of_Kartvelian_version_. Accessed 10 Dec 2019.
Tuskia, Manana. 2010. *saxeluri da saxelzmnuri carmoeba k'art'ulši (Noun and verbal noun derivation in Georgian)*. Tbilisi: Georgian Academy of Sciences.
Uturgaidze, Tedo. 1976. *k'art'uli enis p'onematuri struk'tura (The phonematic structure of the Georgian language)*. Tbilisi: mec'niereba (Science).
———. 1986. *k'art'uli enis saxelis morp'onologiuri analizi (Morphophonological analysis of Georgian noun)*. Tbilisi: mec'niereba (Science).
———. 2001. *gramatikuli kategoriebisa da mat'i urt'iert'mimart'ebisat'vis k'art'ul zmnaši (Grammatical categories and their interrelationship in Georgian verb)*. Tbilisi: k'art'uli ena (Georgian language).
Vogel, Petra, and Bernard Comrie. 2000. *Approaches to the typology of word classes*. Berlin: Mouton de Gruyter.
Vogt, Hans Karmstup. 1961. *k'art'uli enis p'onematuri struk'tura (The phonematic structure of the Georgian language)*. Tbilisi: t'bilisis saxelmcip'o universiteti (Tbilisi State University).
———. 1968. brunvat'a sistema żvel k'art'ulši (Case system in Old Georgian). Reviewer, 251–284.
———. 1971. *Grammaire de la langue géorgienne*. Oslo: Universitetsforlaget.
Wier, Thomas. 2011a. *Georgian morphosyntax and feature hierarchies in natural language*. Chicago: ProQuest LLC.
———. 2011b. Khevsur and Tush and the status of unusual phenomena in corpora. *Annual meeting of the Berkeley Linguistics Society* 37 (2): 96–110.
Zgenti, Serge. 1956. *k'art'uli enis p'onetika (Phonetics of Georgian language)*. Tbilisi: t'bilisis saxelmcip'o universiteti (Tbilisi State University).
———. 1965. *k'art'velur enat'a p'onetikis sakit'xebi: rč'euli šromebi (Phonetic questions of the Kartvelian languages)*. Tbilisi: ganat'leba (Education).
Zurabishvili, Tinatin. 1956. emp'atikuri -a axal k'art'ulši (Extension vowel -a in Modern Georgian). saxelis brunebis istoriisat'vis k'art'velur enebši (To the history of declension in Kartvelian languages), 224–234.
———. 1972. emp'atikuri xmovani t'anamedrove k'art'ulši (Extension vowel in Modern Georgian). Questions of Georgian word culture, 44–57.
Zwicky, Arnold. 1977. *On clitics*. Bloomington: Indiana University Linguistics Club.
———. 1985a. Clitics and particles. *Language* 61: 283–305.
———. 1985b. *How to describe inflection. Proceedings of the eleventh annual meeting of the Berkeley Linguistics Society*, 372–386. Berkeley: Berkeley.
. 1990. Inflection as a (sub)component of morphology. In *Contemporary morphology*, ed. W.E. Dressler, 217–236. Berlin, New York: Mouton de Gruyter.

Chapter 3
Computational Modeling

Abstract This chapter briefly describes finite-state automata, finite-state transducers and regular expressions before focusing on the architecture of the tokenizer and wide-coverage morphological analyzer and generator for Georgian implemented using Xerox Finite-State Tools like *xfst* and *lexc*. The computational modelling of Georgian presented here covers the morphotactics of words and issues encountered during the processing of texts with foreign words, numbers and punctuation marks, abbreviations and multiword expressions. The chapter comprises four sections, the first of which is a short introduction on natural language processing issues from the point of view of finite-state technology. Section 3.2, 'Tokenization', provides an overview of the tokenizer, including issues relating to sentence and word splitting. Section 3.3, 'The morphological analyzer', describes the implementation of a morphological analyzer and generator for Georgian using finite-state tools. Section 3.4 summarizes the information provided in the preceding sections.

Keywords Finite-State Tools · Tokenizer · Morphological analyzer for Georgian

3.1 Introduction

Natural language processing systems combine computational techniques with language description and, generally speaking, retranslate linguistic data into a format comprehensible to a computer. While the morphological processing of languages is carried out using a variety of approaches, the majority of methods used can be divided into two types: rule-based and statistical methods. The rule-based approach requires scrupulous description of morphemes and their combinatorial rules (Koskenniemi 1983; Sproat 1992; Karlsson 1994; Karlsson and Karttunen 1997 and others), while the statistical approach requires corpora and the ability to analyse and calculate word frequencies for data-training purposes (Karlsson and Karttunen 1997; Jurafsky and Martin 2000; Goldsmith 2001 and others).

One of the most popular approaches to morphological processing employs language-independent finite-state technology. This method has its theoretical

I. Lobzhanidze, *Finite-State Computational Morphology*,
https://doi.org/10.1007/978-3-030-90248-3_3

background in the phonological rewriting rules first described by Johnson (1972) and built upon by Kaplan and Kay (1994), researchers from Palo Alto and, ultimately, the algorithms for finite-state computing developed by Beesley and Kartunnen (2003).

Finite-state technology can essentially be described as a set of states and arcs used to connect the states (Jurafsky and Martin 2000; Beesley and Karttunen 2003 and others) forming networks. Finite-state automata describe languages, while finite-state transducers are focused on the relations between languages. Finite-state transducers are bi-directional and generate output on the basis of a given input; this means that they can be used to control applications both in parsing and generation.

Finite-state technology is based on two levels: a surface and a lexical representation of words. Combining these two levels makes it possible to describe linguistic phenomena in the form of finite state morphology (Kaplan and Kay 1994; Beesley and Karttunen 2003), which supports a division of complex morphological processes into a cascade of intermediate operations and the regulation of a design in a systematic way, mapping of a surface representation to its lexical representation and the composition of a single transducer based on a cascade of the aforementioned operations.

The majority of natural language processing systems are based on one hand on Turing's abstract model of computation (Turing 1936), which describes a computing device in terms of a control unit containing rules, which processes symbols taken form a finite list called an 'alphabet', and on the other, on the well-known Chomsky-Schützenberger hierarchy (Chomsky 1956; Chomsky and Schützenberger 1963; Schützenberger 1961), which describes a containment hierarchy of formal grammars according to the class of language it generates, the type of automata that recognize it and the form of its rules. The hierarchy of languages is as follows (Table 3.1):

Table 3.1 Chomsky-Schützenberger hierarchy

Class	Languages	Grammar	Automata
Type 0	Turing-recognizable	Unrestricted	Turing machine (TM)
Type 1	Context sensitive	Context sensitive	Linear bound automata (LBA)
Type 2	Context free	Context free	Pushdown automata (PDA)
Type 3	Regular	Regular	Finite-state automata (FSA)

This hierarchy forms the basis for different grammatical frameworks such as Generalized Phrase Structure Grammar (GPSG) (Gazdar et al. 1985), Lexical Functional Grammar (LFG) (Kaplan and Bresnan 1982) and Head-Driven Phrase Structural Grammar (HPSG) (Pollard and Sag 1994), and for different computational tools like Xerox Finite-State Tools (2013) (Karlsson and Karttunen 1997).

The machine described by Turing proceeds until the sequence of input symbols is finished and reaches its final state by accepting or rejecting other states. The accepted sequence of symbols forms a word and the set of such words constitutes the language of the machine. The most important type for the purposes of the book comprises so-called 'regular grammars' and the associated finite-state automata (FSA) also known as finite-state machines. A FSA is a system that must always be in one of a finite number of states, and a regular language accepted by a FSA can be encoded as a regular expression. More formally, a finite-state automaton can be defined by the following five parameters (Table 3.2):

Table 3.2 Parameters of an FSA described on the base of Jurafsky and Martin (2000)

$Q = q_0 q_1 q_2 \ldots q_{n-1}$	a finite set of *n* states
Σ	a finite list of input symbols, or 'alphabet'
q_0	the initial state which is a member of Q
$\delta : S \times \Sigma \rightarrow S$	the transition matrix with two arguments: a state and an input symbol, which returns a new state
F	the set of final states which is a subset of Q

We can consider a transition network for Georgian in the form of a simple FSA using the following stated above:

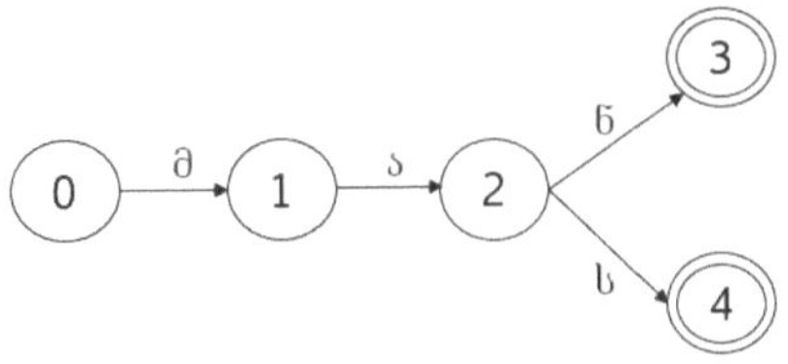

$FSA = (Q, \Sigma, \delta, q_0, F)$
$Q = \{0,1,2,3,4\}$
$\Sigma = \{\text{ა}, \text{მ}, \text{ნ}, \text{ს}\}$
$\delta = \{(0, \text{მ}, 1), (1, \text{ა}, 2), (2, \text{ნ}, 3), (2, \text{ს}, 4)\}$
$q_0 = 0$
$F = \{3,4\}$

Fig. 3.1 FSA for *man* 's/he/it' and *mas* 'for him/her/it' (A)

Figure 3.1 depicts a finite-state automaton that recognizes the following sequences of symbols: *man* and *mas* as corresponding to the regular expression ma[n|s], in which *m* is followed by *a* and followed by either *n* or *s*. The FSA receives and generates language starting from its initial state {0} and finishing on its final states {3, 4}. An important constraint is that the Georgian alphabet is finite, comprising 33 letters, which means that strings are to be associated with this finite quantity of symbols.

A variation on the finite-state automaton is a Mealy Machine, which is a deterministic finite-state transducer (Mealy 1955) which defines relations between strings and can not only accept or reject an input, but also convert it to an output.

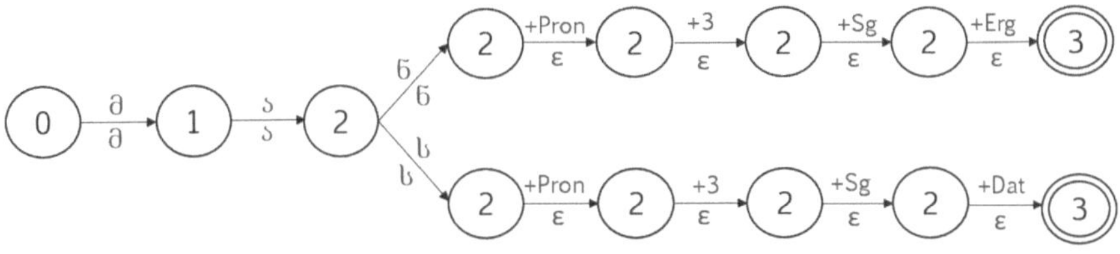

Fig. 3.2 FSA for *man* 's/he/it' and *mas* 'for him/her/it' (B)

As shown in Fig. 3.2, the FST accepts *man* and *mas* on its lower side and converts them into the strings *man+Pron+3+Sg+Erg* and *mas+Pron+3+Sg+Dat* on its upper side. In this way, the transducer creates a mapping between lexical (upper) and surface (lower) languages and can work in either direction.

The use of FST for language description is associated with the question of whether regular or irregular patterns are the more interesting from the point of view of description. It is well known that regular and irregular varieties of inflectional morphology differ from one another; Regular types are generally defined as those that involve predictable transformations, which include such processes as affixation, while irregular types involve at least partially idiosyncratic transformations, which include stem changes.

Traditionally, the languages of the world are classified as analytic, in which case they are characterized by a small number of affixes with grammatical relationships encoded primarilly by word order and auxiliary words, or as synthetic, in which case they are subdivided into fusional and agglutinative languages. Fusional languages are characterized by a greater number of affixes representing several functions (as can be found for instance in Russian). By contrast, in agglutinative languages, words are composed of different affixes, each of which has a unique grammatical and/or semantic function. Agglutinative languages generally represent one grammatical category per affix, while fusional languages can represent multiple categories with a single affix. Furthermore, in contrast with fusional languages, agglutinative languages, and Georgian especially, are characterized by a high degree of word order variation which affects the composition of tree-banks and predicts a sparseness of lexical data which influences statistical analysis of the language as a whole. This kind of challenge can be solved at the level of morphology-based parsing, which can disambiguate and determine dependencies between words.

Finite-state automata, which compose networks, encode regular languages, while transducers encode regular relations. An FST as described by Beesley and Karttunen (2003) is therefore generally used for the morphological analysis of languages, and has been in our case for Georgian. The Xerox Finite-State Tools *xfst* and *lexc*, which were developed by the Xerox Research Centre Europe (XRCE) and the Palo Alto Research Centre (PARC) and are fully described in (Beesley and Karttunen, 2003) are language independent and have been successfully tested on many languages, including Georgian (Meurer 2007; Kapanadze 2009) performing a variety of purposes, including normalization, morphological guessing, sentence splitting, and tokenization.

In the case of Georgian, the possibilities of finite-state tools have been applied to tokenization, sentence splitting, morphological analysis and named entity recognition.

3.2 Tokenization

The tokenizing transducer for Georgian consists of two components. The first is used to split texts into sentences, while the second is used to split sentences into words by taking into consideration white spaces, punctuation marks, and multiword expressions, initials and abbreviations, among other phenomena. The tokenizing transducer applied to Georgian is based on the finite-state tokenizer developed by Anne Schiller (Karttunen et al., 1997; Beesley and Karttunen, 2003). Tokenizing transducers of this kind are defined with the purpose of recognizing language-specific information using *xfst*. At the time of writing, the tokenizer for Georgian is 440.3 Kb in size and consists of 702 states and 35,501 arcs.

The tokenizer depends on the presence of white spaces, punctuation marks consisting of a single symbol or a sequence of symbols, letters and numeric expressions in the text. As defined by (Manning et al. 2008), a token is an instance of a sequence of characters in a given document that is grouped as a unit important for processing.

In Modern Georgian tokens are separated regularly by white spaces if they are not preceded or followed by punctuation marks, while in Old Georgian tokenization is an irregular process, in that tokens are sometimes separated by white spaces and sometimes not, and in some cases, depending on the century, may also be separated by paragraph separators (჻). The cases in which punctuation marks are not separated from adjacent symbols are as follows:

(a) Full stop used in initials (*arn. č'ik'obava* 'Arnold Chikobava' and others) and in abbreviations (*a.š.* 'etc.', *e.i.* 'i.e.', etc.), as shown in Fig. 3.3.

```
define INIT [LETTER %.]+;
define ABBR [{ა.შ.}|{ე.ი.}|{სხვ.}|{იხ.}|{გვ.}]; ! All
abbreviations are not listed here.
```

Fig. 3.3 Tokenization: Abbreviations

(b) Full stop or comma used in numeric expressions (*1.2, 0.5*, etc.), as shown in Fig. 3.4.

```
define DIGIT [%0|%1|%2|%3|%4|%5|%6|%7|%8|%9] ;
define NUMOP [%-|%+|%*|%/|%=|%:] ;
define NUMSEP [%.|%,] ;
define NUM [[DIGIT|NUMOP|NUMSEP]+ & $[DIGIT]] ;
```

Fig. 3.4 Tokenization: Numeric expressions

(c) Punctuation marks used in lists, as shown in Fig. 3.5.

```
define LIST [[LETTER %)]|[%( LETTER %)]|[DIGIT %)]|[%(
DIGIT %)]] ;
```

Fig. 3.5 Tokenization: Punctuation marks in lists

(d) Punctuation marks used in foreign words to identify email addresses or websites (*http://*, *.com*, etc.), as shown in Fig. 3.6.

```
define WEB [[h t t p %: %/ %/]|[ %. c o m]] ;
define AT [%@] ;
define ALPHABET
[A|B|C|D|E|F|G|H|I|J|K|L|M|N|O|P|Q|R|S|T|U|V|W|X|Y|Z|a|
b|c|d|e|f|g|h|i|j|k|l|m|n|o|p|q|r|s|t|u|v|w|x|y|z|1|2|3
|4|5|6|7|8|9|%0] ;
```

Fig. 3.6 Tokenization: E-mail addresses and web-sites

(e) XML tags (*<div > </div>, <p > </p>, <lb/>*, etc.) determined in accordance with the TEI P5 guidelines (TEI Consortium 2019), as shown in Fig. 3.7.

```
define TG [[%< d i v %>]|[%< %/ d i v %>]|[%< p %>]|[%<
%/ p %>]|[%< l b %/ %>]] ; ! All tags are not listed
here.
```

Fig. 3.7 Tokenization: XML mark-up

Georgian letters are determined in accordance with the Georgian alphabet (*Asomtavruli, Nuskhuri* and *Mkhedruli*) in the following way (Fig. 3.8):

```
define LETTER
[ა|ბ|გ|დ|ე|ვ|ზ|თ|ი|კ|ლ|მ|ნ|ო|პ|ჟ|რ|ს|ტ|უ|ფ|ქ|ღ|ყ|შ|ჩ|ც|
ძ|წ|ჭ|ხ|ჯ|ჰ|ჱ|ჲ|ჳ|ჴ|ჵ|ჶ|Ⴀ|Ⴁ|Ⴂ|Ⴃ|Ⴄ|Ⴅ|Ⴆ|Ⴇ|Ⴈ|Ⴉ|Ⴊ|Ⴋ|Ⴌ|Ⴍ|
Ⴎ|Ⴏ|Ⴐ|Ⴑ|Ⴒ|Ⴓ|Ⴔ|Ⴕ|Ⴖ|Ⴗ|Ⴘ|Ⴙ|Ⴚ|Ⴛ|Ⴜ|Ⴝ|Ⴞ|Ⴟ|Ⴠ|Ⴡ|Ⴢ|Ⴣ|Ⴤ|Ⴥ|Ⴧ|
ⴀ|ⴁ|ⴂ|ⴃ|ⴄ|ⴅ|ⴆ|ⴇ|ⴈ|ⴉ|ⴊ|ⴋ|ⴌ|ⴍ|ⴎ|ⴏ|ⴐ|ⴑ|ⴒ|ⴓ|ⴔ|ⴕ|ⴖ|ⴗ|ⴘ|ⴙ|
ⴚ|ⴛ|ⴜ|ⴝ|ⴞ|ⴟ|ⴠ|ⴡ|ⴢ|ⴣ|ⴤ] ;
```

Fig. 3.8 Tokenization: Letters of the Georgian alphabet

Georgian numerals are not represented in the tokenizer, because it was difficult to separate these from textual data in the case of Old and Middle Georgian texts written in *Asomtavruli* and *Nuskhuri*. Roman numerals, which are separated sometimes by white spaces and sometimes by punctuation marks in Modern Georgian texts, are represented in the following way (Fig. 3.9):

```
define ROMAN [i|v|x|l|c|I|V|X|L|C] ;
define NUMERAL [ROMAN+] ;
```

Fig. 3.9 Tokenization: Roman numerals

The sentence-splitting module depends on the presence of punctuation marks, white spaces at the end of sentences and tabulation marks at the beginning of paragraphs. There are two types of punctuation mark which can be used at the end of sentences in Georgian:

1. Punctuation marks which consist of a single symbol, including a full stop (.), exclamation mark (!), question mark (?), semicolon (;) and paragraph separator (⁖), which is used in Old and Middle Georgian;
2. Punctuation marks which consist of a sequence of symbols, such as a question mark followed by an exclamation mark (?!), an exclamation mark followed by two full stops (!..) and ellipsis (…).

Following the principles described in (Beesley and Karttunen 2003), the sentence splitting module was used to provide structural markups of corpus data determining the boundaries between sentences, as per Fig. 3.10.

```
define SINGLE [%. |%; |%! |%? |%⁖ ] ;
define MULT   [%. %. %.% |%? %!% |%! %. %.%  ] ;
define NL "\n";
define TAB "\t";
define Token [SINGLE|MULT|NL|TAB];
```

Fig. 3.10 Tokenization: Sentence splitting

Evaluation of a tokenizer's output is carried out in two ways: by comparison of its output with 'gold standard' tokenized texts, or by comparison of its output with that of other tokenizers run on the same texts, as proposed by Ui Dhonnchadha (Uí Dhonnchadha 2009). Taking into consideration that no other tokenizers of Georgian are freely available for academic purposes, we checked the tokenizer's output manually and corrected it where necessary. The principal mismatches encountered with respect to the identification of tokens and sentence boundaries were associated with the following:

(a) Irregular use of white spaces in Middle and Old Georgian texts;
(b) Complicated recognition of titles and named entities caused by the absence of majuscules in Georgian and irregular use of *Asomtavruli* letters as majuscules in *Asomtavrul-Nuskhuri* or *Asomtavrul-Mkhedruli* Old and Middle Georgian texts;
(c) The absence of punctuation marks at the end of titles, which impedes identification of titles without additional markup, such as <title></title> etc. The identification of titles in raw texts (.txt, .doc etc. formats) without additional markup (.xml format) is somewhat complicated;
(d) Punctuation marks used in initials (*arn. č'ik'obava* 'Arnold Chikobava' and others) and rare abbreviations (*gr.* 'gram', *kap.* 'copeck', etc.). Both of these problems are caused by the absence of majuscules in Georgian, which does not permit recognition of named entities and sentence boundaries in a way typical for Indo-European languages;
(e) Typographical errors and misspellings in raw texts.

3.3 The Morphological Analyzer

Research groups focusing on the computational modelling of Georgian have adopted varying approaches and implemented them in varying ways. Datukishvili, Loladze and Zakalashvili describe the combination of different morphemes, their use in templatic patterns and the application of the aforementioned patterns to a computational modelling system called a morphological processor (Datukischvili et al. 2005, 2007). Margvelani (1999–2001), who analyses word-forms and their application to spellchecking for Modern Georgian, pays special attention to complicated patterns caused by multihormonic affixes used for different PoS-es and describes a system consisting of roots and an algorithm which constructs correct forms from affixes and roots. Kapanadze (2009) subdivides Georgian verbal patterns into five groups: especially, transitive (C1), intransitive (C2), medial (C3), inversion (C4) and stative, and compiles a transducer with recognition rate of less than 20% which employs a finite-state calculus. Gurevich (2006), who discusses the lexical classes defined by Melikishvili (2001), argues that this classification is too fine, but attempts to identify interdependencies between Future and Conditional or Aorist and Perfect following Shanidze (1973). As a result, she compiles a prototype model of Georgian inflectional morphology that employs finite-state technology. She uses this model to develop an online reference tool for Georgian verb inflection and provides a detailed discussion of the difficulties of this approach with regard to the verbal paradigm caused by screeve formation, root alternation, the use of affixes simultaneously in forms involving long-dependencies, and other issues.

Meurer (2007) uses a similar approach in the compilation of a full-scale computational grammar within the framework of Lexical-Functional Grammar, but in contrast to the attempts noted above he bases his work on a digitized version of Tschenkeli Dictionary (1965) with verbal nouns and, specifically, verbal roots treated as initial lemmas for verbs. This dictionary can be considered a highly useful linguistic reference for the structure of the Georgian verb which includes information on the number and type of arguments associated with a concrete verbal root. The recognition rate of this analyser is improved by means of additional guessers.

Rejecting the capabilities of finite-state calculus and pronouncing it inefficient, Antidze and Gulua (2010) develop their own system by means of a C++ compiler and propose their own ideas with respect to formalism. Their morphological analyzer, which utilizes an STL library, can run on the UNIX and Windows operating systems.

While the computational implementation of these approaches varies, their theoretical background generally speaking follows the description of Georgian grammar made by Shanidze (1973) and amended by others (Hewitt 2005; Makharoblidze 2009 and others). None of the computerized treatments of the Georgian verbal paradigm discussed above follows Melikishvili's (2010) classification of the Georgian verb by diathesis.

To summarize, the computational models described here are based on four main factors:

- The number of morphemes/slots per paradigm;
- Internal changes between or within morphemes/slots;
- The linguistic theory used for reference; and
- The type of dictionary(ies) used.

All of these parameters permit a description of Georgian using finite-state morphology. In the Morphological Analyser and Generator of Georgian (nowadays referred to as Lemmatizer of Georgian by S. Asatiani, E. Magradze and others) compiled by Irina Lobzhanidze within the framework of project AR/320/4-105/11 financed by the Shota Rustaveli National Science Foundation, the morphological rules of Georgian are encoded in a way that enables the generation of Modern Georgian forms from the digitized version of Chikobava's explanatory dictionary Chikobava (1950–1964) amended using the index of verbs proposed by Melikishvili (2001) and the generation of Middle and Old Georgian forms from the dictionary produced by Abuladze (1973). The lexicon used by the analyser is enriched with other words collected from various online and offline sources. Phrase-level syntactic relations, such as those between nouns, specifiers and modifiers, as well as disambiguation issues, are not addressed in this book.

The morphological analyser for Georgian is constructed in such a way as to provide morphological analysis for each token of the input text, and provides lemmatization, assignment of PoS tags and determination of other morphological features. It has been tested on the Georgian Language Corpus (Doborjginidze et al. 2012–2014), which was specially compiled to promote corpus-based approaches to Georgian literary language and to provide documentation of different textual genres. The corpus is freely available online at http://corpora.iliauni.edu.ge/ (Doborjginidze et al. 2012) and includes approximately 13 million words. The coverage of the analyser was improved using extended lexicons, morphological guessers and additional rules.

The analyser was written using two tools: *lexc* and *xfst*. *lexc* is a high-level declarative programming language used as lexicon compiler for defining finite-state automata and transducers, while *xfst* is a compiler for regular expressions used to manipulate networks (automata and transducers) previously described by *lexc*. As such, *lexc* is associated with the morphotactics of a language, while *xfst* is associated with its phonological and orthographical alternation rules.

Each entry in the main lexicon contains lexical items for Old and Modern Georgian. Lexicon data are stored separately to provide appropriate tagging of language varieties at the initial stage. While some types of affixes are associated either with Modern or Old Georgian, the overall activation of the modules depends on the century in which the text was created.

The *lexc* modules consist of lexicons which contain Old, Middle and Modern Georgian varieties and continuation classes represented in accordance with the following syntax:

```
Form        continuation class ;
```

The form is subdivided into two parts: lexical, corresponding to upper level and surface, corresponding to lower level. The lexical part comprises a lemma sign assigned by convention to a concrete PoS or a lemma with multicharacter symbols, including the plus sign or another non-alphabetic character or characters used by the Xerox convention to convey morphological or syntactic features or only a multicharacter symbol with plus sign:

```
უვან                                Loc ;
or
გული+Noun+Com+Inanim:გულ     Nmbr_1 ;
or
+ObjBen1Sg+Subj2Sg+Obj3:0      IndSpeech ;
```

The surface component of the form comprises a lemma sign or an affix used for the further generation of surface forms:

```
+Voc:ო     # ;
```

As discussed, the form itself enables lemmas to be distinguished and the results of the lemmatization to be conveyed back to the user. Lemmatization refers to dictionaries and to the morphological analysis of words presented in dictionaries. According to the Morphosyntactic Annotation Framework (MAF) (ISO 24611 2012):

> A lemma is a lemmatized form class of inflected forms differing only by inflectional morphology. In European languages, the lemma is usually the /singular/ if there is a variation in /number/, the /masculine/ form if there is a variation in /gender/ and the /infinitive/ for all verbs. In some languages, certain nouns are defective in the singular form, in which case the /plural/ is chosen. In Arabic, for a verb, the lemma is usually considered to be the third person singular with the accomplished aspect.

In the case of Georgian, lemmatization represents quite a difficult task. While by convention, the lemma for the nominal paradigm as represented in Georgian dictionaries is the nominative singular, the Georgian verb does not have an infinitive form, and there is no clear convention with regard to the headword used for verbal paradigms in Georgian dictionaries. The majority of Georgian dictionaries employ varying strategies with regard to the headwords of dictionary entries, which in the case of verbal entries can be of the following types:

1. The verbal noun, or *masdar* form, is sometimes referred to as the headword for a verbal entry (Tsotsanidze et al. 2014) or as the infinitive of the verbal paradigm, because some scholars (Chubinashvili 1940) argue that the extraction of an abstract root from the verbal noun is simpler than it is from a finite verb form.

Taking into consideration, however, that some Georgian verbs do not have nominal counterparts, it becomes clear that if a dictionary follows this approach, some verbal entries will not be represented at all, while others will be represented at least twice or more with and/or without preverbs (*mi-svla-∅* 'going', *mo-svla-∅* 'coming', *č'a-svla-∅* 'going down', etc.), and it is rather awkward to use such a list of verbal nouns for the generation of verbs in Natural Language Processing (NLP) systems;

2. The root-based form, or so-called 'abstract root' (Tschenkeli 1965), which represents the headword of entries in the form of an abstract verbal root with appropriate paradigms; if a dictionary follows these principles, the structure of entries is assumed to be very complex, with no direct indication of finite forms for lemmas, but instead with indication of verbal valency. Lists of this kind can be adopted for the needs of NLP systems, but only if a verb is strictly represented in the list and each entry is additionally marked with information with regard to valency. Different opinions exist with regard to this approach from language-learning and teaching perspectives; some scholars argue that this approach is well-suited for non-native speakers (Gippert 2016), while others reject it (Lobzhanidze 2019), arguing that it makes it difficult for dictionary users to find the appropriate meaning of verbs, as they must try to determine their abstract roots without a basic knowledge of the grammatic rules by which verbal paradigms are formed. The digitized version of such dictionary (Tschenkeli 1965) is however used by Meurer (2007) in his computational grammar of Georgian largely because the verbs in the lexicon are accompanied by additional morpho-syntactic information such as valency;
3. The third-person singular in the present or future indicative. This approach is proposed by Chikobava (1950–1964) and adopted by other Georgian lexicographers (Oniani 1966; Rayfield 2006 and others). In such dictionaries, verbal entries are accompanied by grammatical categories such as version, causation, etc. as well as the associated verbal noun. These dictionaries follow the principle of a mixed representation of verbal entries with an increased number of headwords at the expense of verbs used with and/or without preverbs.

Taking into consideration that the majority of Georgian dictionaries follow a mixed approach to verbal entries, the lemma sign of a verbal paradigm is determined in the morphological analyser on the basis of Chikobava's explanatory dictionary (Chikobava 1950–1964) and verbal index provided by Melikishvili (2001). The forms of verbal lemma signs presented in dictionaries is also reduced to the forms of the second-person singular, which are closely associated with verbal stems, while the forms of nominals have remained unchanged.

The fragment of the lexicon shown in Fig. 3.11 represents part of Declension No. 5 for *-a*-final common nouns, which truncate in the genitive and instrumental cases in the singular and in all cases in the *-eb-* plural.

```
Multichar_Symbols
+Noun +Prop +Com +Anim +Inanim +Sg +Pl +Nom +Erg +Dat
+Gen +Ins +Advb +Voc +Emph +Post +Ptcl +Aux

! cases
@U.CASE.NOM@ @R.CASE.NOM@ @D.CASE.NOM@ etc.
! extension vowels
@U.EMP.A@ @D.EMP.A@ etc.
! postpositions
@U.POST.SI@ @R.POST.SI@ @U.POST.TAN@ @D.POST.TAN@
@U.POST.ZE@ @D.POST.ZE@ etc.
! particles
@U.PTCL.C@ @D.PTCL.C@ @U.PTCL.CA@ @U.PTCL.RA@
@R.PTCL.RA@ etc.

! triggers ^S ^P ^NT ^N etc.

LEXICON Root
             Noun_5 ;

LEXICON Noun_5
დედა         Nmbr_1 ;

LEXICON Nmbr_1
+Sg:^S0      Cs1 ;
+Pl:^Pებ     Cs1 ;
+Pl:^Pებთ    CaseD ;
+Pl:^NTნ     CaseNV ;
+Pl:^NTთ     CaseD ;
```

Fig. 3.11 *lexc*: Extract from Lexicon for the fifth Declension Nouns

There are two types of tags declared at the start of text file: (a) tags used to describe morphological features such as +Noun, +Prop etc., (b) triggering tags used to trigger replace rules from *xfst* modules such as ^S ^P, etc. A full list of tags per PoS-es is listed in Appendix A, while a partial list of triggers can be seen in Appendix B. The first type of tags is used at the lexical level, and the second type at the surface. An output from a sample fragment provided below (Table 3.3):

Table 3.3 The lexical and surface levels

Lexical Level	Surface Level	Network
დე და +Noun+Sg	დე და ^S0	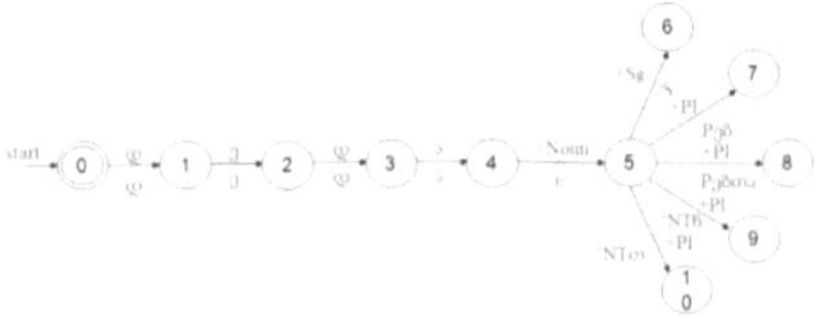
დე და +Noun+Pl	დე და ^Pე ბ	
დე და +Noun+Pl	დე და ^Pე ბ თ	
დე და +Noun+Pl	დე და ^NTნ	
დე და +Noun+Pl	დე და ^NTთ	

If we wish to proceed to other classes of the nominal paradigm, we must implement truncation in the genitive and instrumental cases in the singular and in all cases in the plural with *–eb* marker. It is not sufficient to add the *–eb* plural suffix to the stem *deda* 'mother', for example, as the stem itself must be modified by means of the *xfst* module outside the lexicon to compile a plural nominative form like *ded-eb-i* 'mothers'. This implementation is achieved by means of triggers which ensure the strict implementation of replace rules and enable us to avoid undesirable overgeneration.

Another feature-setting and feature-unification operation of Xerox Finite-State implementation are flag diacritics, which make it possible to store values of variables and to constrain the number of valid paths in a network. Flag diacritics are highly useful for blocking the paths, keeping the transducer small and establishing long dependencies between morphs. In contrast to triggers, flag diacritics are used in *lexc* syntax to avoid overgeneration and overrecognition within a system.

The syntax of flag diacritics follows the rule determined in Beesley and Karttunen (2003) as follows: `@operator.feature.value@`. By convention there are six operators indicating their own action, namely (Table 3.4):

Table 3.4 Operators of flag diacritics as described in Beesley and Karttunen (2003)

Operators	Description
Positive (Re) Setting	Positive (P) shows that the value of the indicated feature is set to the indicated value. Never causes failure or backtracking
Negative (Re) Setting	Negative (N) expresses that the value of the feature is set to the negation of the value. Never causes failure or backtracking
Require Test	Require (R) delivers a successful test result only if the feature is set to the value. If the test fails, the path is blocked and the application finds other solutions.
Disallow Test	Disallow (D) delivers a successful test result only if the feature is set to a value that is incompatible with the given value. Otherwise failure and backtracking result.
Clear Feature	Clear (C) shows that the value of the feature is reset to neutral.
Unification Test	Unification (U) shows that the feature is set to the value if it is neutral or if it is compatible with the current value of the feature.

The system enables operations including Positive setting, Require, Disallow and Unification tests. PoS-es differ with regard to the number of flag diacritics used for them depending on the peculiarities relevant to their formation; generally speaking, the number ranges from 61 in case of pronouns to as many as 167 in the case of verbs. Flag diacritics as well as tags which describe morphological features and trigger replace rules are added to the lexicon, while the replace rules work in the form of regular expressions outside the lexicon.

The *xfst* modules are used to implement replacement rules in accordance with the following syntax:

```
a -> b || L _ R
```

This syntax indicates that a string (a) is replaced by a substitution string (b) only when the left context ends with L and the right context begins with R. This syntax, which may consist of a single or multiple replacement separated by commas, provides the following possibilities:

(a) `a -> b` (a is substituted by b);
(b) `a -> b || c _ d` (a is substituted by b if preceded by c and followed by d),
(c) `a -> b || .#. _ d` (a is substituted by b if followed by d at the absolute beginning of a string),
(d) `a -> b || c _ .#.` (a is substituted by b if preceded by c at the absolute end of a string)

The simple replacement rules used for the fragment mentioned above are shown in Fig. 3.12.

```
define Vowels ა|ე|ი|ო|უ|ჲ ;
define Consonants
ბ|გ|დ|ვ|ზ|თ|კ|პ|ჟ|ს|ტ|ფ|ქ|ღ|ყ|შ|ჩ|ც|ძ|წ|ჭ|ხ|ჯ|ჰ|ჳ|ჴ|ჶ ;
define Sonants ლ|მ|ნ|რ ;
read lexc < nounCom.txt
define Noun ;
Etc.
define R2 [ა|ე|ო -> [] || _ Sonants %^S1 ?* $["^G"]
~$["^NT1"].o. ა|ე|ო -> [] || _ Sonants %^S1 ?* $["^I"]
.o. ა|ე|ო -> [] || _ Sonants %^S1 ?* $["^T"] .o. ა|ე|ო
-> [] || _ Sonants %^P1 ?* ] ;
Etc.
define R12 [%^S1 -> [] .o. %^P1 -> [] .o. %^NT1 -> []
.o. %^G -> [] .o. %^I -> [] .o. %^T -> [] etc. ] ;
read regex [ Noun .o. R1 .o. etc. .o. R12 ] ;
```

Fig. 3.12 *xfst*: Replace rules of Lexicon for the fifth Declension Nouns

As can be seen in Fig. 3.12, this rule defines not only the changes undergone by *-a*-final common nouns, which truncate in genitive and instrumental cases in the singular and in all cases in the plural with the *-eb-* marker, but also those undergone by nouns ending in *-e* or *-o*. Following implementation of the rules, the triggers are removed from the surface level. As discussed, the composed transducer is bidirectional with intermediate levels required to cover morphosyntactic peculiarities and its output are lemmata with morphosyntactic features of Georgian. There are three levels: lexical, intermediate and surface (Table 3.5).

Table 3.5 The lexical, intermediate and surface levels

Lexical	დე და +Noun+Sg+Gen
Intermediate	დე და ^Sი ს
Surface	დე დი ს

An upper level 'a' is mapped to a lower level '0' followed by the trigger '^S' and the genitive case marker *-is*. Accordingly, the '^S' symbol triggers the truncation process and, afterwards, is removed from the surface level. All three levels are covered by the transducer. The morphological analyser consists of different finite-state transducers and replacement rule transducers as given in Fig. 3.13.

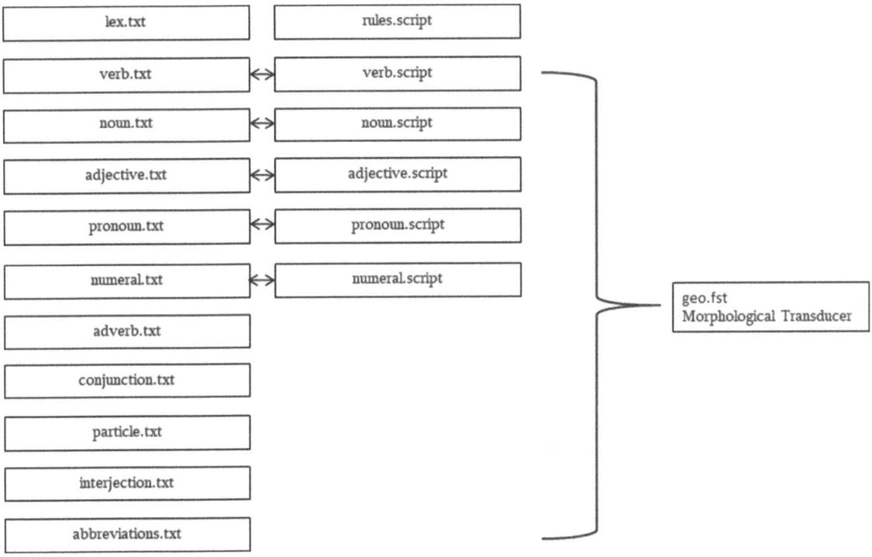

Fig. 3.13 The Georgian morphological transducer

There is a separate lexicon for each class and systematic modifications of verbs, nouns, adjectives, pronouns and numerals are encoded with replacement rule scripts. All other uninflected PoS-es like adverbs, conjunctions, particles, etc. are included in the lexicons without rule scripts.

Stems are assigned to concrete continuation classes depending on their declension or conjugation peculiarities. Each continuation class consists of a stem and the affixes attached to it. Long dependencies are established inside the lexicon by means of flags diacritics, while internal modifications are implemented outside the lexicon by means of regular expressions. Taking into consideration the peculiarities of Georgian already described in the previous chapters, the number of lexicons used by different PoS-es is 499 (Table 3.6).

Table 3.6 The number of continuation classes

PoS	First level continuation classes
Noun	22
Verb	80
Participle	16
Verbal noun	4
Adjective	4
Numeral	4
Pronoun	49
Conjunction	2
Particle	7
Adverb	8
Interjection	1
Postposition	1
Abbreviation	1
Punctuation marks	1

Although grammars of Georgian do not describe these paradigmatic regularities in detail, the complexity of the task obliged us to subdivide existing paradigms into additional groups to reflect all of the peculiarities of their formation. While it was not possible to reduce the number of first-level continuation classes, we attempted to make the transducer as simple as possible without simplifying it. As of the time of writing, the lexicons can be enriched by linguists who are not familiar with programming at all. All of these transducers are subsumed in the morphological analyser as presented in Fig. 3.14.

```
read regex @"nounCom.fst" ;
read regex @"nounProp.fst" ;
read regex @"adjective.fst" ;
read regex @"numeral.fst" ;
read regex @"digits.fst" ;
read regex @"pronoun.fst" ;
read regex @"verb.fst" ;
read regex @"participle.fst" ;
read regex @"masdar.fst" ;
read regex @"functionals.fst" ;
read regex @"punctuation.fst" ;
read regex @"foreign.fst" ;
read regex @"abbr.fst" ;
union net
save stack geo.fst
```

Fig. 3.14 *xfst*: Unification

Although the input text delivered to the morphological analyser depends on the requirements of the application, generally speaking, the input texts as well as the output are generated in the .xml and/or .txt formats.

The output of the analyser is represented in two ways: the surface form represents a written word, while the lexical form represents a morphological description of the surface form in accordance with tags presented in Appendix A. Some tags contain additional information which will be required for future parsing at syntactic level (260–261).

1. *cer-s* 's/he/it writes'

```
წერს:Ipfv+წერ-ს+Verb+Main+IDt+Act+#18+Din+Trans
+Pres+<NomSubj>+<DatObj>+Subj3Sg+Obj3
```

The <NomSubj> and <DatObj> tags refer to the case of subject and object and are used to show agreement between the verb and its arguments, while the +#18 tag represents a verbal class as described by Melikishvili (2010).

2. *ceril-s-a* *grżel-s-a* 'long letter'

```
წერილსა:წერილ-ი+Noun+Com+Inanim+Sg+Dat+Emp
გრძელსა:გრძელ-ი+Adj+Posit+Sg+Dat+Emp
```

The analysis of this example makes it clear that there is agreement between the noun *cerilsa* 'letter' and the adjective *grżelsa* 'long' in number and case and, while the rules of word combination are not given here, this information is important for testing this type of agreement in Georgian nominals at the syntactic level.

3.3.1 The Nominal Lexicon and Replacement Rules

As described in the previous chapter, the inflectional paradigms of Georgian nominals are quite regular and shared by nouns, adjectives, numerals and pronouns. All nominal morphology is encoded in the lexicon, which includes flag diacritics to constrain long-distance dependencies within words and triggers to launch the implementation of rules in *xfst*. The lexicon can be considered a mediator between the lexical and surface levels.

The nominal lexicon is subdivided into two main parts: one for common and one for proper nouns, between which the aforementioned 22 classes are split. The common nouns include 9 classes, while proper nouns include 13. This distribution assists in the recognition of named entities like geographical and personal names. Within their classes, nouns are further sub-categorized in accordance with their formation in terms of number, case etc. A simplified overview of the nominal lexicon is given below (Fig. 3.15):

```
Multichar_Symbols
+Noun +Prop +Com +Anim +Inanim +Sg +Pl +Nom +Erg +Dat
+Gen +Ins +Advb +Voc +Emph +Post +Ptcl +Aux

! cases
@U.CASE.NOM@ @R.CASE.NOM@ @D.CASE.NOM@ etc.
! extension vowels
@U.EMP.A@ @D.EMP.A@ etc.
! postpositions
@U.POST.SI@ @R.POST.SI@ @U.POST.TAN@ @D.POST.TAN@
@U.POST.ZE@ @D.POST.ZE@ etc.
! particles
@U.PTCL.C@ @D.PTCL.C@ @U.PTCL.CA@ @U.PTCL.RA@
@R.PTCL.RA@ etc.

LEXICON Root
  Noun_1 ;

LEXICON Noun_1
ქალ-ი+Noun+Com+Anim:ქალი   Nmbr_1 ;
Etc.

LEXICON Nmbr_1
+Sg:^S0       Case_1 ;
+Pl:^Pებ      Case_1 ;
+Pl:^Pებთ     Case_T ;
+Pl:^NTნ      Case_N ;
+Pl:^NTთ      Case_T ;

LEXICON Case_1
              Nominative ;
              Ergative ;
              Etc. ;

LEXICON Case_N
+Nom:ი        # ;
+Voc:ო        # ;
+Nom:ი        IndSpeech ;
+Voc:ო        IndSpeech ;

LEXICON Case_T
+Dat:0        # ;
+Gen:0        # ;
+Ins:0        # ;
```

Fig. 3.15 *lexc*: Extract from the first declension of the nominal lexicon

```
+Dat:ა         # ;
+Gen:ა         # ;
+Ins:ა         # ;

LEXICON Nominative
+Nom:^Nი@U.CASE.NOM@ # ;
+Nom:^Nი@U.CASE.NOM@ Postposition ;
+Nom:^Nი@U.CASE.NOM@ Particle ;
+Nom:^Nი@U.CASE.NOM@ Auxiliary ;
+Nom:^Nი@U.CASE.NOM@ IndSpeech ;

LEXICON Ergative
+Erg:^Eმა              # ;
+Erg:^Eმან            # ; ! For Old Georgian
+Erg:^Eმა              Particle ;
+Erg:^Eმა              IndSpeech ;

LEXICON Dt1
+Dat:^Dს@U.CASE.DAT@   # ;
+Dat:^Dს@U.CASE.DAT@   Emphatic ;
+Dat:^Dს@U.CASE.DAT@   Postposition ;
Etc.

LEXICON Postposition
+Post(like):ვით@R.CASE.NOM@    # ;
+Post(like):ვით@R.CASE.NOM@    IndSpeech ;
+Post(like):ვით@R.CASE.NOM@    Particle ;
Etc.

LEXICON Emphatic
+Emp:ა                   # ;
+Emp+Dat:ას              # ;
+Emp:ა@R.CASE.DAT@    Particle ;
+Emp:ა                   Auxiliary;
+Emp:ა                   IndSpeech ;
Etc.

LEXICON Particle
+Ptcl:^Veვე@U.PTCL.VE@ # ;
+Ptcl:ვეც@R.POST.VIT1@ # ;
Etc.

LEXICON Auxiliary
+Aux:ა  # ;
+Aux:ა  IndSpeech ;

LEXICON IndSpeech
+IndSpeech1:%-მეთქი # ;
Etc.
```

Fig. 3.15 (continued)

The sample of the nominal lexicon shown in Fig. 3.15 contains one continuation class covering non-syncopating consonant-final common nouns and covers only one lemma: *k'alak'i* 'town' as it is represented in Chikobava's Dictonary (Chikobava 1950–1964), which at the initial stage is marked with type and animacy tags.

`Nmbr_1` contains five continuation classes: the first one is used to generate singulars, the second two – to generate *-eb* plural forms: one for the regular pattern with the *-eb* marker and one for the irregular pattern with *-eb* and *-t'* plural markers used together, and two others, which are used to generate the *-n* and *-t'* plural forms.

Three triggers of the singular and plural markers are modelled which are not activated within this declension type, but are used with other types of declension which involve syncopation or truncation. All of these forms proceed to different continuation classes: `Case_1` is used to attach case markers to singular and *-eb* plural forms, while `Case_T` and `Case_N` are used to attach case markers to the *-t'* and *-n* plural forms respectively. All classes are attached to lexical level tags indicating appropriate cases. The case continuation classes can generate either a complete form of a word or can proceed to other continuation classes like `Postposition, Particle, Emphatic, Auxiliary` and `IndSpeech`. Appropriate flag diacritics are present which are used to establish long-distance dependencies between cases and postpositions on one hand and between postpositions and particles on the other.

The declensions systems for Modern and Old Georgian are slightly different. In the case of Old Georgian, the nominal lexicons include classes for the generation of the secondary cases in the following way:

```
LEXICON Gn1
+Gen:^Gის@U.CASE.GEN@   # ;
+Gen:^Gის@U.CASE.GEN@Emphatic ;
+Gen:^Gჲს@U.CASE.GEN@# ;
+Gen:^Gჲს@U.CASE.GEN@Emphatic ;
Etc.

LEXICON Emphatic
+Emp:ა  Secondary ;
Etc.

LEXICON Secondary
+Nom:ჲ  # ;
+Erg:მან# ;
Etc.
```

Fig. 3.16 *xfst*: Generation of secondary cases

The sample of lexicon shown in Fig. 3.16 contains continuation classes for the generation of doubling and tripling of case markers in the case of Old Georgian as described in Sect. 2.3.1.

The lexicon output for the stem mentioned above at the lexical and intermediate surface levels is as follows (Table 3.7):

Table 3.7 Noun surface and lexical levels

Lexical level	Intermediate Surface level
ქალ-ი+Noun+Com+Anim+Sg+Erg	ქალი^S^Eმა
ქალ-ი+Noun+Com+Anim+Sg+Erg+Ptcl	ქალი^S^Eმა ^Veვე
ქალ-ი+Noun+Com+Anim+Sg+Erg+IndSpeech1	ქალი^S^Eმა -მეთქი
ქალ-ი+Noun+Com+Anim+Sg+Erg	ქალი^S^Eმა ნ
ქალ-ი+Noun+Com+Anim+Sg+Nom	ქალი^S^Nი
ქალ-ი+Noun+Com+Anim+Sg+Nom+Aux	ქალი^S^Nია
ქალ-ი+Noun+Com+Anim+Sg+Nom+Aux+IndSpeech1	ქალი^S^Nია -მეთქი
ქალ-ი+Noun+Com+Anim+Sg+Nom+Ptcl	ქალი^S^Nი^Veვე
ქალ-ი+Noun+Com+Anim+Sg+Nom+Post(like)	ქალი^S^Nივით
ქალ-ი+Noun+Com+Anim+Sg+Nom+Post(like)+Ptcl	ქალი^S^Nივით^Veვე
ქალ-ი+Noun+Com+Anim+Sg+Nom+Post(like)+IndSpeech1	ქალი^S^Nივით' -met'k'i
ქალ-ი+Noun+Com+Anim+Sg+Nom+IndSpeech1	ქალი^S^ი-მეთქი
ქალ-ი+Noun+Com+Anim+Pl+Erg	ქალი^Pებ^Eმა
ქალ-ი+Noun+Com+Anim+Pl+Erg+Ptcl	ქალი^Pებ^Eმა ^Veვე
ქალ-ი+Noun+Com+Anim+Pl+Erg+IndSpeech1	ქალი^Pებ^Eმა -მეთქი
ქალ-ი+Noun+Com+Anim+Pl+Erg	ქალი^Pებ^Eმა ნ
ქალ-ი+Noun+Com+Anim+Pl+Nom	ქალი^Pებ^Nი
ქალ-ი+Noun+Com+Anim+Pl+Nom+Aux	ქალი^Pებ^Nია
ქალ-ი+Noun+Com+Anim+Pl+Nom+Aux+IndSpeech1	ქალი^Pებ^Nია -მეთქი
ქალ-ი+Noun+Com+Anim+Pl+Nom+Ptcl	ქალი^Pებ^Nი^Veვე
ქალ-ი+Noun+Com+Anim+Pl+Nom+Post(like)	ქალი^Pებ^Nივით
ქალ-ი+Noun+Com+Anim+Pl+Nom+Post(like)+Ptcl	ქალი^Pებ^Nივით^Vევე
ქალ-ი+Noun+Com+Anim+Pl+Nom+Post(like)+IndSpeech1	ქალი^Pებ^Nივით-მეთქი
ქალ-ი+Noun+Com+Anim+Pl+Nom+IndSpeech1	ქალი^Pებ^Nი-მეთქი
ქალ-ი+Noun+Com+Anim+Pl+Dat etc.	ქალი^Pებთ etc.
ქალ-ი+Noun+Com+Anim+Pl+Dat etc.	ქალი^Pებთ etc.
ქალ-ი+Noun+Com+Anim+Pl+Dat etc.	ქალი^NTთ etc,
ქალ-ი+Noun+Com+Anim+Pl+Dat etc.	ქალი^NTთ etc.
ქალ-ი+Noun+Com+Anim+Pl+Nom	ქალი^NTნი
ქალ-ი+Noun+Com+Anim+Pl+Nom+IndSpeech1	ქალი^NTნი-მეთქი
ქალ-ი+Noun+Com+Anim+Pl+Voc	ქალი^NTნო
ქალ-ი+Noun+Com+Anim+Pl+Voc+IndSpeech1	ქალი^NTნო-მეთქი

To prepare a stem for further generation, we have to remove the singular nominative marker present at the end of dictionary headwords (Chikobava 1950–1964 and others) and to define variables in the way shown in Fig. 3.17.

```
define Vowels ა|ე|ი|ო|უ|ჱ|ჲ|ჵ ;
define Consonants
ბ|გ|დ|ვ|ზ|თ|კ|პ|ჟ|ს|ტ|ფ|ქ|ღ|ყ|შ|ჩ|ც|ძ|წ|ჭ|ხ|ჯ|ჰ|ჳ|ჴ|ჶ ;
define Sonants ლ|მ|ნ|რ ;
```

Fig. 3.17 *xfst*: Definition of variables

The regular expression which enables the implementation of this process is given in Fig. 3.18.

```
define R1 [ ი|ჲ -> [] || _ [ %^S | %^S1 | %^S2 | %^P |
%^P1 | %^P2 | %^NT | %^NT1 | %^NT2 ] ] ;
```

Fig. 3.18 *xfst*: Removal of final vowels

The triggers operate differently for Modern and Old Georgian declensions. The expression introduced above helps us to remove *-i* at the end of consonant-final headwords of dictionary entries and to remove *-y* at the end of vowel-final Old Georgian entries where theese are followed by the triggers ^P, ^NT, etc. Some triggers mentioned on the surface level are activated in the *xfst* module for this declension type only; others are used in the case of other declensions, but not in the case of this one, i.e. each rule transducer specifies certain constraints and allows other input strings to pass unchanged. For instance, the regular expression used to model the syncopation of nouns with sonant-final stems is shown in Fig. 3.19.

```
define R2 [ა|ე|ო -> [] || _ Sonants %^S1 ?* $["^G"]
~$["^NT1"].o. ა|ე|ო -> [] || _ Sonants %^S1 ?* $["^I"]
.o. ა|ე|ო -> [] || _ Sonants %^S1 ?* $["^T"] .o. ა|ე|ო
-> [] || _ Sonants %^P1 ?* ] ;
```

Fig. 3.19 *xfst*: Syncopation of vowels before sonants

Each trigger is associated with concrete changes which happen before sonants and other triggers in a string. The same triggers are shared between continuation classes and can be activated under different conditions to increase the possibilities of blocking and to avoid overgeneration.

3.3.2 The Adjectival Lexicon and Replacement Rules

The adjectival lexicon shares the majority of its inflectional features with the nominal lexicon, and is subdivided into five declension types, with formation simultaneously dependent on whether or not the adjective produces degrees. In accordance with this possibility there are two main lexicons, the first of which introduces adverbial adjectives and the second relatives. Each of these lexicons has initial continuation classes of its own. The simplified starting point of the adjectival lexicons is shown in Fig. 3.20.

```
Multichar_Symbols
+Adj +Posit +Comp +Sup +Sg +Pl +Nom +Erg +Dat +Gen +Ins
+Advb +Voc +Emph +Post +Ptcl +Aux

! cases
@U.CASE.NOM@ @R.CASE.NOM@ @D.CASE.NOM@ etc.
! extension vowels
@U.EMP.A@ @D.EMP.A@ etc.
! postpositions
@U.POST.SI@ @R.POST.SI@ @U.POST.TAN@ @D.POST.TAN@
@U.POST.ZE@ @D.POST.ZE@ etc.
! particles
@U.PTCL.C@ @D.PTCL.C@ @U.PTCL.CA@ @U.PTCL.RA@
@R.PTCL.RA@ etc.
! degrees
@U.DEGREE.SUP@ @R.DEGREE.SUP@ @U.DEGREE.COM@
@R.DEGREE.COM@ @D.DEGREE.SUP@ @D.DEGREE.COM@
! triggers
^S ^S1 ^S2 ^S3 etc.

LEXICON Root
      Adjectives;

LEXICON Adjectives
      Adverbials ;
      Relatives ;

LEXICON Adverbials
0:უ@U.DEGREE.SUP@  AdjRoots ;
0:მო@U.DEGREE.COM@ AdjRoots ;

LEXICON AdjRoots
ტკბილ-ი:ტკბილი      A1 ;

Lexicon Relatives
ქონიან-ი:ქონიანი    A2 ;

LEXICON A1
+Adj+Posit:^S0@D.DEGREE.SUP@@D.DEGREE.COM@  Nmbr_1 ;
+Adj+Sup:^Sეს@R.DEGREE.SUP@                 Nmbr_1;
+Adj+Dim:^Sო@R.DEGREE.COM@                 Nmbr_2 ;
+Adv:^Sად@D.DEGREE.SUP@@D.DEGREE.COM@        # ;
+Adv:^Sად@D.DEGREE.SUP@@D.DEGREE.COM@ Postposition ;

LEXICON A2
+Adj:^S0              Nmbr_1 ;
+Adv:^Sად              # ;
+Adv:^Sად              Postposition ;
```

Fig. 3.20 *lexc*: Extract from the first declension adjectival lexicon

```
LEXICON Nmbr_1
+Sg:^S0                Case_1 ;
+Pl:^Pებ@U.NUM.EB@     Case_1 ;
+Pl:^NTნ               Case_N ;
+Pl:^NTთ               Case_T ;

LEXICON Nmbr_2
+Sg:^S10               Case_4 ;
+Pl:^P1ებ@U.NUM.EB3@   Case_1 ;
+Pl:^NT1ნ              Case_N ;
+Pl:^NT5თ              Case_T ;
Etc.
```

Fig. 3.20 (continued)

The sample shows the initial stage of the formation of adverbial and relative adjectives. The first adjective, *tkbili* 'sweet', belongs to the adverbial type and forms degrees, while the second adjective, *k'onian-i* 'fatty', does not. In other words, the adjectival lexicon has two entries, one – for adverbial and another – for relative adjectives. The continuation class of adverbial adjectives begins with the degree confixes *-u* and *-mo* and establishes a long-distance dependency with their respective counterparts after the root by means of specially determined flag diacritics. Accordingly, the continuation classes after the root are subdivided into five other classes. One of these connects to `Nmbr_1` class as described in the nominal lexicon, the second generates the superlative degree and, like the previous one, connects to `Nmbr_1`, the third entry is used to generate the *-o* final diminutive degree and continues to the `Nmbr_2` class used for the generation of vowel-final words, and the final two classes have derivational but not inflectional functions, generating adverbs from adjectives with or without postpositions.

Flag diacritics are used to constrain which suffixes can be accepted by the adjectival stem and to provide a mapping between affixes, and specifically for the counterparts of circumfixes; for instance, if the prefix *u-* is presented before the root, the flag diacritic provides its long-distance dependency on its counterpart, the suffix *-es* used after the root, and blocks other suffixes indicating the diminutive or positive degrees or other generational possibilities. U stands for showing of different operation and can be substituted with any other symbol of operations such as R, D etc., while features and values are determined by the developer keeping in mind the requirements of the concrete grammar. The *xfst* module does not contain any of the above-mentioned flags and is used to trigger concrete processes within or at the borders of morphemes in the form of regular expressions. But the scripts of *lexc* modules use them actively.

3.3.3 *The Numeral Lexicon and Replacement Rules*

Numeral inflection generally follows the rules of the nominal paradigm. The lexicon is also used as the starting point for the base-20 system. Its purpose is to generate initial roots of numerals, to separate cardinal, ordinal and fractional numerals, and to proceed to the continuation classes of the nominal paradigm.

Special tags were used to indicate the Arabic (+Digit), Roman (+Roman), alphabetical (+Alpha) and acrophonic (+Letter) numerals described in Sect. 2.3.3. The lexicon is subdivided into three parts, each with different continuation classes. A simplified description of the numeral lexicon is provided in Fig. 3.21.

```
Multichar_Symbols
+Num +Card +Ord +Fract +Approx +Rep +Sg +Pl +Nom +Erg
+Dat +Gen +Ins +Advb +Voc +Emph +Post +Ptcl +Aux

! cases
@U.CASE.NOM@ @R.CASE.NOM@ @D.CASE.NOM@ etc.
! extension vowels
@U.EMP.A@ @D.EMP.A@ etc.
! postpositions
@U.POST.SI@ @R.POST.SI@ @U.POST.TAN@ @D.POST.TAN@
@U.POST.ZE@ @D.POST.ZE@ etc.
! particles
@U.PTCL.C@ @D.PTCL.C@ @U.PTCL.CA@ @U.PTCL.RA@
@R.PTCL.RA@ etc.
! triggers
^S ^S1 ^S2 ^S3 etc.

LEXICON Root
                      Cardinal ;
                      Ordinal ;
                      Irregulars ;

LEXICON Cardinal
                      Ten ;
                      Twelve ;
                      Twenty ;
                      Hundred ;
                      Composites ;

LEXICON Ten
ერთ-ი:ერთ               CardCon ;
Etc.

LEXICON Twelve
თერთმეტ-ი:თერთმეტ     CardCon ;

LEXICON Twenty
ოც-ი:ოც               CardCon ;
ოც:ოც                 And ;
Etc.

LEXICON And
და:და                 Ten ;
და:და                 Twelve ;
Etc.

LEXICON Hundred
ას-ი:ას               CardCon ;
Etc.

LEXICON Composites
ერთ-:ერთ-               Ten ;
Etc.

LEXICON Ordinal
0:მე                  TenOrd ;
```

Fig. 3.21 *lexc*: Extract from the numeral lexicon

```
0:მე                     TwelveOrd ;
0:მე                     TwentyOrd ;
                         TwentyOrd1 ;
0:მე                     HundredOrd ;
ერთ-ი+Num+Ord:პირველ Nmbr_1 ;

LEXICON TenOrd
ერთ-ი:ერთ                  Ord ;

LEXICON TwelveOrd
თერთმეტ-ი:თერთმეტ    Ord ;

LEXICON TwentyOrd
ოც-ი:ოც                  Ord ;

LEXICON TwentyOrd1
ოც-ი:ოც                  AndOrd ;

LEXICON AndOrd
და:დამე                  TenOrd ;
და:დამე                  TwelveOrd ;

LEXICON HundredOrd
ას-ი:ას                  Ord ;

LEXICON Ord
+Num+Ord:^Aე             Nmbr_3 ;
+Num+Fract:ედ            Nmbr_1 ;

LEXICON Irregulars
ბევრ-ი+Num+Ord:ბევრ           Nmbr_1  ;
ერგასის-ი+Num+Ord:ერგასის     Nmbr_1 ;
ცოტა+Num+Ord:ცოტა     Nmbr_2 ;
Etc.
```

Fig. 3.21 (continued)

In contrast with other nominal paradigms, this lexicon contains the roots of numerals distributed between different continuation classes with the purpose of enabling generation not only at the surface, but at the lexical level as well. Accordingly, the *xfst* script was altered slightly with regard to the processing of root-final syllables. The lexicon root consists of three continuation classes: a cardinal continuation class which generates cardinal numerals, an ordinal class which generates ordinals and fractionals, and an irregular class, which generates some numerals that cannot be derived from generated roots.

The cardinal and ordinal continuation classes are in a sense mixed in terms of type, because they are used to generate both roots and paradigms. The cardinal continuation class includes `Ten`, which serves the roots from 1 to 10, `Twelve`, which serves the roots from 11 to 20, `Twenty`, which covers 20, 30, 40, 60, 80, `Hundred`, which covers 100, 200, 300, 400, 500, etc. and `Composites`, which generates composite numerals involving a dash. These classes are interconnected with one another with or without the `And` class, which forms numerals like *oc‘-da-or-i* ‘twenty two’, etc.

The `Ordinal` continuation class begins with the *me-* prefix, proceeds to the formation of roots, represents the formation of the irregular ordinal *pirveli* ‘the first’ and finishes with the suffix *-e* used for the formation of ordinals or the suffix *-ed* used for the formation of fractionals.

There are only three items in the irregular paradigm: *bevri* ‘a lot’, *c‘ota* ‘too little, few’ and *ergasisi* ‘forty’. The first two items are more like adjectives which are treated as numerals, while the final item is a numeral used only in Old Georgian.

The generation of other forms is similar to those already mentioned for other nominal paradigms.

To prepare the stem for further generation, the final *-a* is removed in *rva* ‘eight’ and an ^A trigger activated from within the *xfst* replacement rule transducer as shown in Fig. 3.22 to avoid doubling of the *-e-* vowel.

```
define R1 [ ა -> [] || _ [ %^A ] ] ;
define R2 [ ე -> [] || ?* %^A _ ?* $[ %^I ] ] ;
```

Fig. 3.22 *xfst*: Changes at the borders between morphemes

An additional lexicon is used to map Georgian characters to their numerical values and to translate alphabetic Georgian numerals into their Arabic counterparts. A simplified lexicon for this block is shown in Fig. 3.23.

```
LEXICON Alphabet
            1-10 ;
            10-100 ;
            100-1000 ;
            1000-10000 ;

LEXICON 1-10
1:ა         Tags ;
Etc.

LEXICON 10-100
1%0:ი       Tags ;
1%0:ი       1-10 ;
Etc.

LEXICON 100-1000
1%0%0:რ     Tags ;
1:რ         10-100 ;
1%0:რ       1-10 ;

LEXICON 1000-10000
1%0%0%0:ჩ   Tags ;
1:ჩ         100-1000 ;
1%0:ჩ       10-100 ;
1%0%0:ჩ     1-10 ;

LEXICON Tags
+Num+Alpha:0  # ;
```

Fig. 3.23 *lexc*: Extract from the alphabetical numeral lexicon

This block translates numerals written in the *Mkhedruli* and *Asomtavruli* scripts, because only these scripts were used to represent numerals. The generation principle is similar to that employed for the generation of roots as described above, but in comparison with the previous continuation classes, this class does not generate an inflectional paradigm and accordingly does not contain any flag diacritics or triggers, and can be used only if a text contains appropriate indications, for instance <date></date> tags.

3.3.4 *The Pronominal Lexicon and Replacement Rules*

As with other nominals, pronominal morphology is included in the lexicon, together with mark-up tags and triggers as well as flag diacritics needed to provide constraints on long-distance dependencies between case, postpositions, particles and extension vowels. The pronominal lexicon is organized in accordance with pronoun type as described in Georgian dictionaries and grammars. Its structure is given in Fig. 3.24.

```
LEXICON Pronouns
  Personal ;
  Demonstrative ;
  Possessive ;
  Indefinite ;
  Interrogative ;
  Relative ;
  Reciprocal ;
  Negative ;
  Determinal ;
  Irregulars ;
```

Fig. 3.24 *lexc*: Pronominal continuation classes

The main problem of this lexical separation is that each of these classes encompasses morphologically different declension types and the real number of morphologically stipulated continuation classes is greater. As mentioned above, there are a total of 49 initial morphological level continuation classes e.g. the irregulars comprise the rare third-person plural form *igini* ‘they’: `igin-i+Pron+Pers+3+Pl +Gen:mat'ganis`, which is attested in Georgian dialects. Each of these classes is further sub-divided into sub-types according to declension type in the manner shown in Fig. 3.25.

```
LEXICON Determinal
თვით                    Determinal_1 ;
თვითეულ-ი:თვითეული      Determinal_2 ;
ყველა                   Determinal_3 ;
მავან-ი:მავანი          Determinal_4 ;
სხვა                    Determinal_5 ;
Etc.
```

Fig. 3.25 *lexc*: Determinal pronoun continuation class

`Determinal` includes reflexive pronouns and contains five sub-classes: the first handles consonant-final pronouns with no case indication (for instance *t‘vit‘* ‘oneself’, etc.) and proceeds to particles or extension vowel classes; the second and third classes deal with consonant-final and vowel-final pronouns which do not have *–eb* plural forms (for instance *t‘vit‘euli* ‘each single’, *qvela* ‘all’, etc.); the fourth class comprises a single sonant-final pronoun which can generate syncopating or non-syncopating forms in the genitive, instrumental and adverbial cases in the singular and in all cases in the plural with the *-eb-* marker (*mavani* ‘someone’); and the fifth class comprises standard vowel-final truncating pronouns (for instance *sxva* ‘other’).

The output for the four stems discussed above is approximately 5500 entries. Although pronominal morphology in Georgian is considered to be regular, the irregularities of these paradigms result in an increase in the number of continuation classes, as shown in Fig. 3.26.

```
LEXICON Determinal_1
+Pron+Det+Sg:0        # ;
+Pron+Det+Sg:0        Emphatic_2 ;
+Pron+Det+Sg:0        Ptcl ;

LEXICON Determinal_2
+Pron+Det+Sg:^S10Case_5 ;
+Pron+Det+Pl:^NTნ  CaseN ;
+Pron+Det+Pl:^NTთ  CaseT ;

LEXICON Determinal_3
+Pron+Det+Sg:^A10Case_4 ;
+Pron+Det+Pl:^NTნ  CaseN ;
+Pron+Det+Pl:^NTთ  CaseT ;

LEXICON Determinal_4
+Pron+Det+Sg:^S10Case_5 ;
+Pron+Det+Pl:^P1ებ Case_5 ;
+Pron+Det+Pl:^Aნ   CaseN ;
+Pron+Det+Pl:^Aთ   CaseT ;

LEXICON Determinal_5
+Pron+Det+Sg:^A10Case_4 ;
+Pron+Det+Pl:^P3ებ Case_3 ;
+Pron+Det+Pl:^NTნCaseN ;
+Pron+Det+Pl:^NTთ  CaseT ;
```

Fig. 3.26 *lexc*: Extract from reflexive pronoun continuation classes

Furthermore, some types of pronoun actively use suppletive forms to generate cases. For example, personal pronouns like *es, ese, esa* ‘this’, etc. generate cases by adding case markers to another root: *am* ‘this’; the lexicon used for this purpose is shown in Fig. 3.27.

```
LEXICON Personal
ეს                        Personal_4 ;

LEXICON Personal_4
+Pron+Pers+3+Sg+Nom:0       # ;
+Pron+Pers+3+Sg:^NR0      Personal_8 ;

LEXICON Personal_8
0:ამ                      Case_1 ;
Etc.
```

Fig. 3.27 *lexc*: Extract from personal pronoun continuation classes

The regular expression used for the processing of this lexicon retains *es* 'this' at the lexical level as the lemma indication and removes it from the surface level to use the consonant-final suppletive root for the generation of the paradigm. The regular expression used in this case is given in Fig. 3.28.

```
define R3 [ {ეს} -> [] || _ [ %^NR ] ] ;
```

Fig. 3.28 *xfst*: Replacement rules for suppletive roots

The lexicon output for this case retains the regular form for the nominative case and generates all other cases based on the other root, which is not represented in any Georgian dictionaries.

3.3.5 The Verbal Lexicon and Replacement Rules

Verbs are encoded in accordance with 66 inflectional classes and one additional class for irregularities (so-called 'suppletive verbs', for instance *qop'na* 'to be', *k'mna* 'to do', etc.; verbs with root alternation according to number, for instance *gdeba – qra* 'to throw', *jdoma – sxdoma* 'to sit', etc.; verbs with root alternation according to animacy (*mi/motana – mi/moqvana* 'to take', *k'oneba – qola* 'to have', etc.), as described by Melikishvili (2001). All of these classes use different verbal roots and sometimes share similar roots between paradigms. As a result, the minimum number of forms generated per root is 54 and the maximum is 1076, without taking preverbs into consideration. The majority of these classes are subdivided into object- and *v*-type paradigms which reveal a huge number of long-distance dependencies.

While in the majority of Indo-European languages, the verbal paradigm begins with the verbal root which is then amended by affixes, the Georgian verbal paradigm begins with prefixes, which occupy the four initial slots of a string, and introduces the verbal root only after these. In the analyser, the first two slots are represented in the form of slots with and/or without preverbs.

The headwords of verbal entries cannot be used in the form employed in Georgian dictionaries, because such a representation causes two major problems: firstly, the representation of lemma signs and, secondly, the alphabetization of Georgian offline and/or online dictionaries (Lobzhanidze 2019). All of these problems relate to the position of the verbal root in the verbal template.

As discussed in Sect. 3.3, there are three options: to represent a verb either in the form of a verbal noun, or in the form of a root, or in the form of the third-person singular in the present or future indicative. The focus of our research is closely associated with existing word indexes as with possibility of processing them by means of finite-state automata. As such, it was important for the data in the lexicon to contain forms which permitted generation for the *m*-type inflectional and *v*-type inflectional classes and enabled their further analysis. Taking into consideration that the majority of Georgian dictionaries follow the 'mixed' approach to verbal representation discussed above, the third-person singular in present or future indicative as employed by Chikobava (1950–1964) and Melikishvili et al. (2010) is used as the lemma sign for verbs in the present work. There are however a small number of cases where different lemmata have been seleced for processing convenience—namely, in the case of irregular suppletive verb formation (262–263).

(262) *zis* 'sits', *vzivar* 'I sit', *vijdebodi* 'I was sitting' etc.

```
ზის+Verb+Main+AutAct+Intr+Pres+%<NomSubj%>+Subj1Sg:ვზივ
არ
ზის+Verb+Main+AutAct+Intr+Imperf+%<NomSubj%>+Subj1Sg:ვი
ჯდებოდი
```

(263) *misc'ems* 'gives', *važlevdi* 'I was giving', *mivc'em* 'I will give' etc.

```
მისცემს+Verb+Main+Act+Trans+Imperf+%<NomSubj%>+%<DatObjR
ec%>+%<DatObj%>+Subj1Sg+ObjRec3+Obj3:ვაძლევდი
მისცემს+Verb+Main+Act+Trans+Fut+%<NomSubj%>+%<DatObjRec%
>+%<DatObj%>+Subj1Sg+ObjRec3+Obj3:მივცემ etc.
```

The verbal transducer includes 80 continuation classes with irregularities and consists of different lexicons and replacement-rule transducers compiled in the manner shown in Fig. 3.29.

```
read regex @"verb1.fst" ;
read regex @"verb2.fst" ;
read regex @"verb3.fst" ;
Etc.
read regex @"irregulars.fst" ;
read regex @"participle.fst" ;
read regex @"masdar.fst" ;
union net
save stack verb.fst
```

Fig. 3.29 *xfst*: Compilation of verbal transducers

The lexicons include declarations of multicharacter symbols, flag diacritics and triggers. The list of Multichar_Symbols declares not only morphological-level tags such as +Verb +Aux + Intr, etc., but also syntactic-level tags such as +%<ErgSubj% > +%<DatSubj% > +% < NomSubjBen%>, etc. used to indicate the subject-object agreement of a verb. The list of flag diacritics comprises items on preverbs, for instance @P.PV.MI@ @P.PV.A@ @P.PV.AG@, etc., which enable the establishment of long-distance dependencies between the verbal root and concrete preverbs; in comparison with other flag diacritics, this type of flag is not activated very often. There are also flag diacritics for subject and object markers, for instance @U.SUBJSG.1@ @U.SUBJSG.2@ @U.SUBJSG.3@, etc., screeves, for instance @U.PRS.0@ @R.PRS.0@ @U.PRS.A@, etc., causation, for instance @U.CAUS.0@ @U.CAUS.IN@ @U.CAUS.EVIN@, etc., thematic suffixes, for instance @U.TS.0@ @U.TS.EB@ @U.TS.AV@, etc., extension markers, for instance @U.EM.0@ @U.EM.D@ @U.EM.OD@, etc. and valency, for instance @U.VAL.II@ @R.VAL.II@ @D.VAL.II@, etc.

A simplified overview of the verbal lexicons (positioned at the *v*-type set) is shown in Fig. 3.30.

```
LEXICON Subject_28
                    Preverb_S ;

LEXICON Preverb_S
Ipfv+:0@P.PV.0@Paradigm1S ;
Pfv+:მი@P.PV.MI@ Paradigm2S ;
Etc.

LEXICON Paradigm1S
                    S1PrS ;
                    S1FutS ;
                    S2AorS ;
                    S3PerfS ;

LEXICON Paradigm2S
                    S1FutS ;
                    S2AorS ;
                    S3PerfS ;

LEXICON S1PrS
0:ვ@U.SUBJSG.1@     PresS ;
0:0@U.SUBJSG.2@     PresS ;
0:0@U.SUBJSG.3@     PresS ;
0:ვ@U.SUBJPL.1@     PresS ;
0:0@U.SUBJPL.2@     PresS ;
0:0@U.SUBJPL.3@     PresS ;
Etc.

LEXICON S3PerfS
0:მ@U.ObjSG.1@      PerfS ;
Etc.
0:მ@U.ObjSG.1@      PluPerfS ;
Etc.

LEXICON PresS
0:ა@U.PRS.A@        R1S ;
0:ი@U.PRS.I@        R1S ;
0:უ@U.PRS.U@        R1S ;
Etc.

LEXICON PerfS
0:ი@U.PERF.I@@D.ObjSG.3@@D.ObjPL.3@   R1S ;
0:უ@U.PERF.U@@D.ObjSG.1@@D.ObjSG.2@@D.ObjPL.1@@D.ObjPL.
2@                  R1S ;

LEXICON PluPerfS
0:ე@U.PLUPERF.E@    R1S ;

LEXICON R1S
აშენებ-ს:^O3შენ@R.PV.0@@P.VAL.II@   V28S ;
აშენებ-ს:^O3შენ@R.PV.0@@P.VAL.III@V28S ;

LEXICON V28S
+Verb+Main+IDt+Act+%#28+Din+Trans+Pres+%<NomSubj%>+%<Da
tObj%>+%<DatObjLoc%>:0@R.PRS.A@@D.VAL.II@@R.VAL.III@
  Pres1S ;
+Verb+Main+IDt+Act+%#28+Din+Trans+Pres+%<NomSubj%>+%<Da
tObj%>:0@R.PRS.A@@R.VAL.II@  Pres1S ;
```

Fig. 3.30 *lexc*: Extract from 28th paradigm, *v*-type inflectional class

```
+Verb+Main+IDt+Act+%#28+Din+Trans+Pres+%<NomSubjBen%>+%
<DatObj%>:0@R.PRS.I@ Pres1S ;
+Verb+Main+IDt+Act+%#28+Din+Trans+Pres+%<NomSubj%>+%<Da
tObj%>+%<DatObjBen%>:0@R.PRS.U@ Pres1S ;
Etc.

+Verb+Main+IDt+Act+%#28+Din+Trans+Res2+%<DatSubj%>+%<No
mObj%>:0@R.PLUPERF.E@  Pluperf1S ;
Etc.

LEXICON Pres1S
0:ებ             Subject1S ;
Etc.

LEXICON Pluperf1S
0:ებინ           Subject9S ;

LEXICON Subject1S
+SubjBen1Sg+Obj3:0@R.SUBJSG.1@@R.PRS.I@ # ; ! Pres
+SubjBen1Sg+Obj3:0@R.SUBJSG.1@@R.PRS.I@ IndSpeech ;
Etc.
+Subj1Sg+ObjLoc3:0@R.VAL.II@@R.SUBJSG.1@@R.PRS.A@# ;

+Subj1Sg+ObjLoc3:0@R.VAL.II@@R.SUBJSG.1@@R.PRS.A@
  IndSpeech ;
Etc.
+Subj1Sg+ObjLoc3+Obj3:0@D.VAL.II@@R.SUBJSG.1@@R.PRS.A@
  # ;
+Subj1Sg+ObjLoc3+Obj3:0@D.VAL.II@@R.SUBJSG.1@@R.PRS.A@
  IndSpeech ;
Etc.
+Subj1Sg+Obj3+ObjBen3:0@R.SUBJSG.1@@R.PRS.U@  # ;
+Subj1Sg+Obj3+ObjBen3:0@R.SUBJSG.1@@R.PRS.U@  IndSpeech
;
Etc.

LEXICON Subject9S
+Subj1Sg+Obj3:ა@R.ObjSG.1@     # ;
+Subj2Sg+Obj3:ა@R.ObjSG.2@     # ;
+Subj3Sg+Obj3:ა@R.ObjSG.3@     # ;
+Subj1Pl+Obj3:ა@R.ObjPL.1@     # ;
+Subj2Pl+Obj3:ათ@R.ObjPL.2@    # ;
+Subj3Pl+Obj3:ათ@R.ObjPL.3@    # ;
+Subj1Sg+Obj3:ა@R.ObjSG.1@     IndSpeech ;
Etc.

LEXICON IndSpeech
+IndSpeech1:%-მეთქი          # ;
Etc.
```

Fig. 3.30 (continued)

The final syllables of the verb, which consist of thematic suffixes and the third-person marker, as represented in the headwords of dictionary entries, are removed before the appropriate suffixes are added to the root; this is achieved using special triggers. The sample given below shows the surface levels without the aforementioned markers and only one trigger: ^O3, which is used for the generation of third-person object forms in Modern Georgian and in Old Georgian in the case of *Sannarevi* texts in accordance with the replacement rules shown in Fig. 3.31.

```
define R2 [ [..] -> ს || [ %^OS ] ?* _ [ %^O3]
[დ|თ|ტ|ძ|ც|წ|ჯ|ზ|ჭ]] ;
define R3 [ [..] -> ჰ || [ %^OS ] ?* _ [ %^O3]
[ბ|ფ|პ|გ|ქ|კ|ყ]] ;
define R4 [ [..] -> [] || [ %^OS ] ?* _ [ %^O3]
[ვ|ჩ|ლ|მ|ნ|ჟ|რ|ს|ღ|შ|ხ|ჰ|ა|ე|ი|ო|უ]] ;
```

Fig. 3.31 *xfst*: Replacement rules for the third person object markers

The regular expression replaces the ∅ marker with *-s* in the third-person singular if it precedes the ^O3 trigger before `d|t'` etc., or with the *-h* marker before `b|p'`etc., and leaves it unreplaced in all other cases.

The preverbal lexicon provides a choice of twenty-one routes based on the ability of verbs to begin with or without preverbs indicating perfective and imperfective aspects; taking into consideration that the majority of preverbs are used with the future, aorist and perfective screeves, these routes lead to two paradigms of screeves which either need or do not need preverbs for generation. The first paradigm comprises the Present (`S1PrS`), Future (`S1FutS`), Aorist (`S2AorS`) and Perfective (`S3PerfS`) continuation classes, while the second paradigm comprises Future, Aorist and Perfective continuation classes. It should be noted that the `S1PrS` continuation class is used as the starting point for the Present Indicative, Imperfect Indicative and Present Subjunctive screeves, `S1FutS` for the Future Indicative, Future Conditional and Future Subjunctive, `S2AorS` for the Aorist Indicative, Aorist Subjunctive and Aorist Imperative and, `S3PerfS` for the Perfect Indicative, Pluperfect and Perfect Subjunctive.

All of these continuation classes move to the indication of subject markers for the singular and plural forms, with flag diacritics at the surface level to provide a mapping to their counterparts used stem-finally. Each of the subject markers is marked with appropriate U-type flag diacritics, meaning that they are unified with their counterparts using different values for similar features. Taking into account that the first and the third series screeves use different sets of subject markers, there is a choice of six routes within each continuation class of paradigms leading to lexicons of object correlation markers that include `PresS, FutS, AorS, PerfS` and `PluPerfS`. It should be noted that the choice of whether to use object correlation markers is constrained by the classes described by Melikishvili (2010); for instance, some monopersonal verb paradigms do not require them at all. In other cases, these pointers sometimes share similar markers, but activate them under different conditions and constrain these classes with flag diacritics; we activate them separately for monopersonal, bipersonal and tripersonal verbal roots. Thecontinuation classes for subject and object correlation markers are not marked with special tags at the lexical level, because their use strictly depends on the valency of the verbal root and/or on their counterparts used after it.

The object continuation classes proceed to the main lexicon. It should be mentioned that in the case of paradigm No 28, some roots can be used for the generation of both bipersonal and tripersonal forms. In order to permit this possibility, we had to enterverbal roots into the main lexicon with flag diacritics indicating verbal valency, such as `@P.VAL.II@`. These flag diacritics are activated in the next continuation class, `V28S`, and provide a choice between different types of morphological markup for verbs with different valencies. Accordingly, the `V28S` class is appended with mark-up tags at the lexical level (Fig. 3.32) including morphological information on diathesis and its subtype, paradigm number, verb subtype, transitivity, tense and mood, and syntactic information on the case and type of subject and objects.

```
+Verb+Main+IDt+Act+%#28+Din+Trans+Pres+%<NomSubj%>+%<Da
tObj%>+%<DatObjLoc%>
```

Fig. 3.32 *lexc*: Fragment from lexical level mark-up

On the other hand, the class is also appended with flag diacritics constraining the use of object correlation markers and the valency of the verb (Fig. 3.33) before moving to the next continuation classes.

```
0@R.FUT.A@@D.VAL.II@@R.VAL.III@  Fut1S ;
```

Fig. 3.33 *lexc*: Fragment of flag-diacritics

At this stage, this continuation class does not add any markers to the root and the string, but points to other classes. For instance, the `Pres1S` class encompasses markers of thematic suffixes and points to subject marker continuation classes such as `Subject1S`, while the `Imperf1S` class encompassing thematic suffixes points to the extension marker class `EM1S`. The route from the extension marker class proceeds to screeve markers, and only after that to the subject marker continuation classes. Each of the screeves follows its own route.

The second counterparts of subject markers are bound to the first two slots of the paradigm united within the subject continuation classes. The structure of these classes differs depending on the valency of the verb and its active participants. Accordingly, recipient, causer, causee, beneficiary and location can be distinguished by means of special mark-up tags at the lexical level. These connections are coordinated by flag diacritics as well. The *v*-type continuation classes are terminated or proceed to the `IndSpeech` continuation class.

The *v*-type inflectional class differs from the *m*-type inflectional classin the representation of subject and object markers, forms with auxiliaries, and other items A simplified version of the verbal lexicons (positioned at the *m*-type set) is as shown in Fig. 3.34.

```
LEXICON Object_28
                    Preverb_O ;

LEXICON Preverb_O
Ipfv+:0@P.PV.0@Paradigm1O ;
Pfv+:მი@P.PV.MI@  Paradigm2O ;

LEXICON Paradigm1O
                    S1PrO ;
                    S1FutO ;
                    S2AorO ;
                    S3PerfO ;

LEXICON Paradigm2O
                    S1FutO ;
                    S2AorO ;
                    S3PerfO ;
                    S4AuxO ;

LEXICON S1PrO
0:მ@U.ObjSG.1@      PresO ;
0:გ@U.ObjSG.2@      PresO ;
0:^OS0@U.ObjSG.3@PresO ;
0:გვ@U.ObjPL.1@     PresO ;
0:გ@U.ObjPL.2@      PresO ;
0:^OS0@U.ObjPL.3@PresO ;
Etc.

LEXICON S3PerfO
0:მ@U.ObjSG.1@      PerfO ;
Etc.
0:მ@U.ObjSG.1@      PluPerfO ;
Etc.

LEXICON S4AuxO
0:ვ@U.SUBJSG.1@  PerfaO ; ! subject paradigm
0:0@U.SUBJSG.2@  PerfaO ;
0:0@U.SUBJSG.3@  PerfaO ;
0:ვ@U.SUBJPL.1@  PerfaO ;
0:0@U.SUBJPL.2@  PerfaO ;
0:0@U.SUBJPL.3@  PerfaO ;
0:ვ@U.SUBJSG.1@  PluPerfO ;
Etc.

LEXICON PresO
0:ა@U.PRS.A@     R1O ;
0:ი@U.PRS.I@     R1O ;
Etc.

LEXICON PerfO
0:ი@U.PERF.I@@D.ObjSG.3@@D.ObjPL.3@ R1O ;
0:უ@U.PERF.U@@D.ObjSG.1@@D.ObjSG.2@@D.ObjPL.1@@D.ObjPL.
2@  R1O ;

LEXICON PluPerfO
0:ე@U.PLUPERF.E@ R1O ;

LEXICON R1O
აშენებ-ს:^O3შენ@R.PV.0@  V28O ;

LEXICON V28O
```

Fig. 3.34 *lexc*: Extract of the 28th paradigm, object lexicon

```
+Verb+Main+IDt+Act+%#28+Din+Trans+Pres+%<NomSubj%>+%<Da
tObjLoc%>+%<DatObj%>:0@R.PRS.A@ Pres1O ;
+Verb+Main+IDt+Act+%#28+Din+Trans+Pres+%<NomSubj%>+%<Da
tObj%>+%<DatObjBen%>:0@R.PRS.I@ Pres1O ;
Etc.
+Verb+Main+IDt+Act+%#28+Din+Trans+Res2+%<DatSubj%>+%<No
mObj%>+%<GenObj(for)%>:0@R.PLUPERF.E@ Pluperf1O ;
Etc.

LEXICON Pres1O
0:ებ        Subject1O ;
Etc.

LEXICON Pluperf1O
0:ებინ       Subject9O ;

LEXICON Subject1O
+ObjLoc1Sg+Subj2Sg+Obj3:0@R.ObjSG.1@@R.PRS.A@ # ; !
Pres
+ObjLoc1Pl+Subj2Sg+Obj3:0@R.ObjPL.1@@R.PRS.A@ # ;
Etc.
+ObjBen1Sg+Subj2Sg+Obj3:0@R.ObjSG.1@@R.PRS.I@ # ; !
+ObjBen1Pl+Subj2Sg+Obj3:0@R.ObjPL.1@@R.PRS.I@ # ;
Etc.
+ObjLoc1Sg+Subj2Sg+Obj3:0@R.ObjSG.1@@R.PRS.A@ IndSpeech
; ! Pres
+ObjLoc1Pl+Subj2Sg+Obj3:0@R.ObjPL.1@@R.PRS.A@ IndSpeech
;
Etc.

LEXICON Subject9O
+Obj1+Subj3Sg:ა@R.SUBJSG.1@       # ;
+Obj2+Subj3Sg:ა@R.SUBJSG.2@       # ;
+Obj1+Subj3Pl:ათ@R.SUBJPL.1@      # ;
+Obj2+Subj3Pl:ათ@R.SUBJPL.2@      # ;
+Obj1+Subj3Sg:ა@R.SUBJSG.1@       IndSpeech ;
Etc.

LEXICON AuxO
+Aux+Subj3+Obj1Sg:ვარ@R.SUBJSG.1@    # ;
+Aux+Subj3+Obj2Sg:ხარ@R.SUBJSG.2@    # ;
+Aux+Subj3+Obj1Pl:ვართ@R.SUBJPL.1@  # ;
+Aux+Subj3+Obj2Pl:ხართ@R.SUBJPL.2@  # ;
+Aux+Subj3+Obj1Sg:ვარ@R.SUBJSG.1@    IndSpeech ;
+Aux+Subj3+Obj2Sg:ხარ@R.SUBJSG.2@    IndSpeech ;
+Aux+Subj3+Obj1Pl:ვართ@R.SUBJPL.1@  IndSpeech ;
+Aux+Subj3+Obj2Pl:ხართ@R.SUBJPL.2@  IndSpeech ;

LEXICON IndSpeech
+IndSpeech1:%-მეთქი  # ;
Etc.
```

Fig. 3.34 (continued)

The preverbal lexicon of the object paradigm provides a choice of twenty-one routes based on the ability of verbs to begin with or without preverbs indicating perfective and imperfective aspects and pointing to two paradigms of screeves: Paradigm1O and Paradigm2O. The first does not require preverbs for generation, while the second does.

The first paradigm encompasses the Present (S1PrO), Future (S1FutO), Aorist (S2AorO) and Perfective (S3PerfO) continuation classes, while the second comprises the Future, Aorist, Perfective continuation classes and parallel Perfective forms with Auxiliaries (S4AuxO). These classes begin generation from object markers occupying the second slot of a paradigm after preverbs in the singular and plural, which is bound on their counterparts stem-finally. The surface level of this class is marked with flag diacritics to provide a mapping to their counterparts used after the root and screeve markers. There is a choice of six routes within each continuation class arriving at lexicons of object correlation markers including PresO, FutO, AorO, PerfO and PluPerfO. Taking into consideration that the use of object markers depends on the valency of the verbal root, these classes are not marked with special tags at the lexical level, but are constrained by flag diacritics at the surface level. All of these classes point directly to the main lexicon containing verbal roots, which is sometimes constrained by preverbs.

The next class, V28O, is appended with mark-up tags at the lexical level that include morphological information on the diathesis and its subtype, paradigm number, verb subtype, transitivity, tense and mood, and syntactic information on the case and type of subject and objects. These flag diacritics enable binding with the object correlation markers mentioned above (Fig. 3.35) by means of flag diacritics.

```
+Verb+Main+IDt+Act+%#28+Din+Trans+Pres+%<NomSubj%>+%<Da
tObjLoc%>+%<DatObj%>:0@R.PRS.A@
```

Fig. 3.35 *lexc*: Fragment of the lexical level mark-up

This continuation class (Fig. 3.34) does not add any markers to the root, and the string arriving at this stage points to other classes. For instance, Pres1O, like Pres1S, points to thematic suffixes and then to subject continuation classes such as Subject1O. These continuation classes are generally bound on their counterparts occupying the second and the third slots of the paradigm. Like the *v*-type inflectional class, the structure of the *m*-type inflectional class depends on the valency of the verb and represents active participants using different mark-up tags at the lexical level.

The formation of the AuxO continuation class is somewhat different from the others, because it generates forms of the perfect indicative of the third series by attaching forms of the auxiliary ‘to be’ to the slots of thematic suffixes and screeve markers. This class, which belongs to the subjective paradigm, has four terminating states indicating the first and the second person in the singular and plural and four routes pointing to indirect speech markers.

Replacement rules represented in the form of regular expressions act upon the output of the lexicon and, generally speaking, handle the removal of final syllables with the purpose of implementing the formation of screeves, changes in third-person object markers dependent on the next character, root vowel alternation in Aorist and Perfect screeves, and other such modifications.

The lexicon and rule transducers are composed and united together to create a single, large morphological transducer for verbs. As noted, while the majority of stems follow the rules of the paradigms described by Melikishvili (2010), a small number of so-called 'irregular' verbs exists which employ verbs with different structures to fill in missing screeves within their paradigms.

In order to avoid creating complicated irregular exceptions, these irregular verbs are represented in the form of an additional lexicon which, in combination with a replacement rule script, makes up `irregulars.fst`. The structure of the lexicon consists of a lexicon with verbal lemmas (Fig. 3.36).

```
LEXICON Root
  უნდა ;
  დევს ;
Etc.
```

Fig. 3.36 *lexc*: Fragment from the irregular lexicon

The verbs represented in this class generally employ suppletive forms in their formation and cannot be treated as minor exceptions to the main paradigms. As such, they are processed separately in accordance with screeve continuation classes including Present Indicative (`S1Pr`), Imperfect Indicative (`S1Imperf`), Present Subjunctive (`S1PresSbj`), etc.

3.3.6 The Participial and Verbal Noun Lexicons

Taking into consideration the formation principles of participles and verbal nouns, these are composed separately in the form of two transducers: `participle.fst` and `masdar.fst`. These transducers describe features similar to verbal and adjectival or verbal and nominal paradigms. The tags used at the lexical level of the participial and verbal noun lexicons are described in detail within the verbal morphosyntactic tagset in Appendix A. The verbal noun transducer includes information on five types of declension, and the participial transducer on three types of declension distributed between appropriate continuation classes.

A simplified overview of the participial lexicon is shown in Fig. 3.37.

```
Multichar_Symbols
+VerbalAdj +Act +Pass +Pres +Imperf +Fut +Neg +Sg +Pl
+Nom +Erg +Dat +Gen +Ins +Advb +Voc +Emph +Post +Ptcl
+Aux

! flag diacritics
@U.CASE.NOM@ @R.CASE.NOM@ @D.CASE.NOM@ etc.
! triggers
^S ^S1 ^S3 ^S4 etc.

LEXICON Root
                         VerbalAdj ;

LEXICON VerbalAdj
დამლევ-ი:დამლევი         VA1 ;
Etc.

LEXICON VA1
+VerbalAdj+Pres:^S0      Nmbr_1 ;
+Adv:^Sად                # ;
+Adv:^Sად                Postposition ;
Etc.

LEXICON Nmbr_1
+Sg:^S0                  Case_1 ;
+Pl:^Pებ@U.NUM.EB@       Case_1 ;
+Pl:^NTნ                 Case_N ;
+Pl:^NTთ                 Case_T ;
Etc.
```

Fig. 3.37 *lexc*: Extract from the first Declension of the participial lexicon

As can be seen from the extract, the participial lexicon generally speaking follows the principles already determined for the operation of the adjectival transducer. The primary distinction is that the participial lexicon does not contain a continuation class required for the formation of degree as is present in the adjectival lexicon. Upon arriving at the `VA1` continuation class, the verbal root has a choice of three routes. The first connects to `Nmbr_1`, while the second two are used for the formation of adverbs from participles with or without postpositions. The declaration of PoS from within the `VA1` continuation class depends upon the ability of adjectives and participles to form adverbs.

The category of tense is another morphological feature which is not peculiar to adjectives, but represented in the participial lexicon. The mark-up given at the lexical level, such as `+VerbalAdj+Pres`, `+VerbalAdj+Aor`, etc. depends on the indication of time. Although the possibility of generating verbal adjectives directly from present, future and aorist stems was tested on the previous version of the transducer, at the time of writing this subdivision is based on the grammatical description attached to headwords in Chikobava's Dictionary (Chikobava, 1950–1964).

As in the case of adjectives, flag diacritics are used to constrain which suffixes can be accepted by the participle during generation and to provide a mapping between them. The *xfst* module is used to trigger processes within and/or at the boundaries of morphemes in the form of regular expressions. A simplified overview of the verbal noun lexicon is given in Fig. 3.38.

```
Multichar_Symbols
+VerbalNoun +Pres +Fut +Aor +Sg +Pl +Nom +Erg +Dat +Gen
+Ins +Advb +Voc +Emph +Post +Ptcl +Aux

! flag diacritics
@U.CASE.NOM@ @R.CASE.NOM@ @D.CASE.NOM@
! triggers
^S ^S1 ^S2 ^S3 Etc.

LEXICON Root
                        Preverb ;

LEXICON Preverb
Ipfv+:0@P.PV.0@         Masdars ;
Pfv+amo:ამო@P.PV.AMO@Masdars ;
Etc.

LEXICON Masdars
სუნთქვა                 Nmbr_4 ;
Etc.

LEXICON Nmbr_4
+Sg:^S0                 Case_2 ;
+Pl:^Pებ                Case_1 ;
+Pl:^Pებთ               Case_T ;
+Pl:^NTნ                Case_N ;
+Pl:^NTთ                Case_T ;
Etc.

LEXICON Case_1
                        Nominative ;
Etc.

LEXICON Case_2
                        Nominative_2 ;
Etc.

LEXICON Nominative
+Nom:^No@U.CASE.NOM@ # ;
+Nom:^No@U.CASE.NOM@ Postposition ;
+Nom:^No@U.CASE.NOM@ Particle ;
+Nom:^No@U.CASE.NOM@ Auxiliary ;
+Nom:^No@U.CASE.NOM@ IndSpeech ;

LEXICON Nominative_2
+Nom:0@U.CASE.NOM@    # ;
+Nom:0@U.CASE.NOM@    Postposition ;
+Nom:0@U.CASE.NOM@    Particle ;
+Nom:0@U.CASE.NOM@    Auxiliary ;
+Nom:0@U.CASE.NOM@    IndSpeech ;
Etc.
```

Fig. 3.38 *lexc*: Extract from the third declension of the verbal noun lexicon

The sample shown from the verbal noun lexicon represents the continuation class of truncating vowel-final verbal nouns and covers only one lemma: *sunt'k'va* 'breathing', as it is represented in Chikobava's Dictionary (1950–1964). Unlike the nominal lexicon, the verbal noun lexicon begins with preverbs. The preverb continuation class provides a choice of twenty-one routes, which point to the `Masdars` class. All preverbs are marked with flag diacritics such as `@P.PV.AMO@`, which are activated if their use is relevant to the formation of preverbal forms.

`Nmbr_4` contains five continuation classes: the first is used to generate singulars, the second to generate the regular pattern with the *-eb* plural marker, the third to generate the irregular pattern with the *–eb* and *-t'* plural markers used together, the fourth to generate the regular pattern with the *–n* plural marker used in the nominative and vocative, and the fifth to generate the regular pattern with *-t'* plural forms. All of these forms proceed to different continuation classes: `Case_4` is used to attach case markers to the singular and `Case_1` to attach them to *-eb* plural forms, while `Case_T` and `Case_N` are used to attach case markers to *-n* and *-t'* plural forms separately. The case continuation classes can either generate a complete word-form, or can proceed to another continuation class such as `Postposition`, `Particle`, `Auxiliary` or `IndSpeech`. Similarly to the processing of other nominals, the continuation classes are equipped with flag diacritics with the purpose of establishing dependencies between cases and postpositions and/or between postpositions and particles.

The truncation of vowel-final verbal nouns represented in the extract of the third declension takes place outside the lexicon in the manner shown in Fig. 3.39.

```
define R5 [ ა -> [] || _ %^P .o. ა -> [] || _ %^S ?*
$["^G"] .o. ა -> [] || _ %^S ?* $["^I"] ] ;
```

Fig. 3.39 *xfst*: Syncopation of vowels before sonants

The triggers activated from within the *xfst* module are used to remove final *–a* in the genitive and instrumental cases in the singular and in all cases in the *-eb-* plural.

3.3.7 Closed Word-Classes: Adverbs, Conjunctions, Particles, Interjections and Postpositions

A morphological description of any language includes a variety of functional words which are used to represent grammatical relations between words in a sentence. These functional words belong to so-called 'closed' classes of items, meaning that their generative possibilities are minimal, although the frequency of use of the words is high. The transducer which we designed specifically for functional words includes continuation classes for adverbs, conjunctions, particles, interjections and adpositions. Conjunctions, particles, interjections and postpositions are predominantly expressed using forms found in Georgian dictionaries, where they are listed together with their morphosyntactic description. Structurally, adverbs can be used together with postpositions, extension vowels, particles and indirect speech markers. These forms are generated by means of continuation classes from within *lexc*.

The functional lexicon which provides access to all functional continuation classes is organized as shown in Fig. 3.40.

```
Multichar_Symbols
+Adv +Loc +Temp +Mod +Quan +Caus +Spec +QA +RelA +Emph
+Ptcl +Aux +Post +Dat +Gen +Itj +Conj +Coord +Subord
+Part +Ques +RelP +Proh +Wor +Pos +Negat +IntP

! flag diacritics
@U.POST.C@ @R.POST.C@ @U.POST.V@ @R.POST.V@

LEXICON Root
  Adverb ;
  Postposition ;
  Interjection ;
  Conjunctions ;
  Particle ;
Etc.
```

Fig. 3.40 *lexc*: Functional word-classes

The number of flag diacritics used within this module is very small and is constrained only by the possibility of using postpositions with or without particles.

In accordance with the rules of derivation, some adverbs can be generated directly from within adjective and participle lexicons by adding the adverbial case marker *-ad* to the nominal root, but there is a huge number of adverbs which cannot be generated in this way (see Sect. 3.3.2). These are represented in Georgian dictionaries separately and are distributed between local, temporal, manner and other groups of items. A sample from the adverbial continuation class is given in Fig. 3.41.

```
LEXICON Adverb
ადრე                 Temp ;
Etc.

LEXICON Temp
+Adv+Temp:0          # ;
+Adv+Temp:0          Emphatic ;
+Adv+Temp:0          Particle ;
+Adv+Temp:0          IndSpeech ;

LEXICON Emphatic
+Emph:ა              # ;
+Emph:ა              Particle ;
+Emph:ა              Auxiliary ;
+Emph:ა              IndSpeech ;

LEXICON Particle
+Ptcl:ც          # ;
Etc.
+Ptcl:ცა             Auxiliary ;
Etc.
+Ptcl:ც              IndSpeech ;
Etc.

LEXICON Auxiliary
+Aux:ა               # ;
+Aux:ა               IndSpeech ;
Etc.
```

Fig. 3.41 *lexc*: Extract from the functional word lexicon

The `Temp` continuation class, which is represented by the temporal adverb *adre* 'early', is assigned in accordance with adverb type and determines the formation of paradigm, then points to the terminal state or to other continuation classes including `Emphatic`, `Particle` or `Auxiliary`.

The postpositional continuation classes are represented entirely within the nominal transducers in the forms of suffixes attached to case markers or to extension vowels by means of flag diacritics. In addition, they can also be represented separately, in which case they are not attached to the root. A sample of the postposition lexicon is shown in Fig. 3.42.

```
LEXICON Postposition
შინ@U.POST.C@          Dative ;
Etc.
მომართ@U.POST.C@       Genetive ;
გარდა@U.POST.V@        Genetive;
Etc.

LEXICON Dative
+Post+Dat:0                              # ;
+Post+Dat+Ptcl:ც@R.POST.V@               # ;
+Post+Dat+Emph+Ptcl:აც@R.POST.C@         # ;
+Post+Dat:0                              IndSpeech ;
+Post+Dat+Ptcl:ც@R.POST.V@               IndSpeech ;
+Post+Dat+Emph+Ptcl:აც@R.POST.C@         IndSpeech ;

LEXICON Genetive
+Post+Gen:0                              # ;
+Post+Gen+Ptcl:ც@R.POST.V@               # ;
+Post+Gen+Emph+Ptcl:აც@R.POST.C@         # ;
+Post+Gen:0                              IndSpeech ;
+Post+Gen+Ptcl:ც@R.POST.V@               IndSpeech ;
+Post+Gen+Emph+Ptcl:აც@R.POST.C@         IndSpeech ;
Etc.
```

Fig. 3.42 *lexc*: Extract from the postposition lexicon

Conjunctions, particles and interjections belong to closed classes of items. Conjunctions can be subordinating or coordinating, and interjections can be interrogative, relative, prohibitive, affirmative, intensive, infinitive or negative in accordance with the categories determined in Georgian dictionaries. All of these lexicons have the ability to proceed to the final state or to the `IndSpeech` continuation class.

3.3.8 Abbreviations, Foreign Words and Punctuation Marks

The principal determiners of abbreviations are punctuation marks including ‘.’ and ‘-’, which also serve as sentence separators and are not always associated with abbreviations. Some abbreviations do not require these marks at all, however, and act like a word without any additional marks.

In Old Georgian texts, additional abbreviations are represented by means of different titlo diacritics, including ‘͠’ (code: 0360), ‘͛’ (code: 035B), ‘̒’ (code: 0312), ‘̄’ (code: 0304), ‘̇’ (code: 0307) and ‘͂’ (code: 0342). These symbols are used to represent the following types of abbreviations: suspension, contraction and truncation, as described in Sect. 3.3.

If the abbreviation is specified in the tokenizer and additionally in the abbreviation transducer, it can be easily identified at the morphological level. Otherwise, the dot and the dash symbols are processed in accordance with the primary rules as symbols used to demarcate sentence boundaries or composites.

The abbreviation transducer generally speaking follows the rules of nominal inflection for nouns, adjectives and pronouns and describes abbreviations with and/or without punctuation marks. A simplified overview of the abbreviation lexicon is shown in Fig. 3.43.

```
Multichar_Symbols
+Abbr +Prop +Com +Anim +Inanim +Sg +Pl +Nom +Erg +Dat
+Gen +Ins +Advb +Voc +Emph +Post +Ptcl +Aux

! flag diacritics
@U.CASE.NOM@ @R.CASE.NOM@ @D.CASE.NOM@ etc.
! triggers
^S ^S1 ^S2 ^S3 etc.

LEXICON Root
  Abbreviation ;

LEXICON Abbreviation
ამერიკის% შეერთებული% შტატები+Abbr:აშშ    Nmbr_1 ;
ქალბატონი+Abbr:ქ%-ნი         Nmbr_1;
ასე% შემდეგ+Abbr:ა%.შ%.    # ;
Etc.
```

Fig. 3.43 *lexc*: Extract from the abbreviation lexicon

In some cases, foreign words are embedded in Georgian text in the alphabet of the donor language. This peculiarity allows us to distinguish foreign words directly from within the *xfst* module in the way shown in Fig. 3.44.

```
define GreekLetter
Α|Α|α|ά|Β|β|Γ|γ|Δ|δ|Ε|ε|έ|ε|e|Ζ|ζ|Η|η|ή|Θ|θ|Ι|ι ί|Κ|κ|Λ|
λ|Μ|μ|Ν|ν|Ξ|ξ|Ο|ο|ό|ό|Π|π|Ρ|ρ|Σ|σ|ς|Τ|τ|τ|Υ|υ|ύ|y|s|Φ|φ
|Χ|χ|Ψ|ψ|Ω|ω|ώ ;
define GeorgianLetter ს|{მი} ;
define Punct %-|%«|%»|%,|%; ;
define Words [GreekLetter|Punct GreekLetter|GreekLetter
Punct|GreekLetter Punct Punct
GeorgianLetter|GreekLetter Punct GeorgianLetter]+ ;
read regex [ %+Foreign:Words ] ;
save stack foreignGR.fst
```

Fig. 3.44 *lexc*: Extract from the abbreviation lexicon

The system distinguishes full stops, commas, parentheses, hyphens, exclamatory and question marks, colons, semicolons, and other punctuation marks.

3.4 Summary

This chapter has described the tokenizer and the main architecture of the wide coverage morphological analyser and generator of Old, Middle and Modern Georgian morphosyntax.

References

Abuladze, Ilia. 1973. *żveli k'art'uli enis lek'sikoni (Dictionary of Old Georgian Language)*. Tbilisi: mec'niereba (Science).

Antidze, Jemal, and Nana Gulua. 2010. Software tools for computer realization of morphological and syntactic models of Georgian texts. *Computer Science and Telecommunications* 1: 54–63.

Beesley, Kenneth, and Lauri Karttunen. 2003. *Finite-state morphology: xerox tools and techniques*. Stanford: CSLI Publications.

Chikobava, Arnold. 1950–1964. *k'art'uli enis ganmartebit'i lek'sikoni (Georgian Explanatory Dictionary)*. Tbilisi: Academy of Sciences.

Chomsky, Noam. 1956. Three models for the description of language. *IRE Transactions on Information Theory* 2: 113–124.

Chomsky, Noam, and Marcel-Paul Schützenberger. 1963. The algebraic theory of context-free languages. In *Computer programming and formal systems*, ed. P.H. Braffort, 118–161. Amsterdam: North-Holland.

Chubinashvili, David. 1940. *Georgian-Russian-French dictionary*. Saint-Petersburg: Imperial Academy of Sciences.

Datukischvili, Ketevan. 2005–2007. Morphologic processor of Georgian language. In *Tbilisi symposium language, logic, computation*. Batumi: Batumi State University.

Datukishvili, Ketevan. 1997. Some questions of computer synthesis of verb in Georgian. In *The second tbilisi symposium on language, logic and computation*, 83–85. Tbilisi: t'bilisis saxelmcip'o universiteti (Tbilisi State University).

Doborjginidze, Nino, Lobzhanidze, Irina, and Gunia, Irakli. 2012. *Georgian language corpus*. http://corpora.iliauni.edu.ge/. Accessed 30 Oct 2019.

Doborjginidze, Nino, Lobzhanidze, Irina, and Mirianashvili, George. 2014. *Corpus of Georgian chronicles*. http://corpora.iliauni.edu.ge/. Accessed 30 Oct 2019.

Hewitt, George. 2005. *Georgian: a learner's grammar*. New York: Routledge.

Gazdar, Gerald, Ernest Klein, Geoffrey Pullum, and Ivan Andrew Sag. 1985. *Generalized phrase structure grammar*. Oxford: Basil Blackwell.

Gippert, Jost. 2016. Complex morphology and its impact on lexicology: the kartvelian case. In *Proceedings of the XVII EURALEX International Congress*, 16–37. Tbilisi: t'bilisis saxelmcip'o universiteti (Tbilisi State University).

Goldsmith, John. 2001. Unsupervised learning of morphology of a natural language. *Computational Linguistics* 27 (2): 153–197.

Gurevich, Olga. 2006. *Constructional morphology: the Georgian Version*. Berkeley: PhD Dissertation, University of California.

Johnson, C Douglas. 1972. *Formal Aspects of Phonological Description*. The Hague Mouton.

Jurafsky, Dan, and James Martin. 2000. *Speech and language processing: an introduction to natural language processing, computational linguistics, and speech recognition*. Delhi: Pearson Education.

Kapanadze, Oleg. 2009. Describing Georgian Morphology with a Finite-State System. In *Proceedings of the 8th international conference on finite-state methods and natural language processing*, 114–122. Pretoria: Springer.

Kaplan, Ronald, and Joan Bresnan. 1982. Lexical-functional grammar: a formal system for grammatical representation. In *The mental representation of grammatical relations*, 173–281. Cambridge, MA: The MIT Press.

Kaplan, Ronald, and Martin Kay. 1994. Regular models of phonological rule systems. *Computational Linguistics* 20 (3): 331–378.

Karlsson, Fred. 1994. Computational morphology. In *The encyclopedia of language and linguistics*, ed. R.S. Asher. Oxford: Pergamon.

Karlsson, Fred, and Lauri Karttunen. 1997. Sub-sentential processing. In *Survey of the state of the art in human language technology*, ed. R.M. Cole, 96–100. New York: Cambridge University Press.

Karttunen, Lauri, Jean-Pierre Chanod, Gregory Grefenstette, and A. Schiller. 1997. Regular expressions for language engineering. *Natural Language Engineering* 2 (4): 1–24.

Koskenniemi, Kimo. 1983. *Two-level morphology: a general computational model for word-form recognition and production*. Helsinki: University of Helsinki.

Lobzhanidze, Irina. 2019. Computational model of the modern Georgian language and search patterns for an online dictionary of idioms. In *Language, logic, and computation*, Lecture notes in computer science, ed. A. Silva, S. Staton, P. Sutton, and C. Umbach, vol. 11456, 187–208. Lagodekhi, Georgia: TbiLLC 2018.

Makharoblidze, Tamar. 2009. *A short grammar of Georgian*. Munich: Lincom Europe.

Manning, Christopher, Prabhakar Raghavan, and Hinrich Schütze. 2008. *Introduction to information retrieval*. Cambridge: Cambridge University Press.

Margvelani, Lamara. 1999–2001. Subsystem analyzing Georgian word-forms and its application to spellchecking. In *A Proceedings of the 3rd and 4th InternationalSymposium on Language, Logic and Computation*, 1–7. Borjomi: ILLC Scientific Publications.

Mealy, George. 1955. A method for synthesizing sequential circuits. *Bell System Technical Journal* I: 1045–1079.

Melikishvili, Damana. 2001. *k'art'uli zmnis uġlebis sistema (System of Georgian verbal paradigm)*. Tbilisi: Logos Press.

Melikishvili, Damana, Humphries, John, and Kupunia, Maia. 2010. The Georgian Verb: *A Morphosyntactic Analysis*. Hyattsville, MD: Dunwoody Press.

Meurer, Paul. 2007. A computational grammar for Georgian. In *Lecture notes in computer science*, 1–15. Berlin: Springer.

Oniani, Alexander. 1966. *k'art'uli idiomebi (Georgian Idioms)*. Nakaduli: Tbilisi.

Pollard, Carl, and Ivan Andrew Sag. 1994. *Head-driven phrase structure grammar*. Chicago: University of Chicago Press.

Rayfield, Donald. 2006. *A comprehensive Georgian-English dictionary*. London: Garnett.

Schützenberger, Marcel-Paul. 1961. A remark on finite transducers. *Information and Control* 4: 185–196.

Shanidze, Akaki. 1973. *k'art'uli gramatikis sap'u'vlebi, morp'ologia (Foundations of Georgian Grammar, Morphology)*, I. Tbilisi: t'bilisis saxelmcip'o universiteti (Tbilisi State University).

Sproat, Richard. 1992. *Morphology and computation*. Cambridge: MIT.

Standardization, ISO. 2012. *Language Resource Management – Morpho-syntactic Annotation Framework (MAF), No 24611*. https://www.iso.org/standard/51934.html. Accessed 16 Jul 2019.

TEI Consortium, e. 2019 07 16. TEI P5: *Guidelines for Electronic Text Encoding and Interchange*. https://tei-c.org/guidelines/p5/. Accessed 29 November, 2019.

Tschenkeli, Kita. 1965. *Georgisch-Deutsches Wörterbuch*. Zürich: Amirani-Verlag.

Tsotsanidze, George, Nana Loladze, and Ketevan Datukishvili. 2014. *k'art'uli lek'sikoni (Georgian Dictionary)*. Bakur Sulakauri: Tbilisi.

Turing, Alan. 1936. On computable numbers, with an application to the Entscheidungsproblem. *Proceedings of the London Mathematical Society* 2 (42): 230–265.

Uí Dhonnchadha, Elaine. 2009. *Part-of-speech tagging and partial parsing for Irish using finite-state transducers and constraint grammar*. Dublin: DCU Online Research Access Service.

Xerox Finite-State Tools. 2013. Tools: *lexc, xfst, lookup*. https://web.stanford.edu/~laurik/. book2software/. Accessed 30 Nov 2019.

Chapter 4
Testing and Evaluation

Abstract The compilation of the Georgian morphological analyser using Xerox Finite-State Tools for NLP has been followed by testing and error analysis with the purposes of improving language coverage and of checking the consistency of the theoretical prerequisites of the system. The main procedures covered the testing of rule integrity, the ordering of tags and the checking of recognition rates. The present chapter comprises four sections, the first section is a short introduction on the testing and evaluation stages. Section 4.2, "Rule integrity", describes the testing procedures for the overall system with regard to lost and added words. Section 4.3, "Consistency and ordering of tags", provides information on lexical tag grammar and its use for the evaluation of tag ordering in the system with the purpose of providing future integration of the system output with other systems. Section 4.4, "Language coverage test: wordlists and corpus data", includes information on the compilation of the Georgian Language Corpus (GLC) and its application for the evaluation of recognition rates and the carrying out of language coverage tests.

Keywords Testing · Morphosyntactic tagset · Corpus compilation

4.1 Introduction

Testing and error analysis focus on the confirmation of well-formedness, rule integrity and language coverage; while well-formedness and rule integrity can be checked without the use of additional data, the evaluation of language coverage necessitates testing the system against corpora of Old, Middle and Modern Georgian texts.

I. Lobzhanidze, *Finite-State Computational Morphology*,
https://doi.org/10.1007/978-3-030-90248-3_4

4.2 Rule Integrity

The development of the morphological analyser was not carried out in a single stage; its modules were created, compiled and processed separately. The unification of modules, as well as the adding of new rules, can impede and/or destroy codes developed at previous stages, which are problems that can be avoided by using various capabilities of the Xerox calculus, and especially a regression test used within a version-control system. Regression testing is used to compare different versions of the system at the lexical and at the surface levels of a transducer.

In addition, the *lexc* tools offer the 'lookup' and 'lookdown' commands, and the *xfst* tools the commands 'apply up' and 'apply down'. We have used testing against our own version to catch regressions and to find errors in the form of:

(a) Regression testing comparing two versions to find lost words in the form of `words-lost.txt`
(b) Regression testing comparing two versions to find added words in the form of `words-added.txt`.

These types of regression testing were carried out in accordance with script described in Beesley and Karttunen (2003). The system was run and fixed periodically, and where we discovered badly formed words or lost good ones, the system was improved, the files were fixed and the tests were re-run.

4.3 Consistency and Ordering of Tags

Well-formedness of the surface representation of paradigms depends on the ordering of tags, which is predefined with the purpose of providing for their integration into other systems; to this end, the sequence of tags should be consistent and fixed. There are fixed tags to describe different morphological features and a large number of optional tags which can be interchanged with one another; for instance, the case of a noun may be: `+Nom, +Erg, +Dat, +Gen, +Ins, +Advb` or `+Voc`. All of these tags appear in a fixed order. Following Beesley and Karttunen (2003), the best practice for checking the consistency and ordering of tags is to compile a lexical tag grammar and to check it against the network generated by a transducer. The following is a simplified extract from the lexical tag grammar for Modern Georgian (Fig. 4.1):

```
[ა|ე|ი|ო|უ|ჱ|ჲ|ჵ|ბ|გ|დ|ვ|ზ|თ|კ|ლ|მ|ნ|პ|ჟ|რ|ს|ტ|ფ|ქ|ღ|ყ|
შ|ჩ|ც|ძ|წ|ჭ|ხ|ჯ|ჰ|ჳ|ჸ|ჴ|ჶ|ლ|მ|ნ|რ]+
(%+OGE|%+MGE|%+GE)
[%+Noun [[%+Prop (%+Name|%+Geog)
      [%+Anim [%+Sg|%+Pl]
      [%+Nom|%+Erg|%+Dat|%+Gen|%+Ins|%+Advb|%+Voc]
      (%+Emph)
  ([%+Post%(like%)|%+Post%(with/at%)|%+Post%(on%)|%+Pos
t%(in%)|%+Post%(for%)|%+Post%(from%)|%+Post%(with%)|%+P
ost%(to%)|%+Post%(till%)])
      (%+Emph) (%+Ptcl) (%+Emph) (%+Aux)
      ([%+IndSpeech1|%+IndSpeech2|%+IndSpeech3])]
      |
      [%+Inanim [%+Sg|%+Pl]
      [%+Nom|%+Erg|%+Dat|%+Gen|%+Ins|%+Advb|%+Voc]
      (%+Emph)
  ([%+Post%(like%)|%+Post%(with/at%)|%+Post%(on%)|%+Pos
t%(in%)|%+Post%(for%)|%+Post%(from%)|%+Post%(with%)|%+P
ost%(to%)|%+Post%(till%)])
      (%+Emph) (%+Ptcl) (%+Emph) (%+Aux)
      ([%+IndSpeech1|%+IndSpeech2|%+IndSpeech3])]]
    |
      [%+Com [%+Anim [%+Sg|%+Pl]
      [%+Nom|%+Erg|%+Dat|%+Gen|%+Ins|%+Advb|%+Voc]
      (%+Emph)
  ([%+Post%(like%)|%+Post%(with/at%)|%+Post%(on%)|%+Pos
t%(in%)|%+Post%(for%)|%+Post%(from%)|%+Post%(with%)|%+P
ost%(to%)|%+Post%(till%)])
      (%+Emph) (%+Ptcl) (%+Emph) (%+Aux)
      ([%+IndSpeech1|%+IndSpeech2|%+IndSpeech3])]
      |
      [%+Inanim [%+Sg|%+Pl]
      [%+Nom|%+Erg|%+Dat|%+Gen|%+Ins|%+Advb|%+Voc]
      (%+Emph)
  ([%+Post%(like%)|%+Post%(with/at%)|%+Post%(on%)|%+Pos
t%(in%)|%+Post%(for%)|%+Post%(from%)|%+Post%(with%)|%+P
ost%(to%)|%+Post%(till%)])
      (%+Emph) (%+Ptcl) (%+Emph) (%+Aux)
      ([%+IndSpeech1|%+IndSpeech2|%+IndSpeech3])
      ]]]
  |
%+Adj (%+Pos|%+Com|%+Sup)
      [%+Sg|%+Pl]
      [%+Nom|%+Erg|%+Dat|%+Gen|%+Ins|%+Advb|%+Voc]
      (%+Emph)
  ([%+Post%(like%)|%+Post%(with/at%)|%+Post%(on%)|%+Pos
```

Fig. 4.1 Extract from the lexical tag grammar

```
t%(in%)|%+Post%(for%)|%+Post%(from%)|%+Post%(with%)|%+P
ost%(to%)|%+Post%(till%)])
      (%+Emph) (%+Ptcl) (%+Emph) (%+Aux)
      ([%+IndSpeech1|%+IndSpeech2|%+IndSpeech3])
  |
%+Num (%+Alpha|%+Roman|%+Arabic)
      [[%+Card [%+Sg|%+Pl]
      [%+Nom|%+Erg|%+Dat|%+Gen|%+Ins|%+Advb|%+Voc]
      (%+Emph)
  ([%+Post%(like%)|%+Post%(with/at%)|%+Post%(on%)|%+Pos
t%(in%)|%+Post%(for%)|%+Post%(from%)|%+Post%(with%)|%+P
ost%(to%)|%+Post%(till%)])
      (%+Emph) (%+Ptcl) (%+Emph) (%+Aux)
      ([%+IndSpeech1|%+IndSpeech2|%+IndSpeech3])]
      |
      [%+Ord [%+Sg|%+Pl]
      [%+Nom|%+Erg|%+Dat|%+Gen|%+Ins|%+Advb|%+Voc]
      (%+Emph)
  ([%+Post%(like%)|%+Post%(with/at%)|%+Post%(on%)|%+Pos
t%(in%)|%+Post%(for%)|%+Post%(from%)|%+Post%(with%)|%+P
ost%(to%)|%+Post%(till%)])
      (%+Emph) (%+Ptcl) (%+Emph) (%+Aux)
      ([%+IndSpeech1|%+IndSpeech2|%+IndSpeech3])]
      |
      [%+Fract [%+Sg|%+Pl]
      [%+Nom|%+Erg|%+Dat|%+Gen|%+Ins|%+Advb|%+Voc]
      (%+Emph)
  ([%+Post%(like%)|%+Post%(with/at%)|%+Post%(on%)|%+Pos
t%(in%)|%+Post%(for%)|%+Post%(from%)|%+Post%(with%)|%+P
ost%(to%)|%+Post%(till%)])
      (%+Emph) (%+Ptcl) (%+Emph) (%+Aux)
      ([%+IndSpeech1|%+IndSpeech2|%+IndSpeech3])]
      |
      [%+Approx [%+Sg|%+Pl]
      [%+Nom|%+Erg|%+Dat|%+Gen|%+Ins|%+Advb|%+Voc]
      (%+Emph)
  ([%+Post%(like%)|%+Post%(with/at%)|%+Post%(on%)|%+Pos
t%(in%)|%+Post%(for%)|%+Post%(from%)|%+Post%(with%)|%+P
ost%(to%)|%+Post%(till%)])
      (%+Emph) (%+Ptcl) (%+Emph) (%+Aux)
      ([%+IndSpeech1|%+IndSpeech2|%+IndSpeech3])]
      |
```

Fig. 4.1 (continued)

```
      [%+Rep (%+Emph) (%+Aux)
      ([%+IndSpeech1|%+IndSpeech2|%+IndSpeech3])]
      ]
  |
%+Pron [[%+Pers [%+1|%+2|%+3] [%+Sg|%+Pl]
      [%+Nom|%+Erg|%+Dat|%+Gen|%+Ins|%+Advb|%+Voc]
      (%+Emph)
  ([%+Post%(like%)|%+Post%(with/at%)|%+Post%(on%)|%+Pos
t%(in%)|%+Post%(for%)|%+Post%(from%)|%+Post%(with%)|%+P
ost%(to%)|%+Post%(till%)])
      (%+Emph) (%+Ptcl) (%+Emph) (%+Aux)
      ([%+IndSpeech1|%+IndSpeech2|%+IndSpeech3])]
      |
      [%+Dem [%+1|%+2|%+3] [%+Sg|%+Pl]
      [%+Nom|%+Erg|%+Dat|%+Gen|%+Ins|%+Advb|%+Voc]
      (%+Emph)
  ([%+Post%(like%)|%+Post%(with/at%)|%+Post%(on%)|%+Pos
t%(in%)|%+Post%(for%)|%+Post%(from%)|%+Post%(with%)|%+P
ost%(to%)|%+Post%(till%)])
      (%+Emph) (%+Ptcl) (%+Emph) (%+Aux)
      ([%+IndSpeech1|%+IndSpeech2|%+IndSpeech3])]
      |
      [%+Poss [%+1|%+2|%+3] [%+Sg|%+Pl]
      [%+Nom|%+Erg|%+Dat|%+Gen|%+Ins|%+Advb|%+Voc]
      (%+Emph)
  ([%+Post%(like%)|%+Post%(with/at%)|%+Post%(on%)|%+Pos
t%(in%)|%+Post%(for%)|%+Post%(from%)|%+Post%(with%)|%+P
ost%(to%)|%+Post%(till%)])
      (%+Emph) (%+Ptcl) (%+Emph) (%+Aux)
      ([%+IndSpeech1|%+IndSpeech2|%+IndSpeech3])]
      |
      [%+Indf [%+1|%+2|%+3] [%+Sg|%+Pl]
      [%+Nom|%+Erg|%+Dat|%+Gen|%+Ins|%+Advb|%+Voc]
      (%+Emph)
  ([%+Post%(like%)|%+Post%(with/at%)|%+Post%(on%)|%+Pos
t%(in%)|%+Post%(for%)|%+Post%(from%)|%+Post%(with%)|%+P
ost%(to%)|%+Post%(till%)])
      (%+Emph) (%+Ptcl) (%+Emph) (%+Aux)
      ([%+IndSpeech1|%+IndSpeech2|%+IndSpeech3])]
      |
      [%+Int [%+1|%+2|%+3] [%+Sg|%+Pl]
      [%+Nom|%+Erg|%+Dat|%+Gen|%+Ins|%+Advb|%+Voc]
```

Fig. 4.1 (continued)

```
      (%+Emph)
  ([%+Post%(like%)|%+Post%(with/at%)|%+Post%(on%)|%+Pos
t%(in%)|%+Post%(for%)|%+Post%(from%)|%+Post%(with%)|%+P
ost%(to%)|%+Post%(till%)])
      (%+Emph) (%+Ptcl) (%+Emph) (%+Aux)
      ([%+IndSpeech1|%+IndSpeech2|%+IndSpeech3]))
      |
      [%+Rel [%+1|%+2|%+3] [%+Sg|%+Pl]
      [%+Nom|%+Erg|%+Dat|%+Gen|%+Ins|%+Advb|%+Voc]
      (%+Emph)
  ([%+Post%(like%)|%+Post%(with/at%)|%+Post%(on%)|%+Pos
t%(in%)|%+Post%(for%)|%+Post%(from%)|%+Post%(with%)|%+P
ost%(to%)|%+Post%(till%)])
      (%+Emph) (%+Ptcl) (%+Emph) (%+Aux)
      ([%+IndSpeech1|%+IndSpeech2|%+IndSpeech3]))
      |
      [%+Recp [%+1|%+2|%+3] [%+Sg|%+Pl]
      [%+Nom|%+Erg|%+Dat|%+Gen|%+Ins|%+Advb|%+Voc]
      (%+Emph)
  ([%+Post%(like%)|%+Post%(with/at%)|%+Post%(on%)|%+Pos
t%(in%)|%+Post%(for%)|%+Post%(from%)|%+Post%(with%)|%+P
ost%(to%)|%+Post%(till%)])
      (%+Emph) (%+Ptcl) (%+Emph) (%+Aux)
      ([%+IndSpeech1|%+IndSpeech2|%+IndSpeech3]))
      |
      [%+Neg [%+1|%+2|%+3] [%+Sg|%+Pl]
      [%+Nom|%+Erg|%+Dat|%+Gen|%+Ins|%+Advb|%+Voc]
      (%+Emph)
  ([%+Post%(like%)|%+Post%(with/at%)|%+Post%(on%)|%+Pos
t%(in%)|%+Post%(for%)|%+Post%(from%)|%+Post%(with%)|%+P
ost%(to%)|%+Post%(till%)])
      (%+Emph) (%+Ptcl) (%+Emph) (%+Aux)
      ([%+IndSpeech1|%+IndSpeech2|%+IndSpeech3]))
      |
      [%+Det [%+1|%+2|%+3] [%+Sg|%+Pl]
      [%+Nom|%+Erg|%+Dat|%+Gen|%+Ins|%+Advb|%+Voc]
      (%+Emph)
  ([%+Post%(like%)|%+Post%(with/at%)|%+Post%(on%)|%+Pos
t%(in%)|%+Post%(for%)|%+Post%(from%)|%+Post%(with%)|%+P
ost%(to%)|%+Post%(till%)])
      (%+Emph) (%+Ptcl) (%+Emph) (%+Aux)
      ([%+IndSpeech1|%+IndSpeech2|%+IndSpeech3]))]
```

Fig. 4.1 (continued)

```
  |
(Ipfv%+|Pfv%+)
%+Verb [[%+Main [%+IDt|%+IIDt|%+IIIDt]
      [%+AbsStat|%+RelStat|%+Dyn|%+RelDyn]
      [%+Intrans|%+IndTrans|%+Trans]
      [%+Act|%+AutAct|%+Inact|%+Pass|%+MPass]
  [%+Pres|%+Imperf|%+PresSbj|%+Fut|%+FutCond|%+FutSbj|%
+Aor|%+AorSbj|%+AorImp|%+Res1|%+Res2|%+PerfSbj]
  [[%+%<NomSubj%>|%+%<ErgSubj%>|%+%<DatSubj%>|%+%<NomSu
bjBen%>|%+%<ErgSubjBen%>|%+%<DatSubjBen%>|%+%<NomSubjCa
us%>|%+%<ErgSubjCaus%>|%+%<DatSubjCaus%>]
  ([%+%<NomObj%>|%+%<DatObj%>|%+%<DatObjBen%>|%+%<DatOb
jRec%>|%+%<DatObjLoc%>|%+%<DatObjPat%>|%+%<GenObj%(for%
)%>|%+%<DatObjRecCaus%>])
  ([%+%<NomObj%>|%+%<DatObj%>|%+%<DatObjBen%>|%+%<DatOb
jRec%>|%+%<DatObjLoc%>|%+%<DatObjPat%>|%+%<GenObj%(for%
)%>|%+%<DatObjRecCaus%>])]
      (%+Aux)
  [[%+Subj1Sg|%+Subj2Sg|%+Subj3Sg|%+Subj1Pl|%+Subj2Pl|%
+Subj3Pl|%+SubjBen1Sg|%+SubjBen2Sg|%+SubjBen3Sg|%+SubjB
en1Pl|%+SubjBen2Pl|%+SubjBen3Pl|%+SubjCaus1Sg|%+SubjCau
s2Sg|%+SubjCaus3Sg|%+SubjCaus1Pl|%+SubjCaus2Pl|%+SubjCa
us3Pl]
  ([%+Obj1Sg|%+Obj2Sg|%+Obj3Sg|%+Obj1Pl|%+Obj2Pl|%+Obj3
Pl|%+ObjBen1|%+ObjBen1Sg|%+ObjBen1Pl|%+ObjBen2|%+ObjBen
2Sg|%+ObjBen2Pl|%+ObjBen3|%+ObjLoc1|%+ObjLoc1Sg|%+ObjLo
c1Pl|%+ObjLoc2|%+ObjLoc2Sg|%+ObjLoc2Pl|%+ObjLoc3|%+ObjR
ec1|%+ObjRec1Sg|%+ObjRec1Pl|%+ObjRec2|%+Obj2RecSg|%+Obj
2RecPl|%+Obj3Rec|%+ObjRecCaus1|%+ObjRecCaus1Sg|%+ObjRec
Caus1Pl|%+ObjRecCaus2|%+Obj2RecCausSg|%+Obj2RecCausPl|%
+Obj3RecCaus|%+Obj1Pat|%+Obj1PatSg|%+Obj1PatPl|%+Obj2Pa
t|%+Obj2PatSg|%+Obj2PatPl|%+Obj3Pat])
  ([%+Obj1Sg|%+Obj2Sg|%+Obj3Sg|%+Obj1Pl|%+Obj2Pl|%+Obj3
Pl|%+ObjBen1|%+ObjBen1Sg|%+ObjBen1Pl|%+ObjBen2|%+ObjBen
2Sg|%+ObjBen2Pl|%+ObjBen3|%+ObjLoc1|%+ObjLoc1Sg|%+ObjLo
c1Pl|%+ObjLoc2|%+ObjLoc2Sg|%+ObjLoc2Pl|%+ObjLoc3|%+ObjR
ec1|%+ObjRec1Sg|%+ObjRec1Pl|%+ObjRec2|%+Obj2RecSg|%+Obj
2RecPl|%+Obj3Rec|%+ObjRecCaus1|%+ObjRecCaus1Sg|%+ObjRec
Caus1Pl|%+ObjRecCaus2|%+Obj2RecCausSg|%+Obj2RecCausPl|%
+Obj3RecCaus|%+Obj1Pat|%+Obj1PatSg|%+Obj1PatPl|%+Obj2Pa
t|%+Obj2PatSg|%+Obj2PatPl|%+Obj3Pat])]
      ([%+IndSpeech1|%+IndSpeech2|%+IndSpeech3])]
```

Fig. 4.1 (continued)

```
    |
      [%+Aux [%+Intrans|%+IndTrans|%+Trans]
      [%+Act|%+AutAct|%+Inact|%+Pass|%+MPass]
  [%+Pres|%+Imperf|%+PresSbj|%+Fut|%+FutCond|%+FutSbj|%
+Aor|%+AorSbj|%+AorImp|%+Res1|%+Res2|%+PerfSbj]
      [%+%<NomSubj%>|%+%<ErgSubj%>|%+%<DatSubj%>]
  [%+Subj1Sg|%+Subj2Sg|%+Subj3Sg|%+Subj1Pl|%+Subj2Pl|%+
Subj3Pl]
      ([%+IndSpeech1|%+IndSpeech2|%+IndSpeech3])]]
  |
%+VerbalNoun [%+Sg|%+Pl]
      [%+Nom|%+Erg|%+Dat|%+Gen|%+Ins|%+Advb|%+Voc]
      (%+Emph)
  ([%+Post%(like%)|%+Post%(with/at%)|%+Post%(on%)|%+Pos
t%(in%)|%+Post%(for%)|%+Post%(from%)|%+Post%(with%)|%+P
ost%(to%)|%+Post%(till%)])
      (%+Emph) (%+Ptcl) (%+Emph) (%+Aux)
      ([%+IndSpeech1|%+IndSpeech2|%+IndSpeech3])
  |
%+VerbalAdj [%+Sg|%+Pl]
      [%+Nom|%+Erg|%+Dat|%+Gen|%+Ins|%+Advb|%+Voc]
      (%+Emph)
  ([%+Post%(like%)|%+Post%(with/at%)|%+Post%(on%)|%+Pos
t%(in%)|%+Post%(for%)|%+Post%(from%)|%+Post%(with%)|%+P
ost%(to%)|%+Post%(till%)])
      (%+Emph) (%+Ptcl) (%+Emph) (%+Aux)
      ([%+IndSpeech1|%+IndSpeech2|%+IndSpeech3])
  |
%+Adv
[%+Loc|%+Temp|%+Mod|%+Quan|%+Caus|%+Spec|%+Q|%+Rel]

  ([%+Post%(like%)|%+Post%(with/at%)|%+Post%(on%)|%+Pos
t%(in%)|%+Post%(for%)|%+Post%(from%)|%+Post%(with%)|%+P
ost%(to%)|%+Post%(till%)])
      (%+Emph) (%+Ptcl) (%+Emph) (%+Aux)
      ([%+IndSpeech1|%+IndSpeech2|%+IndSpeech3])
  |
%+Conj [%+Coord|%+Subord]
      ([%+IndSpeech1|%+IndSpeech2|%+IndSpeech3])
  |
%+Part [%+Q|%+Rel|%+Proh|%+Aff|%+Int|%+Inf|%+Neg]
      ([%+IndSpeech1|%+IndSpeech2|%+IndSpeech3])
```

Fig. 4.1 (continued)

```
  |
%+Itj
      ([%+IndSpeech1|%+IndSpeech2|%+IndSpeech3])
  |
%+Abr
      ([%+IndSpeech1|%+IndSpeech2|%+IndSpeech3])
];
```

Fig. 4.1 (continued)

The sequence of tags (for the full list of tags see, Appendix A[1]) is predefined in accordance with the morphosyntactic structure already described. For example. The verbal adjective transducer represents the following sequence: string of characters followed by an optional language variety tag followed by a verbal adjective tag followed by a case tag followed by an optional extension vowel tag followed by an optional postposition tag followed by an optional extension vowel tag followed by an optional particle tag followed by an optional extension vowel tag followed by an optional auxiliary tag and followed by an optional indirect speech tag.

The consistency and ordering of tags were checked using projection and subtraction. Projection returns the upper or the lower levels of the network and allows us to extract projections of a transducer; for instance, the upper projection of a verbal noun network can be derived in the way shown in Fig. 4.2.

```
xfst [0]: set char-encoding utf8
set char-encoding utf8
variable char-encoding = UTF-8
xfst [0]: source masdar.script
source masdar.script
Opening input file 'masdar.script'
Etc.
0%>>>>>>>>>>>>>>>>>>>>>>>>>>>>>>>>100%
Closing 'masdar.fst'
Closing file masdar.script...
xfst [1]: define VerbalNoun ;
define VerbalNoun ;
Defined 'VerbalNoun': 183.8 Kb. 4227 states, 9162 arcs,
3906909820 paths.
xfst [0]: read regex VerbalNoun.u ;
read regex VerbalNoun.u ;
215.1 Kb. 4305 states, 11801 arcs, 720574447 paths.
xfst [1]: print words > upper.txt
print words > upper.txt
Opening 'upper.txt'
```

Fig. 4.2 Upper projection of a verbal noun network

[1]The appendix includes the finite-state tagset supplemented by language-specific units added to the MULTEXT-East Morphosyntactic Specifications for European languages in 2021 (Lobzhanidze 2021).

The upper projection of a network can be easily checked against the lexical tag grammar described previously. This checking is performed using subtraction, which allows us to obtain the lexical grammar language from the transducer and returns an empty language if the upper level is fully covered by the lexical grammar. The lexical grammar was changed during the compilation of the system and is checked against the network on an ongoing basis.

4.4 Language Coverage Test: Wordlists and Corpus Data

The language coverage test always depends on "zipfian" distributions (Zipf 1932). These distributions are based on the assumption that, in all languages, a small number of words has a high frequency of use, a larger number has an intermediate frequency of use, and an even larger number has a very low frequency of use which varies from 1 to 2 occurrences, and, that most frequent word is used twice as frequently as the second most frequent word, three times as frequently as the third, and so on. To assess and to improve the coverage and accuracy of the network, it is necessary to test it against wordlists and evaluate it on the basis of corpus data.

While evaluation against wordlists was a task implemented on an ongoing basis during the compilation of the morphological analyser from sources available online, evaluation against corpus data necessitated the compilation of a corpus, piping the corpus data to the tokenizer, breaking normal running text down into individual tokens, and then piping tokens into lookup tool with purpose of analysing them. The development of analyzer was carried out in parallel with the compilation of the corpus, which gave us the opportunity to carry out repeated testing on different kinds of texts.

4.4.1 Corpus Compilation

According to the general definition applied in corpus linguistics, a corpus is a collection of texts 'bound' together through specific parameters and principles. More broadly, a corpus can be defined with reference to the following quotations:

> "A linguistic corpus is a collection of texts which have been selected and brought together so that language can be studied on the computer." (Wynne 2005)

> "A corpus is a collection of texts assumed to be representative of a given language, dialect, or other subset of a language to be used for linguistic analysis." (Francis 1991)

> "A corpus is understood to be a collection of samples of running text. The texts may be in spoken, written or intermediate forms, and the samples may be of any length." (Aarts 1991)

A corpus is simultaneously an output of textual data processing and a tool enabling the study of language data and the application of these data for the further production of dictionaries and grammars of language. In our case, the development and testing of the morphological analyser for Georgian is associated with the compilation of the Georgian Language Corpus (Doborjginidze et al. 2012–2014) freely available online at http://corpora.iliauni.edu.ge/ (last accessed 15 September, 2019). The Corpus was designed in 2013 to support the development of corpus annotation tools for languages with rich morphologies like Georgian (Project No AR/320/4-105/11 implemented under the financial support of the Shota Rustaveli National Science Foundation) and to facilitate interdisciplinary approaches to the study of the Georgian language.

The content of the corpus was chosen to represent the Georgian literary language beginning from the sixth century and ending in 2014 and to test tools on different varieties of literary Georgian. The orientation of the corpus varies over centuries, and although it was constructed to be internally contrastive, it can be considered neither a standard historical corpus representing a unified picture of the language over time, nor a parallel corpus representing only a few texts of Old Georgian manuscripts such as *the Georgian Chronicles* (Abuladze 1973) in parallel.

The GLC was developed based on the following:

- An interdisciplinary approach to the texts, including compilation, systematization and online accessibility of printed and manuscript data;
- A taxonomy of corpus design dealing with selection of sources, obtaining copyright permissions, providing markup and processing of texts;
- Machine-readable standards (ISO No 24614-1 2010, No 24611 2012, No 24610-1 2006, No 24613 2008, No 10646. 2017, etc. and TEI P5 guidelines (TEI Consortium 2019).

The GLC consists of approximately 15 million words of written text without punctuation marks. The corpus texts are represented in a variety of genres, including newspaper and magazine articles, prosaic, scientific and fiction literature, poems, and others.

The GLC is composed of written text because neither the tools nor the time were available to provide appropriate transcriptions to audio files. This gap in corpus design may be filled in the future. The written texts were obtained from books and newspapers to provide representations of different subject areas, including sciences like chemistry and physics. In the majority of cases, the texts were collected and typed by research assistants under the supervision of the collection coordinators: Svetlana Berikashvili (the Parallel Corpus of the Georgian Chronicles), George Tadumadze (Corpus of New and Modern Georgian Language), Tsira Khakhviashvili, and Nato Bilanishvili (Old Georgian Translation Corpus, Pre-Athonite Period); some electronic texts were obtained directly from the copyright owners, but access to these texts is restricted in some ways.

4.4.2 Corpus Processing and Markup

Taking into consideration the challenges associated with the diverse textual material included in the corpus, the corpus pre-processing stages were somewhat time-consuming; these included not only the collection, but also the description and preparation of the texts as follows:

(a) Conversion of texts provided in .pdf, .docx etc. format into plain text format and their encoding in utf-8 format;
(b) Removal of front and end content including tables of contents, bibliographies, references, indices, etc. with the purpose of retaining only plain text starting with the first chapter or introduction and finishing with the last chapter or conclusions and avoiding an artificial increase in number of frequent words. Information contained in front and end content is partially represented in meta-annotation;
(c) Removal of tables, formulas, images, etc. from texts to avoid text interruption with items which are irrelevant from a linguistic point of view. Deletions were marked with <gap/> element. Foreign words were however retained with the purpose of quantifying foreign influence on Georgian;
(d) The ends of lines of poetic and prosaic texts were tagged with the element <lb/> to preserve the structure of text.

The further processing of the corpus texts was associated with the preparation of meta- and inner annotation of texts, especially in the case of unstructured Old Georgian data. For the tags associated with the description of textual material, which generally follows TEI P5 guidelines with regards to text corpora (TEI Consortium 2019), see Appendix C.

4.4.2.1 Header

The texts included in the corpus have been appended with header information. This information was entered manually in the form of a <teiHeader> block with the purpose of representing meta-annotation and for subsequent inclusion in the PhP/MySQL database. Metadata is defined as 'data about data' (Wynne 2005) and provides information about corpus texts in accordance with the TEI P5 Guidelines. It consists of the following four subdivisions:

- <fileDesc> – contains a full bibliographic description of a file's so-called 'main characteristics';
- <profileDesc> – provides a detailed description of the non-bibliographic aspects of a text;
- <encodingDesc> – shows the relationship between an electronic text and the source or sources from which it was derived, and especially describes the editorial rules of publication;
- <revisionDesc> – summarizes the revision history of a file.

These blocks allowed us to prepare complex queries on annotated data subsequently and to manage structured documents. The variety of documents involved, which ranged from handwritten manuscripts to printed books, required a range of different approaches to annotation; according to the type of text in question, all corpus files are equipped with the following information distributed within the aforementioned four subdivisions:

- Project description: funding institution, leading institution, responsible person: first name, last name, responsible person's obligations, institution, project name;

- File description: file author: first name, last name, file source, file language, file size, kB, date of creation, place of creation, information about file revision, etc.;
- Printed text description: text title, author: first name, last name, source language, date of creation, place of origin, publisher, place of publication, date of publication, editor, translator, illustrator, number of volumes/issues, number of pages, text pages from … to …, ISBN/ISSN, availability, distributor, authorized institution, notes;
- Manuscript description: location, name of repository, number of repository, name of collection, additional identification code, catalogue number, manuscript author, copyist or compiler: first name, last name, statement of responsibility, etc., manuscript title;
  - Manuscript language and script: *Asomtavruli* – Majuscule, *Nuskhuri* – Minuscule/Cursive, *Mkhedruli* – Civil;
  - Physical condition of the manuscript: form of the object, material, paper, number of papers, paper size type, height, width, manuscript condition (description of revisions, damage), foliation type (for instance recto, verso, etc.), paper collation type (for instance mixed sequence);
  - Formal description of the manuscript: description of handwriting, script description, description of miniatures and decorations, metatexts;
  - History of manuscript: place of origin, date of origin, provenance from creation to archiving (if any), information about manuscript purchase or donation.

4.4.2.2 Text

After preparation, some of the texts were converted to .xml and some kept in .txt format. These files contained standard annotations of textual data, although some points of annotation were distinct for different types of texts:

- Old and Middle Georgian unpublished manuscripts were represented with 2D00–2D2F and/or 10A0–10FF appended by the 10A0–10FF range, while Modern Georgian texts were represented strictly by the 10A0–10FF range of Unicode Standard;
- The standard markup included information on divisions, page numbers, titles, paragraphs, line breaks, etc.;
- In addition to the standard markup, unpublished manuscripts were equipped with information on marginalia, additions, deletions, damages, highlighted sections and abbreviations;
- Some symbols and specifically titlo diacritics were substituted by special xml characters such as ~ ˜ etc.

4.4.2.3 Summary

Although the compilation of the corpus is not yet finished, and the research group is adding Old and Middle Georgian texts to it on an ongoing basis, two characteristics of the corpus can be noted at this time: (a) .xml files are validated against RELAX

NG and Schematron schemas; (b) the header data allows us to subdivide the texts collected and processed into the following types: fiction, non-fiction, poetry, newspapers, periodicals and others.

4.4.3 Language Coverage

A language coverage test was implemented with the purpose of assessing the lexicon of the transducer from the point of view of frequency. As discussed above, the test was implemented against both wordlists and corpus data. The wordlists were compiled from a number of texts available online and contained a set of words typed one to a line in alphabetical order, while the corpus data were obtained from the GLC. In both cases, special attention was paid to more frequent words. Failures in recognition were stored in separate files which were processed, assigned appropriate continuation classes and added to the lexicon of the transducer. The procedure was carried out according to the following schema: Corpus → Tokenizer → Looku p → Output analysis (Fig. 4.3).

```
type inpute.txt | tokenize tokenizer.fst -utf8 | lookup
-flags mbL:LTT analyzer.fst -utf8 > output.txt
```

Fig. 4.3 Checking of the transducer

A list of the most frequent words was automatically generated from the GLC separately for Modern and for Old Georgian. Taking into consideration the Zipfian distribution, special attention was paid to the 10,000 most frequent words in Modern and Old Georgian. These words were studied from the recognition perspective of inflected words—specifically, nominals and verbs, as well as uninflected words.

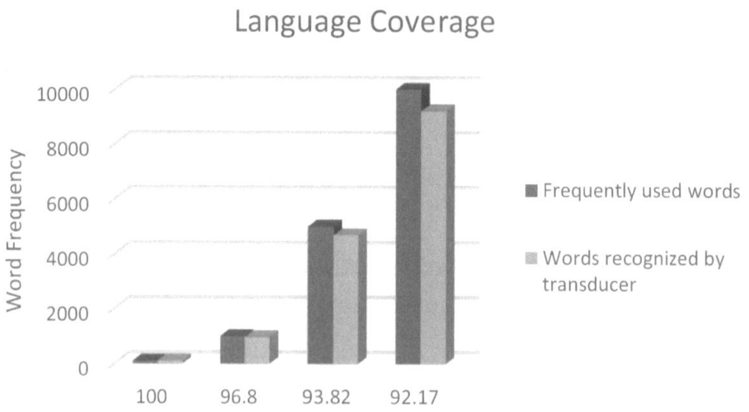

Fig. 4.4 Language coverage test for Modern Georgian (Lobzhanidze 2019)

As can be seen (Fig. 4.4), the transducer for Modern Georgian recognized only 92.17% of the 10,000 most frequently used words. The unrecognized words were analyzed and added to the relevant lexicons. The number of verbs per 1000 most frequent words was 530, including 521 recognized by the transducer and 9 not recognized by the transducer, so that the recognition rate for verbs was 98.31%. This recognition rate enables us to predict approximately 85-90% coverage in a random corpus of Modern Georgian.

At the same time, in analysing the forms recognized by the transducer for Modern Georgian, overlapping must be noted between different paradigms within the first diathesis—namely between classes No. 19 and No. 26 (264)—and between different diatheses, namely between classes No.28, No. 29, No. 30 and No. 47 (265).

(264) *ket-av-s* 'shuts smth.'
shut-TS-3SGSbj:PRS.IND

კეტავს: Ipfv+კეტავ-ს+Verb+Main+IDt+#19+Din+Trans+Act+Pres+<NomSubj>+<DatObj>+Subj3Sg+Obj3

კეტავს: Ipfv+კეტავ-ს+Verb+Main+IDt+#26+Din+Trans+Act+Pres+<NomSubj>+<DatObj>+Subj3Sg+Obj3

(265) *da-int'-o* 'was lit for smb.'
PV.PFV-light-3SGSbj:AOR.IND or PV.PFV-light-3SGSbj:AOR.SUBJ

დაინთო: Pfv+ინთებ-ს+Verb+Main+IDt+#29+Din+Trans+Act+AorSbj+<ErgSubjBen>+<NomObj>+SubjBen2Sg+Obj3

დაინთო: Pfv+ინთებ-ს+Verb+Main+IDt+#30+Din+Trans+Act+Aor+<ErgSubjBen>+<NomObj>+SubjBen2Sg+Obj3+IndSpeech3

დაინთო: Pfv+ინთებ-ს+Verb+Main+IDt+#30+Din+Trans+Act+AorSbj+<ErgSubjBen>+<NomObj>+SubjBen2Sg+Obj3

დაინთო: Pfv+ინთებ-ა+Verb+Main+IIDt+#47+Din+Intr+Pass/AutAct+AorSbj+<NomSubjBen>+SubjBen2Sg

დაინთო: Pfv+ანთებ-ს+Verb+Main+IDt+#28+Din+Trans+Act+AorSbj+<ErgSubjBen>+<NomObj>+SubjBen2Sg+Obj3

დაინთო: Pfv+ინთებ-ს+Verb+Main+IDt+#29+Din+Trans+Act+Aor+<ErgSubjBen>+<NomObj>+SubjBen3Sg+Obj3

დაინთო: Pfv+ინთებ-ს+Verb+Main+IDt+#30+Din+Trans+Act+Aor+<ErgSubjBen>+<NomObj>+SubjBen3Sg+Obj3

დაინთო: Pfv+ინთებ-ა+Verb+Main+IIDt+#47+Din+Intr+Pass/AutAct+Aor+<NomSubjBen>+SubjBen3Sg

These classes generally differ in structure and at the same time generate similar forms for aorist and aorist subjunctive screeves.

In comparison with the transducer for Modern Georgian language, the recognition rate of Middle and Old Georgian is lower (Fig. 4.5).

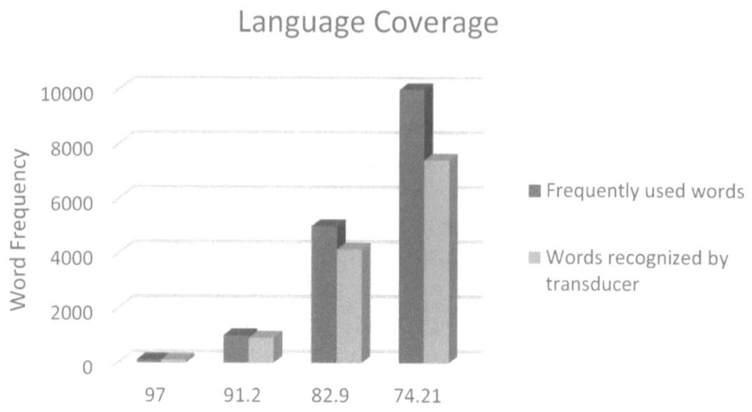

Fig. 4.5 Language coverage test for Old and Middle Georgian

As can be seen, the transducer recognized only 74.21% of the 10,000 most frequently used words in the case of Old and Middle Georgian. While words continue to be added to the relevant lexicons, the lower recognition rate is due predominantly to chaotic spacing between words, the absence of punctuation marks and a large number of abbreviated forms, which we hope to reduce by enabling the tokenizer to calculate the number of syllables in a word and by compiling special lexicon for forms abbreviated with titlo diacritics. The number of verbs per 1000 most frequent words was equal to 166, which included 105 recognized by the transducer and 61 not recognized by the transducer, yielding a recognition rate for verbs of approximately 64%. This recognition rate means that, at the time of writing, we can predict recognition of approximately 65–70% of words in a random corpus of Old and Middle language; as work on these issues is ongoing, this rate will no doubt be improved.

4.5 Summary

The testing results discussed in this chapter allow us to predict possible word recognition rates with regard to the future enrichment of the lexicon. At the time of writing, the lexicon encompasses all major available dictionaries of Old and Modern Georgian and can be added to manually by determining the relevant lexicon class, with the purpose of ensuring the correct generation of inflections. This manual work is being done by linguists and those who are otherwise familiar with the grammatical structure of Georgian.

References

Aarts, J. 1991. Intuition-based and observation-based grammars. In *English Corpus Linguistics*, 44–62. New York: Routledge.

Abuladze, Ilia. 1973. *żveli k'art'uli enis lek'sikoni (dictionary of old Georgian language)*. Tbilisi: mec'niereba (Science).

Beesley, Kenneth, Karttunen, Lauri. 2003. *Finite-state morphology: Xerox tools and techniques*. Stanford: CSLI Publications.

Doborjginidze, Nino, Lobzhanidze, Irina, Gunia, Irakli. 2012. *Georgian language corpus*. http://corpora.iliauni.edu.ge/. Accessed 30 Oct 2019.

Doborjginidze, Nino, Lobzhanidze, Irina, Mirianashvili, George. 2014. *Corpus of georgian chronicles*. http://corpora.iliauni.edu.ge/. Accessed 30 Oct 2019.

Francis, Nelson. 1991. Language corpora B.C. In *Directions in corpus linguistics*, 17–32. Berlin: Mouton de Gruyter.

Lobzhanidze, Irina. 2019. Computational model of the modern Georgian language and search patterns for an online dictionary of idioms. In *Language, logic, and computation*, Lecture notes in computer science, ed. A. Silva, S. Staton, P. Sutton, and C. Umbach, vol. 11456, 187–208. Lagodekhi, Georgia: TbiLLC 2018.

———. 2021. Georgian specifications. In *MULTEXT-east morphosyntactic specifications*, ed. Erjavec T. http://nl.ijs.si/ME/V6/msd/html/msd-ka.html. Accessed 07 July 2021.

Standardization, ISO. 2006. *Language resource management — Feature structures — Part 1: Feature structure representation, No 24610-1*. https://www.iso.org/standard/37324.html. Accessed 16 July 2019.

———. 2008. *Language resource management - lexical markup framework (LMF), No 24613*. https://www.iso.org/standard/37327.html. Accessed 16 July 2019.

———. 2010. *Language resource management — Word segmentation of written texts — Part 1: Basic concepts and general principles, No 24614-1*. https://www.iso.org/standard/41665.html. Accessed 16 July 2019.

———. 2012. *Language resource management – Morpho-syntactic annotation framework (MAF), No 24611*. https://www.iso.org/standard/51934.html. Accessed 16 July 2019.

———. 2017. *Information technology — Universal Coded Character Set (UCS), No 10646*. https://www.iso.org/standard/69119.html. Accessed 16 July 2019.

TEI Consortium, e. 2019. *TEI P5: Guidelines for electronic text encoding and interchange*. https://tei-c.org/guidelines/p5/. Accessed 29 Nov 2019.

Wynne, Martin. 2005. *Developing linguistic corpora: A guide to good practice*. Oxford: Oxbow Books for the Arts and Humanities Data Service.

Zipf, George. 1932. *Selected studies of the principle of relative frequency in language*. Cambridge: Harvard University Press.

Appendix A: Morphosyntactic Tags

The following tables contain two types of tagsets: Tagset 1 contains morphosyntactic tags used in the morphological analyser of Georgian and follows the conventions of finite state morphology[1]; Tagset 2 proposes codes which can be used for Georgian as a component of morphosyntactic specifications already developed for the majority of Indo-European languages.[2] Attribute-value pairs are defined only where a morpho-syntactic description is not sufficiently language specific; otherwise, attribute-values are omitted.

Table A.1 General tags

Variety definition	FS Tag
Old Georgian	+OGE
Modern Georgian	+MGE

Table A.2 Table of categories

PoS	FS Tags	Code	Attributes
Noun	+Noun	N	5
Verb	+Verb	V	11
Adjective	+Adj	A	5
Numeral	+Num	M	4
Pronoun	+Pron	P	5
Conjunction	+Conj	C	1
Particle	+Part	Q	1
Adverb	+Adv	R	2
Adposition	+Post	S	1
Interjection	+Itj	I	-
Abbreviation	+Abr	Y	4
Punctuation Marks	+F	Z	-

[1] Finite-state tagset specially elaborated within the framework of Project on the Compilation of Corpus annotation tools (No. AR/320/4-105/11) financed by the Shota Rustaveli National Science Foundation

[2] The codes are similar to those used in the MULTEXT-East Morphosyntactic Specifications for European languages, available at http://nl.ijs.si/ME/V6/msd/html/msd.html (last accessed September 09, 2019). Georgian, which has been supplemented by language-specific units such as 'z' for ergative case, was added to this specification in 2021 (Lobzhanidze 2021).

I. Lobzhanidze, *Finite-State Computational Morphology*,
https://doi.org/10.1007/978-3-030-90248-3

Table A.3 Noun morphosyntactic tags

		Noun	+Noun	N
Attribute	Add. Attr.	Value	FS Tags	Code
Type		Proper	+Prop	p
		Common	+Com	c
	Sub-type	Personal names	+Name	-
		Geographical Names	+Geog	-
Animacy		Animate	+Anim	y
		Inanimate	+Inanim	n
Number		Singular	+Sg	s
		Plural	+Pl	p
Case		Nominative	+Nom	n
		Ergative	+Erg	z
		Dative	+Dat	d
		Genitive	+Gen	g
		Instrumental	+Ins	i
		Adverbial	+Advb	w
		Vocative	+Voc	v
Clitics		Postposition	+Post	t
	Sub-type	Postpositions, vitʻ, ebr, ebriv, mebr ʻlikeʼ	+Post(like)	-
		Postposition, tʻan ʻwith/atʼ	+Post(with/at)	-
		Postposition, ze ʻonʼ	+Post(on)	-
		Postposition, ši ʻinʼ	+Post(in)	-
		Postposition, tʻvis ʻforʼ	+Post(for)	-
		Postposition, gan, dan ʻfromʼ	+Post(from)	-
		Postposition, urtʻ ʻwithʼ	+Post(with)	-
		Postposition, ken ʻtoʼ	+Post(to)	-
		Postpositions, dmi, mde, mdi, mdin, mdis, da, dam, dami ʻtillʼ	+Post(till)	-
		Indirect Speech, 1st person	+IndSpeech1	-
		Indirect Speech, 2nd person	+IndSpeech2	-
		Indirect Speech, 3rd person	+IndSpeech3	-
		Particle	+Ptcl	Q
		Auxiliary	+Aux	a
		Extension vowel	+Emph	-

Table A.4 Adjective morphosyntactic tags

		Adjective	+Adj	A
Attribute	Add. Attr.	Definition	FS Tags	Code
Degree		Diminutive	+Dim	d
		Positive	+Pos	p
		Comparative	+Com	c
		Superlative	+Sup	s
Number		Singular	+Sg	s
		Plural	+Pl	p
Case		Nominative	+Nom	n
		Ergative	+Erg	z
		Dative	+Dat	d
		Genitive	+Gen	g
		Instrumental	+Ins	i
		Adverbial	+Advb	w
		Vocative	+Voc	v
Clitics		Postposition	+Post	t
	Sub-type	Postpositions, *vit‘, ebr, ebriv, mebr* ‘like’	+Post(like)	-
		Postposition, *t‘an* ‘with/at’	+Post(with/at)	-
		Postposition, *ze* ‘on’	+Post(on)	-
		Postposition, *ši* ‘in’	+Post(in)	-
		Postposition, *t‘vis* ‘for’	+Post(for)	-
		Postposition, *gan, dan* ‘from’	+Post(from)	-
		Postposition, *urt‘* ‘with’	+Post(with)	-
		Postposition, *ken* ‘to’	+Post(to)	-
		Postpositions, *dmi, mde, mdi, mdin, mdis, da, dam, dami* ‘till’	+Post(till)	-
		Indirect Speech, 1st person	+IndSpeech1	-
		Indirect Speech, 2nd person	+IndSpeech2	-
		Indirect Speech, 3rd person	+IndSpeech3	-
		Particle	+Ptcl	Q
		Auxiliary	+Aux	a
		Extension vowel	+Emph	-

Table A.5 Numeral morphosyntactic tags

		Numeral	+Num	M
Attribute	Add. Attr.	Value	FS Tags	Code
Type		Cardinal	+Card	c
		Ordinal	+Ord	o
		Fractional	+Fract	f
		Approximative	+Approx	a
		Multiple	+Mul	m
Form		Alphabetic	+Alpha	c
		Roman	+Roman	r
		Digit	+Digit	d
		Letter	+Letter	l
Number		Singular	+Sg	s
		Plural	+Pl	p
Case		Nominative	+Nom	n
		Ergative	+Erg	z
		Dative	+Dat	d
		Genitive	+Gen	g
		Instrumental	+Ins	i
		Adverbial	+Advb	w
		Vocative	+Voc	v
Clitics		Postposition	+Post	t
	Sub-type	Postpositions, *vit‘, ebr, ebriv, mebr* ‘like’	+Post(like)	-
		Postposition, *t‘an* ‘with/at’	+Post(with/at)	-
		Postposition, *ze* ‘on’	+Post(on)	-
		Postposition, *ši* ‘in’	+Post(in)	-
		Postposition, *t‘vis* ‘for’	+Post(for)	-
		Postposition, *gan, dan* ‘from’	+Post(from)	-
		Postposition, *urt‘* ‘with’	+Post(with)	-
		Postposition, *ken* ‘to’	+Post(to)	-
		Postpositions, *dmi, mde, mdi, mdin, mdis, da, dam, dami* ‘till’	+Post(till)	-
		Indirect Speech, 1st person	+IndSpeech1	-
		Indirect Speech, 2nd person	+IndSpeech2	-
		Indirect Speech, 3rd person	+IndSpeech3	-
		Particle	+Ptcl	Q
		Auxiliary	+Aux	a
		Extension vowel	+Emph	-

Table A.6 Pronoun morphosyntactic tags

		Pronoun	+Pron	P
Attribute	Add. Attr.	Value	FS Tags	Code
Type		Personal	+Pers	p
		Demonstrative	+Dem	d
		Possessive	+Poss	s
		Indefinite	+Indf	i
		Interrogative	+Int	q
		Relative	+Rel	r
		Reciprocal	+Recp	y
		Negative	+Neg	z
		Determinal	+Det	m
Person		First	+1	1
		Second	+2	2
		Third	+3	3
Number		Singular	+Sg	s
		Plural	+Pl	p
Case		Nominative	+Nom	n
		Ergative	+Erg	z
		Dative	+Dat	d
		Genitive	+Gen	g
		Instrumental	+Ins	i
		Adverbial	+Advb	w
		Vocative	+Voc	v
Clitics		Postposition	+Post	t
	Sub-type	Postpositions, *vit‘, ebr, ebriv, mebr* ‘like’	+Post(like)	-
		Postposition, *t‘an* ‘with/at’	+Post(with/at)	-
		Postposition, *ze* ‘on’	+Post(on)	-
		Postposition, *ši* ‘in’	+Post(in)	-
		Postposition, *t‘vis* ‘for’	+Post(for)	-
		Postposition, *gan, dan* ‘from’	+Post(from)	-
		Postposition, *urt‘* ‘with’	+Post(with)	-
		Postposition, *ken* ‘to’	+Post(to)	-
		Postpositions, *dmi, mde, mdi, mdin, mdis, da, dam, dami* ‘till’	+Post(till)	-
		Indirect Speech, 1st person	+IndSpeech1	-
		Indirect Speech, 2nd person	+IndSpeech2	-
		Indirect Speech, 3rd person	+IndSpeech3	-
		Particle	+Ptcl	Q
		Auxiliary	+Aux	a
		Extension vowel	+Emph	-

Table A.7 Verb morphosyntactic tags

		Verb	+Verb	V
Attribute	Add. Attr.	Value	FS Tags	Code
Type		Main	+Main	m
		Auxiliary	+Aux	a
	Sub-type	Absolute Stative	+AbsStat	-
		Relative Stative	+RelStat	-
		Dynamic	+Dyn	-
		Relative Dynamic	+RelDyn	-
VForm		Indicative	+Ind	i
		Subjunctive	+Subj	s
		Imperative	+Imp	m
		Causative	+Caus	z
		Participle	+VerbalAdj	p
		Gerund, Masdar	+VerbalNoun	g
Tense &		Present Indicative	+Pres	p
mood		Imperfect Indicative	+Imperf	i
		Present Subjunctive	+PresSbj	-
		Future Indicative	+Fut	f
		Future Conditional	+FutCond	-
		Future Subjunctive	+FutSbj	-
		Aorist Indicative	+Aor	a
		Aorist Subjunctive	+AorSbj	-
		Aorist Imperative	+AorImp	-
		Perfect Indicative	+Res1	n
		Pluperfect	+Res2	l
		Perfect Subjunctive	+PerfSbj	-
Aspect		Progressive, imperfective	Ipfv+	p
		Perfective	Pfv+	e
Number		Singular	+Sg	s
		Plural	+Pl	p
Transitivity		Intransitive	+Intrans	-
		Indirect transitive	+IndTrans	-
		Transitive	+Trans	-
Subject &		First Subject, Singular	+Subj1Sg	-
object		Second Subject, Singular	+Subj2Sg	-
correlation, person, number		Third Subject, Singular	+Subj3Sg	-
		First Subject, Plural	+Subj1Pl	-
		Second Subject, Plural	+Subj2Pl	-
		Third Subject, Plural	+Subj3Pl	-
		First Subject, Singular, Beneficiary	+SubjBen1Sg	-
		Second Subject, Singular, Beneficiary	+SubjBen2Sg	-

(continued)

Table A.7 (continued)

		Verb	+Verb	V
		Third Subject, Singular, Beneficiary	+SubjBen3Sg	-
		First Subject, Plural, Beneficiary	+SubjBen1Pl	-
		Second Subject, Plural, Beneficiary	+SubjBen2Pl	-
		Third Subject, Plural, Beneficiary	+SubjBen3Pl	-
		First Subject, Singular, Causer	+SubjCaus1Sg	-
		Second Subject, Singular, Causer	+SubjCaus2Sg	-
		Third Subject, Singular, Causer	+SubjCaus3Sg	-
		First Subject, Plural, Causer	+SubjCaus1Pl	-
		Second Subject, Plural, Causer	+SubjCaus2Pl	-
		Third Subject, Plural, Causer	+SubjCaus3Pl	-
		First Object, Singular	+Obj1Sg	-
		Second Object, Singular	+Obj2Sg	-
		Third Object, Singular	+Obj3Sg	-
		First Object, Plural	+Obj1Pl	-
		Second Object, Plural	+Obj2Pl	-
		Third Object, Plural	+Obj3Pl	-
		First Object, Beneficiary	+ObjBen1	-
		First Object, Singular, Beneficiary	+ObjBen1Sg	-
		First Object, Plural, Beneficiary	+ObjBen1Pl	-
		Second Object, Beneficiary	+ObjBen2	-
		Second Object, Singular, Beneficiary	+ObjBen2Sg	-
		Second Object, Plural, Beneficiary	+ObjBen2Pl	-
		Third Object, Beneficiary	+ObjBen3	-
		First Object Locative	+ObjLoc1	-
		First Object Locative, Singular	+ObjLoc1Sg	-
		First Object Locative, Plural	+ObjLoc1Pl	-
		Second Object Locative	+ObjLoc2	-
		Second Object Locative, Singular	+ObjLoc2Sg	-
		Second Object Locative, Plural	+ObjLoc2Pl	-
		Third Object Locative	+ObjLoc3	-
		First Object Recipient	+ObjRec1	-
		First Object Recipient, Singular	+ObjRec1Sg	-
		First Object Recipient, Plural	+ObjRec1Pl	-
		Second Object Recipient	+ObjRec2	-
		Second Object Recipient, Singular	+Obj2RecSg	-
		Second Object Recipient, Plural	+Obj2RecPl	-
		Third Object Recipient	+Obj3Rec	-
		First Object Recipient, Causee	+ObjRecCaus1	-
		First Object Recipient, Causee	+ObjRecCaus1Sg	-
		First Object Recipient, Causee	+ObjRecCaus1Pl	-
		Second Object Recipient, Causee	+ObjRecCaus2	-
		Second Object Recipient, Causee	+Obj2RecCausSg	-
		Second Object Recipient, Causee	+Obj2RecCausPl	-

(continued)

Table A.7 (continued)

		Verb	+Verb	V
		Third Object Recipient, Causee	+Obj3RecCaus	-
		First Object Patient	+Obj1Pat	-
		First Object, Singular, Patient	+Obj1PatSg	-
		First Object, Plural, Patient	+Obj1PatPl	-
		Second Object Patient	+Obj2Pat	-
		Second Object, Singular, Patient	+Obj2PatSg	-
		Second Object, Plural, Patient	+Obj2PatPl	-
		Third Object Patient	+Obj3Pat	-
Voice		I diathesis	+IDt	-
		II diathesis	+IIDt	-
		III diathesis	+IIIDt	-
	Sub-type	Active	+Act	a
		Autoactive	+AutAct	c
		Inactive	+Inact	i
		Passive	+Pass	p
		Mediopassive	+MPass	d
Case		Nominative	+Nom	n
		Ergative	+Erg	z
		Dative	+Dat	d
		Genitive	+Gen	g
		Instrumental	+Ins	i
		Adverbial	+Advb	w
		Vocative	+Voc	v
Subject &		Subject Nominative	+<NomSubj>	-
object		Subject Ergative	+<ErgSubj>	-
cases		Subject Dative	+<DatSubj>	-
		Subject Nominative, Beneficiary	+<NomSubjBen>	-
		Subject Ergative, Beneficiary	+<ErgSubjBen>	-
		Subject Dative, Beneficiary	+<DatSubjBen>	-
		Object Nominative	+<NomObj>	-
		Object Dative	+<DatObj>	-
		Object Dative, Beneficiary	+<DatObjBen>	-
		Object Dative, Recipient	+<DatObjRec>	-
		Object Dative, Locative	+<DatObjLoc>	-
		Object Dative, Patient	+<DatObjPat>	-
		Object Genitive	+<GenObj(for)>	-
		Subject Nominative, Causer	+<NomSubjCaus>	-
		Subject Ergative, Causer	+<ErgSubjCaus>	-
		Subject Dative, Causer	+<DatSubjCaus>	-
		Object Dative, Causee	+<DatObjRecCaus>	-
Clitics		Postposition	+Post	t
	Sub-type	Postpositions, *vit'*, *ebr*, *ebriv*, *mebr* 'like'	+Post(like)	-

(continued)

Table A.7 (continued)

		Verb	+Verb	V
		Postposition, *t'an* 'with/at'	+Post(with/at)	-
		Postposition, *ze* 'on'	+Post(on)	-
		Postposition, *ši* 'in'	+Post(in)	-
		Postposition, *t'vis* 'for'	+Post(for)	-
		Postposition, *gan, dan* 'from'	+Post(from)	-
		Postposition, *urt'* 'with'	+Post(with)	-
		Postposition, *ken* 'to'	+Post(to)	-
		Postpositions, *dmi, mde, mdi, mdin, mdis, da, dam, dami* 'till'	+Post(till)	-
		Indirect Speech, 1st person	+IndSpeech1	-
		Indirect Speech, 2nd person	+IndSpeech2	-
		Indirect Speech, 3rd person	+IndSpeech3	-
		Particle	+Ptcl	Q
		Auxiliary	+Aux	a
		Extension vowel	+Emph	-

Table A.8 Adverb morphosyntactic tags

		Adverb	+Adv	R
Attribute	Add. Attr.	Value	FS Tags	Code
Type		Local	+Loc	l
		Temporal	+Temp	t
		Modifier	+Mod	m
		Quantitative	+Quan	u
		Causal	+Caus	c
		Specifier	+Spec	s
		Interrogative	+Q	i
		Relative	+Rel	l
Clitics		Postposition	+Post	t
	Sub-type	Postpositions, *vit', ebr, ebriv, mebr* 'like'	+Post(like)	-
		Postposition, *t'an* 'with/at'	+Post(with/at)	-
		Postposition, *ze* 'on'	+Post(on)	-
		Postposition, *ši* 'in'	+Post(in)	-
		Postposition, *t'vis* 'for'	+Post(for)	-
		Postposition, *gan, dan* 'from'	+Post(from)	-
		Postposition, *urt'* 'with'	+Post(with)	-
		Postposition, *ken* 'to'	+Post(to)	-
		Postpositions, *dmi, mde, mdi, mdin, mdis, da, dam, dami* 'till'	+Post(till)	-
		Indirect Speech, 1st person	+IndSpeech1	-
		Indirect Speech, 2nd person	+IndSpeech2	-
		Indirect Speech, 3rd person	+IndSpeech3	-

Table A.9 Conjunction morphosyntactic tags

		Conjunction	+Conj	C
Attribute	Add. Attr.	Definition	FS Tags	Code
Type		Coordinating	+Coord	c
		Subordinating	+Subord	s

Table A.10 Particle morphosyntactic tags

		Particle	+Part	Q
Attribute	Add. Attr.	Definition	FS Tags	Code
Type		Interrogative	+Q	-
		Relative	+Rel	-
		Prohibitive	+Proh	-
		Affirmative	+Aff	-
		Intensive	+Int	-
		Infinitive	+Inf	-
		Negative	+Neg	-

Table A.11 Interjection morphosyntactic tags

		Interjection	+Itj	I
Attribute	Add. Attr.	Value	FS Tags	Code

Table A.12 Adposition morphosyntactic tags

		Adposition	-	Y
Attribute	Add. Attr.	Value	FS Tags	Code
Type		Postposition	+Post	t

Table A.13 Abbreviation morphosyntactic tags

		Abbreviation	+Abr	Y
Attribute	Add. Attr.	Value	FS Tags	Code
Type		Nominal	+Noun	-
		Verbal	+Verb	-
		Adjectival	+Adj	-
		Adverbial	+Adv	-
Number		Singular	+Sg	s
		Plural	+Pl	p
Case		Nominative	+Nom	n
		Ergative	+Erg	z
		Dative	+Dat	d
		Genitive	+Gen	g
		Instrumental	+Ins	i
		Adverbial	+Advb	w
		Vocative	+Voc	v
Clitics		Postposition	+Post	t
	Sub-type	Postpositions, vit‘, ebr, ebriv, mebr ‘like’	+Post(like)	-
		Postposition, t‘an ‘with/at’	+Post(with/at)	-
		Postposition, ze ‘on’	+Post(on)	-
		Postposition, ši ‘in’	+Post(in)	-
		Postposition, t‘vis ‘for’	+Post(for)	-
		Postposition, gan, dan ‘from’	+Post(from)	-
		Postposition, urt‘ ‘with’	+Post(with)	-
		Postposition, ken ‘to’	+Post(to)	-
		Postpositions, dmi, mde, mdi, mdin, mdis, da, dam, dami ‘till’	+Post(till)	-
		Indirect Speech, 1st person	+IndSpeech1	-
		Indirect Speech, 2nd person	+IndSpeech2	-
		Indirect Speech, 3rd person	+IndSpeech3	-
		Particle	+Ptcl	Q
		Auxiliary	+Aux	a
		Extension vowel	+Emph	-

Table A.14 Punctuation marks morphosyntactic tags

		Punctuation marks	+F	Z
Attribute	Add. Attr.	Value	FS Tags	Code
Type		Dot	+Period	-
		Comma	+Comma	-
		Parenthesis	+Paren	-
		Hyphenation	+Hyphen	-
		Exclamation point	+ExclPoint	-
		Interrogation point	+IntPoint	-
		Colon	+Colon	-
		Semicolon	+Semicolon	-
		Ellipsis	+Ellipsis	-
		Quotation mark	+Quote	-
		Star	+Star	-
		Any symbol	+Symbol	-

Appendix B: Triggers

The following markup tags are added to the surface level with the purpose of activating phonological processes.

Table B.1 Replacement rule surface triggers shared between nouns, adjectives, verbal nouns, verbal adjectives, numerals, and pronouns

Trigger	Description
^S	Singular marker used to remove *-i/-y* from consonant-final non-syncopating nominals
^S1	Singular marker used to remove *-a/-e/-o* vowels in *-l, -r, -m, -n*-final nominals which syncopate in the genitive, instrumental and adverbial cases
^S2	Singular marker used to provide alternation between *-o-* and *-v-* in the genitive, instrumental and adverbial cases
^S3	Singular marker used to remove *-a* vowel in the genitive and instrumental cases
^S4	Singular marker used to remove *-i* vowel in the genitive in the case of non-truncating *-o* and *-u*-final nominals
^S5	Singular marker used to remove *-e* vowel in the genitive and instrumental cases
^S6	Singular marker used to remove *-a/-e* vowels from *-e* and *-a*-final nominals which syncopate in the genitive, instrumental and adverbial cases in the singular and truncate in the genitive and instrumental cases in the singular
^P	Plural marker used to remove *-i/-y* from consonant-final non-syncopating nominals before the *-eb* plural marker
^P1	Plural marker used to remove *-a/-e/-o* vowels before the *-eb* plural marker in *-l, -r, -m, -n*-final nominals which syncopate in the genitive, instrumental and adverbial cases
^P2	Plural marker used to provide alternation between *-o-* and *-v-* before the *-eb* plural marker in the genitive, instrumental and adverbial cases
^P3	Plural marker used to remove *-a* vowel before the *-eb* plural marker in the genitive and instrumental cases
^P5	Plural marker used to remove *-i* vowel before the *-eb* plural marker in the genitive in the case of non-truncating *-o* and *-u*-final nominals
^P6	Plural marker used to remove *-e* vowel before the *-eb* plural marker in the genitive and instrumental cases

(continued)

I. Lobzhanidze, *Finite-State Computational Morphology*,
https://doi.org/10.1007/978-3-030-90248-3

Trigger	Description
^NT	Plural marker used to remove *-i/-y* before second plural markers from consonant-final non-syncopating nominals
^NT1	Plural marker used to remove *-a/-e/-o* vowels before second plural markers in *-l, -r, -m, -n*-final nominals which syncopate in the genitive, instrumental and adverbial cases
^NT2	Plural marker used to provide alternation between *-o-* and *-v-* second plural markers in the genitive, instrumental and adverbial cases
^NT3	Plural marker used to remove *-a* vowel before second plural markers in the genitive and instrumental cases
^NT5	Plural marker used to remove *-i* vowel before second plural markers in the genitive in the case of non-truncating *-o* and *-u*-final common nouns
^NT6	Plural marker used to remove *-e* vowel before second plural markers in the genitive and instrumental cases
^N	Nominative case marker
^E	Ergative case marker
^D	Dative case marker
^G	Genitive case marker
^I	Instrumental case marker
^A	Adjective marker
^NR	Special marker to trigger suppletion in pronouns

Table B.2 Replacement rule surface tags for verbs

Trigger	Description
^O	Marker of *m*-type inflectional class used to insert *s-* in front of *-d, -t‘, -t, -ż, -c‘, -c, -j, -č‘, -č*, consonant *h-* in front of *b-, p‘-, p-, g-, k‘-, k-, q-*
^E	Special marker used to insert *-a-* in the aorist, aorist subjenctive, aorist imperative, pluperfect and perfect subjenctive
^E1	Special marker used to provide *e/i* root vowel alternation in monopersonal verbs in the future and aorist
^E2	Special marker used to provide *ϕ/e* root vowel alternation in the aorist
^E3	Special marker used to provide *ϕ/a* root vowel alternation in the aorist
^I	Special marker used to remove *-i-* in the pluperfect and perfect subjenctive
^TS	Thematic suffix marker used to substitute *-av* suffix with *-eb* suffix in the future indicative
^TS1	Thematic suffix marker used to remove *-eb* suffix in the aorist
^TS2	Thematic suffix marker used to remove *-ob* suffix in the aorist
^TS3	Thematic suffix marker used to remove *-il/ul-ob* in the aorist
^TS4	Thematic suffix marker used to remove *-en/-ev* in the aorist
^TS5	Thematic suffix marker used to remove *-am/av* in the aorist
^TS6	Thematic suffix marker used to substitute *-ev* with *-v* in the aorist
^Fut	Marker of future indicative
^Aor	Marker of aorist indicative
^AorSbj	Marker of aorist subjunctive
^AorImp	Marker of aorist imperative
^PluPerf	Marker of pluperfect
^PerfSbj	Marker of perfect subjunctive

Appendix C: Structural Markup

The structural markup of the files available in the GLC, and especially in its Middle and Old Georgian collections, follows the recommendations of the TEI P5 guidelines with regards to language corpora (TEI Consortium 2019). While it is beyond the scope of this publication to describe each tag precisely, this annex in most cases contains samples with project headers and text-level annotations.

```
<?xml version="1.0" encoding="UTF-8"?>
<teiCorpus xmlns="http://www.tei-c.org/ns/1.0">
    <teiHeader xml:lang="kat">
        <fileDesc>
            <titleStmt>
                <title></title>
                <funder></funder>
                <principal></principal>
            </titleStmt>
            <extent>
                <measure quantity="430" unit="kB"/>
                <measure      type="words"      quanti-
ty="79942"/>
            </extent>
            <publicationStmt>
                <authority>  ->
                    <persName role="site"></persName>
                    <name></name>
                </authority>
                <idno type="URL"></idno>
                <availability status="free">
                    <p></p>
                </availability>
                <date></date>
            </publicationStmt>
            <sourceDesc>
```

Fig. C.1 Structural markup

I. Lobzhanidze, *Finite-State Computational Morphology*,
https://doi.org/10.1007/978-3-030-90248-3

```
                <p></p>
            </sourceDesc>
        </fileDesc>
        <encodingDesc>
            <projectDesc>
                <p></p>
            </projectDesc>
            <tagsDecl>
                <namespace        name="http://www.tei-
c.org/ns/1.0">
                    <tagUsage gi="text"/>
                    <tagUsage gi="body"/>
                    <tagUsage gi="div"/>
                    <tagUsage gi="pb"/>
                    <tagUsage gi="head"/>
                    <tagUsage gi="seg"/>
                    <tagUsage gi="lg"/>
                    <tagUsage gi="l"/>
                    <tagUsage gi="w"/>
                    <tagUsage gi="pc"/>
                    <tagUsage gi="fLib"/>
                    <tagUsage gi="fs"/>
                    <tagUsage gi="f"/>
                </namespace>
            </tagsDecl>
            <editorialDecl>
                <correction method="silent">
                    <p></p>
                </correction>
                <normalization method="silent">
                    <p></p>
                </normalization>
                <segmentation>
                    <p></p>
                </segmentation>
                <hyphenation>
                    <p></p>
                </hyphenation>
                <interpretation>
                    <p></p>
                </interpretation>
                <stdVals>
```

Fig. C.1 (continued)

```
                    <p></p>
                </stdVals>
            </editorialDecl>
        </encodingDesc>
        <profileDesc>
            <creation>
                <date from="2010" to="2020"></date>
                <rs type="city"></rs>
            </creation>
            <langUsage>
                <language ident="kat"></language>
                <language ident="eng"></language>
            </langUsage>
            <textClass>
                <keywords>
                    <term>Fiction</term>
                    <term>Manuscript</term>
                </keywords>
            </textClass>
        </profileDesc>
        <revisionDesc>
            <change>
                <date></date>
                <name></name>
            </change>
        </revisionDesc>
    </teiHeader>
    <TEI
        xmlns:xi="http://www.w3.org/2001/XInclude"
        xmlns:svg="http://www.w3.org/2000/svg"
        xmlns:math="http://www.w3.org/1998/Math/MathML"
        xmlns="http://www.tei-c.org/ns/1.0">
        <teiHeader
xmlns:tg="http://corpora.iliauni.edu.ge/qats/index.php"
xml:lang="eng">
            <fileDesc>
                <titleStmt>
                    <title></title>
                    <author></author>
                    <principal></principal>
                    <respStmt>
                        <resp></resp>
```

Fig. C.1 (continued)

```
                <persName></persName>
            </respStmt>
        </titleStmt>
        <extent>
            <measure quantity="852" unit="kB"/>
            <measure type="paragraphs" quanti-
ty="256"/>
            <measure type="words" quanti-
ty="47265"/>
        </extent>
        <publicationStmt>
            <authority></authority>
            <availability>
                <p></p>
            </availability>
            <date></date>
            <distributor></distributor>
        </publicationStmt>
        <notesStmt>
            <note type="ilustrator"></note>
        </notesStmt>
        <sourceDesc>
            <biblFull>
                <titleStmt>
                    <title></title>
                    <author></author>
                </titleStmt>
                <extent></extent>
                <publicationStmt>
                    <publisher></publisher>
                    <pubPlace></pubPlace>
                    <date when="1937"></date>
                    <idno type="vol"></idno>
                    <idno type="ISBN"></idno>
                    <availability sta-
tus="free"><p></p>
                    </availability>
                    <availability sta-
tus="restricted"><p></p>
                    </availability>
                    <availability sta-
tus="unknown"><p></p>
```

Fig. C.1 (continued)

```
                            </availability>
                        </publicationStmt>
                    </biblFull>
                    <msDesc>
                        <msIdentifier>
                            <settlement></settlement>
                            <repository></repository>
                            <idno></idno>
                            <altIdentifier>
                                <idno></idno>
                            </altIdentifier>
                        </msIdentifier>
                        <msContents>
                            <msItem>
                                <locus        from="1r"
to="2r"></locus>
                                <editor
role="compiler"></editor>
                                <editor
role="illustrator"></editor>
                                <title></title>
                            </msItem>
                        </msContents>
                        <physDesc>
                            <objectDesc form="codex">
                                <supportDesc    materi-
al="paper">
                                    <support>
                                        <p></p>
                                    </support>
                                    <extent>
                                        <dimensions
scope="all" type="leaf" unit="inch">

<height></height>

<width></width>
                                        </dimensions>
                                    </extent>
                                    <folia-
tion></foliation>
                                    <colla-
```

Fig. C.1 (continued)

```
tion></collation>
                                    <condi-
tion></condition>
                                </supportDesc>
                                <layoutDesc>
                                    <layout          col-
umns="1">
                                        <p></p>
                                    </layout>
                                </layoutDesc>
                            </objectDesc>
                            <handDesc>
                                <p></p>
                            </handDesc>
                            <decoDesc>
                                <p></p>
                            </decoDesc>
                            <additions>
                                <date  notBefore="1800"
notAfter="1900">
                                </date>
                            </additions>
                        </physDesc>
                        <history>
                            <origin>
                                <p>
                                    <origPlace>
</origPlace>
                                    <origDate        no-
tAfter="1600" notBefore="1700"></origDate>
                                </p>
                            </origin>
                            <provenance>
                                <p></p>
                            </provenance>
                            <acquisition>
                                <p>
                                    <name
type="place"></name>
                                    <name
type="person"> </name>
                                </p>
```

Fig. C.1 (continued)

```
                                </acquisition>
                            </history>
                        </msDesc>
                    </sourceDesc>
                    </fileDesc>
                <profileDesc>
                    <textDesc>
                        <channel mode="s"/>
                        <constitution type="composite"/>
                        <derivation type="original"/>
                        <domain type="religious"/>
                        <factuality type="mixed"/>
                        <interaction type="complete"/>
                        <preparedness type="none"/>
                        <purpose     type="inform"     de-
gree="unknown"/>
                    </textDesc>
                </profileDesc>
            </teiHeader>
                        <text>
                            <body>
                                <div n="1" type="chapter">
                                    <pb n="1" />
                                    <head></head>
                                    <cb n="1"/>
                                    <p>
                                    </p>
                                </div>
                            </body>
                        </text>
    </TEI>
</teiCorpus>
```

Fig. C.1 (continued)

Glosses[3]

1, 2, 3	First, second, third person.
ADV	Adverbial
AOR	Aorist
AUX	Auxiliary
CAUS	Causative
COND	Conditional
DAT	Dative
DIM	Diminutive
DObj	Direct object
EM	Extension marker
EMPH	Extension vowel
ERG	Ergative
FRACT	Marker of fractional numeral
FUT	Future
GEN	Genitive
IMP	Imperative
IMPFV	Imperfect
IND	Indicative
INST	Instrumental
IObj	Indirect object
IPFV	Imperfective aspect
NOM	Nominative
NNOM	Not nominative
Obj	Object
ORD	Marker of ordinal numeral
PASS	Passive voice marker

[3] The glossing, generally, follows the conventions established in the Leipzig Glossing Rules (Comrie et al. 2008) and Eurotyp Guidelines (Bakker et al. 1993)

I. Lobzhanidze, *Finite-State Computational Morphology*,
https://doi.org/10.1007/978-3-030-90248-3

PF	Perfect
PFV	Perfective aspect
PL	Plural
PLUP	Pluperfect
POSS	Possessive
pref	Prefix
PRS	Present
PRV	Preradical vowel
PTCL	Particle
PV	Preverb
QUOT	Speech marker
RFL	Reflexive
SBJ	Subject
SG	Singular
SUBJ	Subjunctive
suff	Suffix
SUP	Superlative
TM	Tmesis
TS	Thematic suffix
VOC	Vocative

Author Index

I. Lobzhanidze, *Finite-State Computational Morphology*,
https://doi.org/10.1007/978-3-030-90248-3

Subject Index

I. Lobzhanidze, *Finite-State Computational Morphology*,
https://doi.org/10.1007/978-3-030-90248-3